the adjacent buildings are probably a bit too high, and the peculiar "points" and buttresses on the building in the foreground may be artistic license.
Courtesy of the Daughters of the Republic of Texas Library.

One of the earliest known drawings of the
Alamo in 1845. Allowing for the damage
inflicted by the Mexican Army in 1836
and by the effects of time, this is probably
close to the original appearance of the
fortress, although the "Long Barrack" and

THE ALAMO

THE ALAMO

and the Texas War for Independence
September 30, 1835 to April 21, 1836

Heroes, Myths and History

ALBERT A. NOFI

DA CAPO PRESS

Cataloging in Publication data is available from the Library of Congress.

Second Da Capo Press Edition 2001
ISBN 0-306-81040-9

Published by Da Capo Press
A Member of the Perseus Books Group
http://www.perseusbooksgroup.com

1 2 3 4 5 6 7 8 9 10——05 04 03 02 01

Acknowledgments

It is not possible to undertake a work of this sort without the help and advice of many people.

Several Alamo descendants provided interesting and useful information about their heroic ancestors, and I would like to thank them by name: Kevin L. Wornell, several times grandson of Henry Warnell; Myra DeVee Vanderpool Gormley, descendant of Micajah Autry; and Jack Mitchell, several times grand-nephew of Isaac G. Baker and grandson-in-law of Gordon C. Jennings; and Jack Coffee, the several times great grandson of Jesse B. Bowman. In addition, Shannon Elder was able to provide information about his several times great grandfather, Josias Bradley Beall, who perished with Fannin's men.

Many other people provided general advice on matters from the area of the Presidio La Bahia to the nature of a Blue Norther. These include Prof. John Boardman, of Brooklyn College, Austin Bay, Dennis Casey, Steve Cole of F.Y.E.O., Robert Hall, William S. Gross, Steve Petrick, Bob Dennis, Paul Morgan, Roger Covington, D. Mohney, Chris Goodey, Mark Turnage, R. Watson, Karen L. Myers, Dave Zincavage, M. Raymond, James Dingman, Jaime Delsen, Frank Deis, Jim Woolsey, Judith A. Trolinger, and Rhonda McLure.

This project benefited enormously from the existence of GENIE, General Electric's electronic mail network. The management of both the military and the genealogical bulletin boards were generous in permitting me to make use of their facilities, and many of their patrons are included in the list above.

The Daughters of the Republic of Texas were very cooperative in locating and providing access to materials.

Happy Shahan, of the Alamo Village, in Brackettville,

Texas, and Richard L. Curilla, of G.T.T. (Gone to Texas) Films, were both very generous with their time and advice, as well as permitting me to wander through the recreated Alamo during a visit not long ago.

Prof. Helga Feder and the staff of the C.U.N.Y. Graduate Library were enormously helpful in locating materials, as were the people of the New York Public Library.

Particular thanks are in order to Robert Pigeon and John Cannan, of Combined Books, for making this project possible, and to Robert Pigeon, III, for executing the maps and diagrams.

Special thanks must go to Carlotta Wright, whose Brackettville connections proved immensely valuable to the completion of this book.

As always, special thanks are of course in order to my wife, Mary S. Nofi, and my daughter, Marilyn J. Spencer, who both suffered through the writing of this book.

Albert A. Nofi
Brooklyn
6 March 1992

Contents

Maps

CHAPTER I

The Coming of War

It was a small war as such things go, probably no more than 2,500 men were ever engaged in a single action, both sides taken together. It was a short one too, lasting only about seven months. And it was certainly fought in what was at the time one of the most obscure corners of the world. Yet for all that, the Texas War for Independence was an heroic struggle of legendary character.

For centuries, Texas was an almost empty land. Along the coast a few small Indian tribes eked out a bare living, while much further inland the fierce Comanche battled with their neighbors. Although Spain imposed its authority in the sixteenth century, she proved unable effectively to colonize the region, her time-honored mission system failing to stimulate settlement. The region was hardly touched by history until the onset of the nineteenth century, when perhaps 4,000 settled souls inhabited it, about half of them in the vicinity of San Antonio de Bexar. But with the new century, change began to come to Mexico, and, more slowly but perhaps more decisively, to Texas.

In 1810, with Spain engaged in a life and death struggle against Napoleon, revolution broke out in Mexico. A long and bitter struggle ensued between Revolutionaries advocating independence, and Royalists holding out for the authority of the Spanish Crown. For the Revolutionaries it was a struggle for rather vaguely defined Enlightenment-style liberal ideals, including land for the Indian and *mestizo* peasantry and economic and political opportunity for the *mestizo* and *criollo* bourgeoisie and intelligentsia. The Royalists, led by Spanish officials, and the *criollo* aristocracy of Mexico largely fought for the maintenance of the status quo. On both sides, the armies were composed primarily of peasants dragooned into service with little notion of the questions at issue. A decade of brutal warfare followed.

These events had an impact upon thinly populated Texas. One reason for this was the desire of Mexican Revolutionaries to secure material aid from the United States. As a result, there were several composite Mexican-American expeditions into the vast territory during the Revolutionary era.

In August of 1813, for example, a column of several hundred men invaded Texas from Louisiana. Raised in the U.S. by one of the leading Mexican rebels, Bernardo Gutierrez de Lara, the Republican Army of the North included more Americans than Mexicans and was under the operational command of an American, Augustus W. Magee, a former U.S. Army officer. But the purpose of the expedition was to secure Texas for the Revolution, and it did attract considerable support from the small *Tejano* population. In what was an arduous campaign lasting about nine months, the expedition secured control of southern Texas, defeating the Royalist forces and in April of 1814 occupying San Antonio. Although the American members of the expedition attempted to adhere to the rules of war, their Mexican counterparts, reflecting the brutalities characteristic of the war further south in Mexico proper, massacred all prisoners. In the spring of 1814 a Royalist expedition of some 3,000 men undertook a counteroffensive, entering Texas partially overland and partially by sea. The Royalist column was commanded by Major General Joaquin Arredondo, a tough, seasoned campaigner, with a reputation for brutally crushing resistance. In some preliminary encounters the Revolutionaries came off second best. Then in August, the Royalist Army inflicted a crushing defeat on the rebels at the Medina River, near San Antonio. Perhaps

Mexicans: *Indios, Mestizos,* and *Criollos*

Although the racial divisions in their own society are familiar to Americans, a similar situation prevailed in Mexico. Under Spanish rule a very rigid racial hierarchy had been established. There were four principal groups. At the top were the *peninsulares,* the Spanish-born, who were held to have special qualities of character and intellect. While the *criollos,* or Mexican-born persons of "pure" European blood, deprecatingly referred to them as *gaupinches,* under Spanish rule the *peninsulares* were at the top of the heap, securing the most important civil, military, ecclesiastical, and judicial posts, leaving only the crumbs for the *criollos.* But at least the *criollos* got that, and many were wealthy landowners. Below the *criollos* were the *mestizos,* persons of mixed Indian and European ancestry. Although some *mestizos* were quite wealthy, owning estates to compete with those of the *criollos,* most were tradesmen and members of the middle class, and they staffed the lower ranks of the church and government. At the very bottom were the *Indios,* the Indians, who comprised the bulk of Mexico's population. *Indios* were mostly peons, effectively serfs, working for landed aristocrats, being dragooned into the army, and

being subjected to abuses which would have brought social ostracism to a slaveholder in the southern United States. Although Mexico's black population was rather small, a similar vocabulary existed to describe persons of mixed Indian and black—*lobo*—or black and white—*mulatto*—ancestry, as well as all sorts of combinations in between, such as the offspring of *mestizos* and *mulattoes* or of *lobos* and *mulattoes* and so forth.

As there was considerable social advantage to belonging to a higher racial class, it was not unusual for pregnant European women in Mexico to make the arduous journey to Spain, so that they could deliver a *gaupinche* child. Meanwhile, *mestizos* often strove mightily to be accepted as *criollos,* as did, by some accounts, Brig. Gen. Juan Urrea.

Independence brought an end to the *gaupinches,* who either settled down or returned to Spain, thus putting the *criollos* in charge. But the *criollos* were being pressed by the *mestizos.* A great deal of the political life of Mexico was defined by this racial tension. *Criollos,* like Santa Anna, tended to be more conservative, while *mestizos,* like Zavala, tended to be more radical.

a third of the 1,500-1,800 rebels, about half of whom were American volunteers, were killed outright in a battle lasting some four hours. Most of the rest were captured over the next

Texans: *Tejanos*, Texians, and Texicans

The term "Texan" was not in common use prior to attainment of independence by Texas. Until then several different terms were in use. *"Tejano"* referred to a resident in Texas who was of Hispanic background. "Texians" was the term commonly used to designate the American settlers in Texas. For a time the term "Texican" found some favor, and, indeed, continued in use until at least the Civil War. However, soon after the Texas Declaration of Independence, the term "Texan" began to be heard, and its use spread rather rapidly after San Jacinto.

few days; only a few hundred managed to escape back to the United States. Arredondo then proceeded to slaughter his prisoners in the most brutal fashion possible, while inflicting massacre and rape on the citizens of San Antonio and its environs. Among the officers who distinguished themselves in this campaign was a young lieutenant, Antonio Lopez de Santa Anna, who received a decoration for his courage. Needless to say, the Arredondo expedition brought peace and stability of a sort to Texas.

However, just four years later, in 1818, there was yet another such expedition, about 300 men under a Dr. James Long, who held a commission from one of the Republican factions in Mexico. After occupying Nacogdoches, Dr. Long put his men on ships and landed them down the coast. He then marched inland for Goliad and San Antonio. Royalist reaction was swift, however. After a brief skirmish, Long and his men were all captured and sent to Mexico City, where they were incarcerated. Although Dr. Long himself was eventually shot, most of the men with him were released when the Mexican Republic came into existence.

The defeat of the two filibustering expeditions put Texas securely under Royalist control. However, it was a poor prize. The two campaigns had inflicted great suffering upon the *Tejanos*, and the population had fallen by about half, so that, Indians aside, by 1820 there were apparently only some

2,000 settled residents in Texas. Reflecting upon this, the Spanish government did a curious thing. It offered extensive lands in Texas to anyone who would agree to bring in a certain number of settlers. And then it specifically extended the offer to citizens of the United States. A number of Americans took up the offer, the first of whom was a Spanish-speaking merchant named Moses Austin who had lived in Missouri when it was Spanish territory. Austin was granted 200,000 acres with the proviso that he settle several hundred American families in Texas. Of course actual settlement of these lands would take time, particularly in the light of the ongoing revolutionary struggle in Mexico.

By 1820, after a decade of brutal and bloody struggle, the Royalists had more or less managed to hold their own against the Revolutionaries in Mexico. Given time, they would probably have been able to crush all resistance. However, in that year a politically explosive development occurred. In 1820 a liberal government came to power in Spain, with a program which largely endorsed the political platform of the Revolutionaries in Mexico and Spain's other restive American colonies. This development put the Royalists on the horns of a dilemma: by continuing to uphold the authority of Madrid, they would be endorsing the very principles against which they had fought since 1810. Agustin Iturbide, the Spanish commander in Mexico and a prominent *criollo*, consulted with the leadership of the conservative faction and his principal aides, who included a Lt. Col. Antonio Lopez de Santa Anna. Early in 1821 he announced a plan for the reform of the government of Mexico, one which seemed to have something for everyone, promising a monarchy under a Spanish Bourbon prince, the continuation of the authority of the Church, and political equality. After a brief consultation with revolutionary leaders, Iturbide proclaimed a constitutional monarchy, assuming the regency until a suitable prince could be found; the flag of the new state—green, white, and red—was designed to symbolize its three guiding principles, green for independence, white for religion, and red for the unity of the

European and Amerindian races. Shortly afterwards, Iturbide announced that he had assumed the "throne of Moctezuma." He was not yet 38, less than five years older than his hero Napoleon when he had assumed the throne of France. The newly crowned monarch did not last very long. Agustin I proved an inept ruler, with strong inclinations towards tyranny. Things not all going as expected, in late 1822 the newly minted Brigadier General Antonio Lopez de Santa Anna, once among Iturbide's most enthusiastic supporters, issued his Plan of Vera Cruz, which proclaimed a republican regime based on liberal, federalist principles, a move which was almost immediately seconded by the bulk of the former Revolutionaries. By the spring of 1823 Iturbide had fled and a republic proclaimed, but it would require more than a century before the nature of that republic was firmly established. In the ensuing decades, Mexico underwent frequent changes of government, as political and military leaders vied for power, while the bulk of the impoverished populace sought only bread and peace.

These developments were watched with concern by Moses Austin, and then, when he died in 1821, by his son Stephen F. Austin. But both the government of Agustin I and that of the Republic which succeeded him confirmed the Austin land grant, and, indeed, made further grants to Mexican and American *empresarios* alike, though no one managed to secure as much land as did the Austins. For various reasons, most notably superior financial resources and organizational skills, the American *empresarios* proved much more successful in enticing settlers to Texas than did their Mexican counterparts. As a result, within a few years, there was a large and growing American expatriate colony in Texas, by 1834 there were apparently some 15,000-16,000 Americans in Texas and only some 3,000-4,000 Mexicans. Americans, including Austin, who accepted land in Texas were legally obliged by their grants to adopt Roman Catholicism, assume Mexican citizenship, learn Spanish, and bring no slaves into the territory. Many, particularly those among the earliest arrivals in

Population of Texas in 1836

According to a survey conducted by Col. Juan Almonte in 1834, the population of Texas north of the Neuces River seems to have been about 36,000 people. These comprised several different groups:

Americans:	Whites	15,400
	Blacks	2,000
Indians:	Settled	4,500
	"Wild"	10,500
Mexicans		3,600

Of the settled population, only about 4,000 lived in the southern and western portions of the territory, the Department of Bexar, with San Antonio, at about 2,400 people, the largest settlement. About 10,000 more lived in the Department of the Brazos, in which San Felipe de Austin was the largest settlement, at 2,900, but with sizable communities at Columbia, Matagorda, Gonzales, and Mina, all between 1200 and 1650. The Department of Nacogdoces, constituting the portion of Texas from the Trinity River to the U.S. frontier, had slightly more than 10,000 inhabitants, with Nacogdoches itself having some 4,000 people, and with San Augustine, Liberty, and Johnsburg all having between 1,000 and 2,900 people.

It is unclear how many people lived in the area between the Neuces River and the Rio Grande, at that time not considered part of Texas, but where there were already some American settlers.

Although most of the "Wild" Indian population lived west of the settled areas, there were some tribes still living along the middle reaches of the Trinity River, between more settled areas in the Departments of Brazos and Nocagdoches. It is likely that Almonte seriously underestimated the numbers of unsettled Indians, since some estimates place them at upwards of 25,000.

Texas, including Austin, went along with this. But some resented the loosely enforced requirements, and made only a sham compliance. This was by no means difficult, and was, indeed, even winked at by the Mexican authorities. Priests, for example, were rather thinly spread over the countryside, so conversion to Catholicism could be superficial indeed, particularly since Republican Mexico was at times anti-clerical. The provisions regarding slaves, could be evaded by simply bringing them into Texas in the guise of contract laborers with 99-year indentures, which was legal under Mexican law.

Even if both sides had carried on with the best possible intentions, there would have been serious problems. There were, after all, significant cultural, religious, and psychological differences between Americans and Mexicans. Then too, there were important differences in the way Mexicans and Americans looked at economic enterprise. Technically liberal, that is capitalistic, the Mexican Republic was the heir to a highly centralized and essentially feudalistic economic philosophy which clashed with the free enterprise attitude of the American settlers. Even more significant were the differences in political outlook between the two groups. Rooted in the relatively democratic and decentralized English tradition, American attitudes towards law and government differed markedly from those of Mexico, rooted in the centralized and essentially absolutist Spanish tradition. And, of course, relations between the two groups was further eroded by the inherent instability of Mexican political institutions. Conflict was almost certain, even given the best of intentions. Nor was serious conflict long in coming.

Late in 1826 a band of about 30 Americans, mostly new arrivals in Texas, occupied Nacogdoches. Arresting the *alcalde* and other local officials, among them several Americans, the rebels proclaimed the Republic of Fredonia. They quickly concluded a treaty with some renegade Cherokees, promising them half of Texas in return for an alliance. However, the bulk of the people of Texas, Americans as well as Mexicans, opposed the rebellion. Within less than a fortnight, about 300 Mexican troops from San Antonio, reinforced with several score American settler militiamen from Austin's colony at San Felipe, marched on Nacogdoches while the leaders of the Cherokees acted quickly to repudiate the actions of a handful of malcontents. The rebellion collapsed without bloodshed, its leaders fleeing to the United States.

Although the vast majority of the American settlers had actively opposed the Fredonian Rebellion, many Mexican political leaders began to view their presence in Texas with suspicion. As a result, Mexico began to consider ways to strengthen its control over the area. After much discussion, in 1828 Brig. Gen. Jose Manuel Rafael Simeon de Mier y Teran, a distinguished soldier and scholar, and a liberal, was given command of an expedition to survey Texas and make recommendations for its further development. Mier y Teran spent nearly a year in this work, in the process developing a close friendship with Stephen F. Austin. The general's recommendations were simple: to increase Mexican settlement through grants to Mexican citizens, while limiting those to Americans. In consequence of Mier y Teran's proposals, garrisons, hitherto limited to some *presidiales*, frontier guards, were enlarged, more grants were made to Mexicans, including Mier y Teran and several other soldiers, and other measures were taken. In addition, customs houses were erected and regulations issued limiting the entry of ships to a handful of ports. While land grants to Mexican citizens were expanded it became more difficult for Americans to obtain such. Save for the imposition of import duties, none of these measures was particularly severe, and certainly all were within the purview of the legitimate exercise of government power. But many of the American settlers, particularly the later arriving ones, found them irksome. Tensions began to rise and incidents between the American settlers and the Mexican government became more frequent. Nor were relations between the Mexican residents of Texas and their government very much better.

Under Spanish rule Texas had been a separate province of Mexico, with its capital at San Antonio. The creation of a federal republic in 1824 changed this. Lumped together with Coahuila to form the state of Coahuila-Texas, Texas lost its separate political identity. Relatively autonomous under Royal rule, the small *Tejano* community had few ties with the distant and far more populous Coahuila. Sentiment for the creation of a state of Texas grew among the *Tejanos*, particularly the old leading families, which had been prominent in the territory for several generations, such as the Menchacas and the Seguins, whose importance continued as the citizens of Texas elected them to the national congress in Mexico City. And the *Tejanos* had benefited from the suspension of import duties, the reimposition of which Mier y Teran observed was a gross violation of the government's good faith since most land holders were supposed to have immunity from such. So both Mexican and American Texans, and at least initially the two groups got along fairly well with each other, had problems with the government in Mexico City.

Meanwhile, Mexico's political instability took several turns which tended to further exacerbate the situation in Texas. The liberal regime established under the Constitution of 1824 struggled with many problems, none of which President Guadalupe Victoria was able to solve. The economy proved unable to recover from the damage inflicted during the long years of revolution, and the state sank deeper and deeper into debt. An ongoing threat from Spain, which retained control

---

Stephen F. Austin

Stephen F. Austin (1793-1836) was born in Virginia into a slave-holding family with mining interests. In 1798 the family moved to Missouri, at that time a sparsely populated region under Spanish control. At the age of 17 young Austin left college in the U.S. to return to Missouri, by which time the territory had passed from Spanish to French, and then from French to American control. He went into business, doing moderately well as a merchant and land speculator, while serving as a militia officer and member of the territorial legislature in Missouri. However, ill luck caused the family's fortunes to crash: worth some $160,000 in 1812, by the end of the decade the Austins had little left. The family relocated to Arkansas, where Austin was elected a judge. Knowing nothing of the law, he went to New Orleans to read law, supporting himself by editing a newspaper. Meanwhile, in the hope of recouping the family fortune, Moses Austin (1761-1821), Stephen's father, applied for and received a grant permitting him to settle some 300 American families in Texas. The elder Austin died before he could act under the terms of the grant, whereupon the younger Austin took it up. Austin applied for a renewal and expansion of his grant upon the fall of the ephemeral Empire of Agustin Iturbide in 1823. He soon proved to be the most successful of several Texas land grantees and eventually set-of the island-fortress of San Juan de Ulua, off Vera Cruz, into 1825 and seized Tampico briefly in 1829, necessitated the maintenance of a large armed force, the cost of which was twice that of all other government expenditures taken together. Attempts at reform were continuously frustrated by vested interests, notably the Church, the landowners, and the army, which had one politically-well connected general for every 230 men, and one officer or non-commissioned officer for every two privates. The first attempted *coup d'etat* against the new regime occurred in 1824, when the erstwhile Emperor Agustin I made an unsuccessful bid to regain power, leading to his execution. Surprisingly, it was not until 1827 that someone attempted another *coup*, when Vice-President Nicolas Bravo, allying himself with the old revolutionary general Vicente Guerrero, tried, only to be put down quickly. Victoria's term of office expiring in 1829, Manuel Gomez Pedraza,

tled over 1,000 families. Meanwhile he worked for the fuller integration of the American settlers into Mexican society. He served for a time in the Coahuila-Texas legislature, and was a member of various commissions and delegations.

An honest, energetic man who displayed remarkable powers of leadership, Austin sincerely believed that Texas ought to remain a part of Mexico and worked hard toward establishing a separate state of Texas within Mexico. Unfortunately he was caught between the proverbial "rock and a hard place," on the one hand having to deal with the strong annexationist feelings among many Americo-Texans, and on the other struggling to cope with the chaotic politics of Mexico. He was unable to work out a modus vivendi with Mexicans of any

political outlook and was tossed in jail for about 18 months in 1834. Upon his release, Austin threw in with the Independence movement and was elected Provisional President of Texas. After the revolution, he briefly served as Secretary of State in Houston's cabinet, but died of pneumonia. "Texas" was among his last words.

Austin was a man of considerable character, and great personal charm. Not only was he a personal friend of such prominent Mexicans as Vicente Filisola and Manuel de Mier y Teran, both of whom had commanded in Texas at various times, but he was also able to get along with the frequently rough-hewn American farmers and frontiersmen who migrated to Texas and the native *Tejano* community as well.

Liberal and Conservative in a Mexican Context.

In the political life of Mexico during the nineteenth century, the terms "liberal" and "conservative" may roughly be translated as "federalist" and "centralist." Liberals tended to favor a loose relationship between the several states of the Mexican Republic, a laissez faire approach to economics, anti-clericalism, and intellectual freedom. Conservatives tended to favor a more authoritarian, centralized regime, supportive of the Church, hostile to "foreign" ideas, and rigidly in control of the economy. Two additional differences between the two factions was that *criollos* tended to support the Conservatives and *mestizos* the Liberals. Further complicating matters were internal conflicts within the federalist and centralist factions, so that, for example, the *puro* or "pure" federalists had little regard for the *moderado* or "moderate" federalists, who returned the sentiments, generally with a ferocity equal to that with which either faction regarded the conservatives. None of the parties or factions had much use for the *indios*.

a moderate liberal, won the election of 1828. In December, before his inauguration, Gomez Pedraza illegally used military forces in an attempt to overthrow the liberal government of the state of Mexico. The governor, the extreme liberal Lorenzo de Zavala, fought back, aided by troops under Antonio Lopez de Santa Anna. As a result, Gomez Pedraza fled and Vicente Guerrero was illegally installed as President, with Anastasio Bustamante as Vice-President, in a sop to the conservatives. Unfortunately, although a brilliant guerrilla leader, Guerrero proved an inept chief executive. In 1830 Bustamante staged a *coup* of his own, assuming the presidency in turn and, after a complex series of betrayals and treacheries, executed his predecessor. Bustamante then proceeded to overturn the Constitution of 1824, imposing a conservative, even reactionary regime. Bustamante's high-handed rule sparked unrest and insurrection in many parts of Mexico, notably in the fringe areas, where federalist sentiments—and the reach of Mexico City—were strongest, such as Zacatecas,

Lorenza de Zavala

Lorenzo de Zavala (1788-1836) was born into a prosperous *mestizo* family in Yucatan. Originally educated for the priesthood, he left the seminary because he disputed the authority of St. Thomas Aquinas and became a physician instead. An ardent liberal, indeed during the revolutionary years 1810-1821 he was widely regarded as a "Jacobin," he became an important political figure while still in his mid-20s, serving in various municipal and regional posts. Elected to the liberal Spanish *Cortes* of 1814, he was arrested en route to Madrid by agents of the reactionary King Fernando VII and imprisoned in the island fortress of San Juan de Ulua, off Vera Cruz until 1817. For a time he practiced medicine, but in 1820 he was elected secretary of the Yucatan provincial legislature and was sent to the new liberal *Cortes* which had just assumed power in Spain. He returned the following year, after Mexico had secured its independence. Zavala was a member of the constituent assembly of 1823-1824, which drew up the liberal federal constitution of 1824. He was elected to the first Senate in 1824 and governor of the State of Mexico in 1827, resigning in 1829 to become Minister of Finance in the liberal Vicente Guerrero administration, which he helped bring to power by suppressing a coup by the legitimately elected conservative President-elect Manuel Gomez Pedraza.

Zavala's connection to Texas began in 1829, when he received a grant to settle 500 families in the area. He did not, however, act upon this grant immediately. When the conservative Anastasio Bustamante took power later that same year, Zavala went into exile. He spent the next three years in Europe and the United States. In 1832 he returned to Mexico. Elected to Congress and then as governor of Mexico once again, he quickly established himself as one of the most prominent liberal leaders. In 1833 the newly installed and allegedly federalist and liberal President Santa Anna made Zavala Minister to France. However, as Santa Anna moved rapidly to a centralist position, Zavala broke with him. Resigning his post, he went to Texas in 1835 and quickly became one of the most active revolutionary leaders.

Zavala took part in the "Consultation" of October-November 1835 and was a signer of the Texas Declaration of Independence. Elected vice-president in the provisional government of the Republic, he resigned due to ill health in October, and died soon after.

A proud, principled man, Zavala possessed remarkable energy, considerable political skills, and a keen intellect, and found time to write several histories.

Zavala's eldest son, also Lorenzo, served in the Texas cavalry during the Revolution, and his granddaughter, Adina, was a noted preservationist and historian.

Durango, Yucatan, New Mexico, California, San Luis Potosi, Oaxaca, and Guerrero. Among these was Texas, where the American settlers were particularly annoyed by a ban imposed on further settlement of foreigners.

In late 1830 Col. John D. Bradburn, an American who had been in Mexican service since 1817, was sent with about 75 men to establish a garrison and customs house on the northern edge of Galveston Bay, at a place which he named Anahuac Nauatl for "Place by the Water." Bradburn's instructions were to control trade and collect customs duties, supervise the settlers, and deal with the unauthorized movement of additional Americans into Texas. Soon afterwards there arrived Col. George Fisher, assigned as collector of customs for the Galveston area. A Serbian who had become a citizen of the U.S. in 1822, and then of Mexico in 1829, Fisher, like Bradburn, was an arbitrary, self-important, and egotistical sort. The two men soon had the entire American colony in an uproar, and not a few of the native *Tejanos* as well. Mier y Teran, by this time commanding general of all of Northern Mexico, intervened to cancel the collection of customs on the grounds that such violated the terms of most of the land grants in Texas, which specified immunity from import duties for about ten years. Fisher, however, chose to ignore Mier y Teran's authority. With local officials such as these, it is by no means surprising that tensions rose through 1831 and into 1832. This was also the period during which Bustamante proved increasingly arbitrary and dictatorial as President, which further exacerbated the situation. Things came to a head in the spring of 1832.

For various essentially political reasons, Bradburn unlawfully arrested several American settlers in the growing town around Anahuac. William B. Travis, a recent settler who was already an acknowledged leader of those among the American settlers who were thinking in terms of separating Texas from Mexico, was in town at the time to petition for the return of two runaway slaves. When Travis and others asked Bradburn to release those under arrest, the latter threw them in jail as well. Things began to get ugly, as the Americo-Texans talked of mob action. Col. Domingo de Ugartechea, commanding the garrison at Velasco, concluded that the settlers had a legitimate grievance, and sent an officer to urge Bradburn to release the prisoners. At first Bradburn refused, and even fired upon the officer messenger, but he shortly promised to cooperate. Then he reneged on his promise, and the Americans remained incarcerated. Meanwhile, at Vera Cruz, far to the south, Maj. Gen. Antonio Lopez de Santa Anna, a leading liberal, had raised the standard of revolt against conservatism and Bustamante in favor of liberalism and the Constitution of 1824. So when in late June a considerable mob of American settlers marched on Anahuac, they did so with Santa Anna's name on their lips. Since this was open rebellion against the authority of the President of Mexico, Ugartechea marched to the relief of the post, reaching it shortly before the mob invested the place on 26 June. After a three day siege, and several deaths on both sides, Ugartechea concluded that he was outgunned and surrendered on the 29th. A day or two later the liberal Col. Jose de las Piedras arrived from Nacogdoches with a small contingent of troops. Recognizing the legitimacy of the settler's demands, and probably noting that they considerably outnumbered his own troops, de las Piedras essentially approved of their actions and removed Bradburn from command. Moreover, since de las Piedras was a liberal and supporter of Santa Anna, he did not necessarily see the skirmish at Anahuac as contrary to the interests of Mexico. With the approval of Mier y Teran, himself also a supporter of Santa Anna, as soon as he had settled things at Anahuac, de las Piedras set sail for Mexico with all his troops, effectively leaving Texas without a garrison north of San Antonio.

The desultory war between Santa Anna and Bustamante dragged on through the balance of 1832. Like other northern states, Coahuila-Texas sided with the popular liberal general. Late in the year Bustamante gave up, fleeing into exile. The presidency having suddenly fallen vacant, the moderate lib-

Antonio Lopez de Santa Anna Perez

Antonio Lopez de Santa Anna Perez de Lebron (1794-1876), to give him his full name, better known to Americans as Santa Anna, was a *criollo*. His family were recent settlers in Mexico, having taken up residence at Jalapa near Vera Cruz in the mid-eighteenth century. In 1810, shortly after the beginning of Mexico's long war for independence, the then 14-year old Santa Anna enlisted as a cadet in the Regiment of Vera Cruz. During the Mexican Revolution (1810-1821), Santa Anna served the Royalist cause with some distinction, rising to lieutenant of Grenadiers by 1815. Six years later he had risen to lieutenant colonel, largely on the strength of his abilities at pacification, and was attached to the staff of General Agustin Iturbide, chief of the Royalist armies in Mexico. By this time the revolutionary cause in Mexico was in desperate straits. However, back in Spain a liberal government had come to power.

In 1821 Santa Anna was among those who urged Iturbide to proclaim the independence of Mexico, and as a reward was made a brigadier general—at the age of 27—by his grateful sovereign. Within a few months, Santa Anna had put himself at the head of the republican faction, proclaiming the Republic of Mexico, defeating the Imperial forces, and sending Iturbide into exile. As a reputed Liberal, Santa Anna helped write the widely admired federal Constitution of 1824 and immediately went into retirement. He then dominated Mexican political and military life for more than 30 years, sometimes as President (1833-1834, 1834-1835, 1841-1844, 1847, 1853-1855), sometimes as stage manager, and sometimes as rebel.

In 1835, Santa Anna abolished the Constitution of 1824, imposing in its place a centralist document, a move which was one of the causes of the Texas Revolution. He shortly afterwards resigned the presidency in order to more effectively prosecute the Texas War.

Officially out of office over the next half-dozen years, Santa Anna remained a power in the land, as political boss of Vera Cruz. During the 1838 "Pastry War" with France, he lost a leg in the defense of Vera Cruz, an amputation which enhanced his political career, as he ever afterwards would refer to the loss as evidence of his patriotism. The next few years found him in and out of power. By 1846 the rough and tumble of Mexican politics found him in exile when the Mexican-American War broke out. Contacting American authorities he gave them some tips on strategy ("Occupy Vera Cruz and Tampico") and suggested that given enough support he might be able to return to power and thereby bring about a quick end to the war on terms favorable to the United States. With American funding he returned to Mexico, became President yet again, and promptly began energetic efforts to mobilize Mexico's considerable resources against the *gringos*. The disastrous consequences of Santa Anna's defeats at the hands of Zachary Taylor and Winfield Scott had little effect upon his political career, and he returned to the presidency for one final time in 1853, only to be ousted again in 1855, and sent into exile.

Much of the rest of his life Santa Anna spent in exile, with occasional efforts at making a comeback. He several times approached various foreign powers—Spain and France in particular—with schemes for turning Mexico into a colony once again. During the French Intervention and the ephemeral reign of the Emperor Maximilian (1861-1867) he tried to secure a command, but was ignored. Settling at Nassau, in the Bahamas, in the 1870s, he wrote some wonderfully creative and self-serving memoirs. In extreme old age, he was permitted to return to Mexico and spent his last few years in strained circumstances at his beloved hacienda above Vera Cruz.

Although Santa Anna was a man of considerable talents and some impressive accomplishments, he nevertheless remains something of an enigmatic figure in the history of Mexico, where he is universally detested. As a soldier he could be remarkably energetic and resourceful, with an extraordinary ability to raise and equip armies virtually from nothing. A meticulous planner when he wanted to be, he frequently had brilliant insights, but he never let his talents work to his best advantage. He was too often loyal to inept subordinates, many of whom were selected for their political connections rather than their military skills, and he often let ambition or lethargy get in the way of clear thinking and decisive action. During one of his numerous tenures as President, he let his Vice-President run things while he led an easy life in his mountain hacienda. Self-styled "The Napoleon of the West," he could hardly be said to have come close to the Corsican in talent or accomplishments, though he might have made an able marshal.

Santa Anna was a tall, well proportioned man of considerable charm and intellect. He wore uniforms well and often. Fond of pretty women, he had dozens of affairs, often with girls as young as 13. He also liked good living: he wore three shirt studs worth over $5,000; indulged often in opium; wagered enormous sums at cockfighting; and wielded power with enormous indifference to its consequences. Albeit a man of great intelligence and considerable charm, Santa Anna was wholly unethical. He bore his sins well, never regretting anything.

Santa Anna is a wonderful case of a man who was both born great and had greatness thrust upon him, and then chose to forfeit that greatness.

eral Gomez Pedraza, who had been elected President in 1828, but then forced from office even before his installation after attempting a *coup* against the more extreme liberals, was brought back to complete the last six months of his original term of office under the restored Constitution of 1824. Gomez Pedraza's principal accomplishment was to hold new presidential elections according to the constitutional prescription. Not surprisingly, the elections of 1832 saw Antonio Lopez de Santa Anna swept into office by an overwhelming majority. Then the ambitious and vainglorious general did something remarkable.

In January of 1833, shortly before his inauguration, Santa Anna announced that he would not take his seat as President, citing a desire to return to the simple life at his *hacienda*, leaving the business of government to men more qualified than himself. Santa Anna's gesture raised his popularity even more, but was a well calculated political move; whoever was President of Mexico was not likely to remain popular very long, since the problems of the country were overwhelming. So as Santa Anna returned to Jalapa, Valentin Gomez Farias, his Vice-President, an extreme liberal, was left to run the country as acting president.

Gomez Farias proved an energetic, idealistic Liberal. His administration launched a spate of reforms, and the resistance from the vested interests, army, Church, landowners, and, above all, grafters of all political stripes, was swift and dogged. Making matters worse, the global cholera epidemic of 1828 finally reached Mexico with devastating effect. Criticism of Gomez Farias' administration grew bolder. A stream of disaffected religious and military officials passed through Jalapa to lay their grievances at Santa Anna's feet. Although the general, still legally President, took no action on any of the grievances, his sympathetic attitude won him many supporters among the conservative elements, while losing none among the liberals.

Meanwhile, Gomez Farias' federalist reputation sparked the hope among the American settlers and many native *Te-*

janos of establishing a separate state of Texas within the Mexican Republic. In April of 1833 Stephen F. Austin, Sam Houston, and about 55 other delegates from all over Texas gathered at San Felipe de Austin to write a draft constitution for the proposed state. Surprisingly, when he met with Santa Anna on 5 November, the latter proved rather impressed by the sincerity of Austin's protestations. He agreed that the Texians had much to complain about, and that a ban on further immigration from the United States was perhaps unfair. However, when, soon afterwards, Austin presented this proposal to Gomez Farias, the Acting President proved notably uninterested. Indeed, he was openly opposed to the notion. Quite aside from the fact that, even counting Indians, Texas had far fewer than the 80,000 inhabitants required for a new state by the Constitution of 1824, or that the problems of Texas seemed minor compared to the deteriorating political situation which faced him, Gomez Farias was one of an increasing number of Mexicans, liberals and conservatives alike, to question the wisdom of permitting the settlement of Americans in Mexico, and in fact was not particularly fond of Americans in any circumstances. Frustrated, Austin wrote home suggesting that preparations be made any way for the assumption of statehood, apparently on the theory that if the Texians could prove their capacity for self-rule the Mexican government might relent. He could hardly have been more wrong. His letters were intercepted by Gomez Farias. By Mexican standards, this was treason. Austin was thrown in jail and forgotten. Meanwhile the political situation in Mexico grew worse. Mexico was drifting towards renewed civil war. Carefully watching the way the wind was blowing, in April of 1834 Santa Anna concluded that it was time once more to come to the rescue of the *patria*.

Still legally President, Santa Anna made a triumphal march on Mexico City and removed Gomez Farias from office. Invoking the emergency provisions of the Constitution of 1824, he began to rule by decree, dissolving Congress, rescinding Gomez Farias' anti-clerical legislation, and canceling other

Martin Perfect de Cos

Martin Perfect de Cos (1802-1854) was a *criollo* from Tehuantepec. At an early age he ran away from home to join the Revolutionary forces under Jose Morelos. He rose steadily in Revolutionary ranks, and upon the attainment of Mexican independence passed into the new regular army, rising to brigadier general, a rank for which he was wholly unsuited. Nevertheless, he was one of Santa Anna's closest advisers due to his two primary assets: he had married the general's sister in the early 1820s and he had enormous political influence in his native Tehuantepec.

Cos, who wore tiny gold earrings, was a moderately tall, dark haired man, with long sideburns, a dashing mustache, and "remarkably short fingernails." By no means a capable soldier, he could lead a battalion with some success, but certainly ought never to have been entrusted with so delicate a political and military command as Texas in 1835.

liberal legislation as well. As liberals fled in every direction, President and Major General Santa Anna adopted a conservative and centralist political platform. Opposition was swift. The state of Zacatecas, a notable liberal stronghold, mobilized its militia, on paper some 17,000 men, many well trained and seasoned veterans of various civil wars. Santa Anna marched north late in 1834. In May of 1835 he smashed the Zacatecans in a bloody battle, slaughtering some 4,000 in the process. Meanwhile, internal disorders having broken out in Coahuila, with which Texas was linked in statehood, in January of 1835, Santa Anna sent his brother-in-law, Col. Martin Perfecto Cos, into Coahuila with an infantry battalion and some additional forces, plus a brevet commission as a brigadier general and instructions to "restore order," "put an end to corruption," and pick up various fugitive liberals in the bargain. As Cos took up his command at Leona Vicario (now Saltillo), tension grew in Texas. A "war party" emerged among the Texians, mostly Americans but including some *Tejanos*, who were immediately nicknamed "The War Dogs," and were opposed by a peace party, as the confused settlers sought solutions to their difficulties. In early June Cos arrested the duly elected governor and various other officials and prominent citizens of Coahuila-Texas, dissolved the state legislature, and closed the state courts. Many of those who escaped arrest, such as the distinguished liberal Lorenzo de Zavala and James Bowie, a member of the legislature, fled to Texas, where they spread the word of Santa Anna's high-handed treatment of dissenters. Meanwhile, Santa Anna re-imposed customs duties on Texas, in renewed violation of the terms of the original contracts under which many Americans had acquired lands in the region, further exacerbating tensions.

In late June Cos attempted to calm the situation by dispatching a courier to Capt. Antonio Tenorio, the local commander at Anahuac, bearing two messages. One was for public consumption. In it, the general announced that with "order" restored in Coahuila calm had returned to northern Mexico, and normal life could resume. The second message was a confidential one. In it, Cos informed Tenorio that he should hold on patiently, for reinforcements, including veterans of the Zacatecas Campaign, were on their way, and that upon their arrival "the affairs of Texas will definitely be settled." Cos' first message was read to the populace of San Felipe de Austin on 28 June, and it might have had a calming effect, but for an unfortunate incident. Some rowdy American settlers managed to seize the dispatch case, in which they soon found Cos' second message. Whatever hope there was that tensions might be eased dissolved as the settlers began to demand immediate action to overthrow Santa Anna's tyranny. Several settlers delivered inflammatory speeches. Then the local political boss, J.B. Miller, moved that William B. Travis be authorized to occupy Anahuac. The motion passed unanimously, and many of those who voted on it immediately placed themselves at Travis' disposal and demanded to be led against Anahuac immediately.

Travis rummaged up an old 6-pounder cannon, piled it and his men aboard the sloop *Ohio*, and set sail across Galveston Bay. Accompanied by one or two other small vessels, the little expedition made a pre-dawn landing at Lynchburg, where the local American community proved remarkably lacking in enthusiasm for the venture. Despite this dampening experience, and the fact that some of his men had second thoughts and deserted the expedition, Travis persevered. Later that day the ships made a brief landing for another round of inflammatory speeches and a few jugs of whiskey, in the process electing Travis as captain. Then they shoved off again. Approaching Anahuac in late afternoon, *Ohio* grounded briefly on a mud flat about a mile offshore. While the smaller vessels accompanying the expedition prepared to land his men, Travis let go a round at the little fort. Then he headed for shore with his little army, now reduced to only about 16 men. As they reached shore amid a crowd of curious onlookers, Travis was handed a message from the *alcalde*, an American named William Duncan, with the request that the group not cause any disturbances. Ignoring this, Travis sent a message to Tenorio, demanding that he surrender immediately. By now it was about sunset, and without awaiting a reply Travis decided to move against the fort immediately, taking advantage of the moonlight. Much to his surprise, he found it empty, Tenorio having withdrawn his men into a nearby forested area.

Travis ordered his 6-pounder into action. After several rounds, Tenorio decided to parley. He sent two messengers, both Americans, to request that Travis meet him alone. Travis agreed to meet, but secretly arranged for three men to cover him from a concealed position. Apparently catching wind of this, Tenorio declined to expose himself, and demanded that Travis enter the woods so that they could talk. After some hesitation, Travis did so. As it transpired, although Tenorio's men were both more numerous and better equipped than Travis', he was inclined to surrender on terms. When Tenorio expressed a desire to do this at dawn, Travis demanded that he surrender immediately. After dithering over details for about an hour, Tenorio agreed to surrender his command, on condition that his men be paroled as quickly as possible.

William Barret Travis

William Barret Travis (1809-1836) was born on a plantation in South Carolina, but from the age of nine was raised in rural Alabama, where his family endured considerable hardship until they became established. Moderately well educated for his day, he taught school for a time, read law and was admitted to the Alabama bar shortly before he turned 20. Marrying, Travis practiced law and published a little newspaper, while attempting to make useful political connections, joining the militia and becoming a Mason. In 1831 Travis abandoned his wife, then pregnant with their second child in as many years, and headed for Texas. His reasons for doing so are unclear. Boredom and ambition have been suggested, but in his family the oral tradition is that he killed a man who had made advances towards his wife.

Settling in Nacogdoches, "Buck" Travis soon acquired a considerable reputation as a lawyer, fashion-plate, gambler, and womanizer (he meticulously recorded his many "conquests"—most of whom appear to have been prostitutes or slaves—in his diary, along with a detailed account of the progress of his various venereal conditions). And he quickly became involved in the separatist movement, being involved in the 1832 "Anahuac War" and playing a leading role in the events which led to the final break between Texas and the central government. On the outbreak of the Texas Revolution, Travis was commissioned a lieutenant colonel in the then virtually non-existent Texas "Cavalry Corps" and sent to command the Alamo, a feat which he accomplished with some dignity, dying heroically.

Travis was a big man, about six feet tall and around 175 pounds, good looking and well proportioned; an intense, almost fanatical young man with an urge to greatness, though with little qualifications for it.

Travis agreed, exulting in his triumph. His elation did not last long, however.

Much to his astonishment, Travis' feat of arms did not go over well with the bulk of the American settlers in Texas. When he brought his prisoners to Harrisburg and later San Felipe, he found a very cold welcome; indeed, it was Tenorio who was lionized by most of the settlers. Moreover, on 17 July a meeting of prominent Texians held at San Felipe de Austin, roundly condemned Travis' actions at Anahuac. But Travis' fortunes were soon to change. When word of Travis' feat reached Cos, the latter ordered his immediate arrest, along with that of a number of other men, including the liberal Zavala, who had taken no part in the Anahuac affair. Opinions about Travis promptly turned favorable, as Texians feared Cos was about to impose martial law. With memories of the recent bloody treatment which Santa Anna had inflicted on Zacatecas still fresh, Texians, began to consider collective action. Some settler communities began to organizes committees of safety, on the model of those organized in the Thirteen Colonies on the eve of the American Revolution. On 20 August the Columbia committee of safety proposed that representatives of all communities meet in a Consultation at San Felipe in October. Meanwhile, some bolder souls began collecting arms, while others circulated appeals for aid among acquaintances in the United States. Texas hovered on the brink of open rebellion. All that was need was a spark. And that spark was provided by Stephen F. Austin.

Austin was released from his Mexico City jail cell on 13 July 1835, in a general amnesty proclaimed by Santa Anna as a good will gesture. Ill and weakened by his two year imprisonment, Austin immediately took ship for New Orleans. From there he sailed to Texas, arriving at Velasco aboard the armed schooner *San Felipe* on 2 September, having barely escaped recapture by the Mexican armed transport *Correo de Mejico*. Austin was a changed man, and a dying one, having apparently acquired tuberculosis while in his Mexican jail cell. After preaching conciliation and cooperation for more than a dozen years, Austin, the most widely respected man in Texas, issued a call to arms. Openly declaring that a peaceful solution to the issues which divided Texas and Mexico was no longer possible, he urged the annexation of Texas by the United States and called upon Americans to come to the aid of their kinsmen. Even as Cos landed at Copano Bay with a column of 400 reinforcements for the garrison at San Antonio, Austin declared, "Every man in Texas is called upon to take up arms in defence of his country and his rights," adding, "War is our only recourse...war in full!"

CHAPTER II

The Outbreak of the Texas Revolution

September-December 1835

Austin's call to arms was greeted with considerable unanimity by all Texians, Mexican and American alike. Even those most committed to cooperation with the government of Mexico were moved by his appeal. After all, if Austin, the man most committed to cooperation, had decided such a policy was no longer possible, there seemed little choice but to resort to arms. People had already begun collecting weapons, and now towns and villages began organizing militia companies. Arrangements were made for a Consultation to be held in October to decide on further action. Despite the Anahuac incident, an open break with Mexico had yet to occur. Not even secession from Mexico was inevitable. To be sure, the people of Texas were clearly at odds with the government of Santa Anna, but this was no different from the resistance offered to his dictatorship from Zacatecas or Yucatan. However, given that most of the people in Texas were American settlers, after Austin's "War is our only recourse...war in full," secession from Mexico was only a matter of time. Meanwhile an uneasy peace prevailed in Texas, needing only a spark to ignite an open rebellion. That spark was not long in coming.

Aware that most Texians were preparing for war, Col. Domingo de Ugartechea, who was now commanding at San Antonio, decided that a show of force was in order. In 1831 the little town of Gonzales, about 60 miles east of San Antonio, had been given a small cannon, a light infantry gun, for use in the event of an Indian attack. The old piece, which had been captured during the Guttierez de Lara expedition in 1814, had been badly repaired after being spiked, and did not even have a proper carriage. Although it could make a useful noise which might perhaps frighten off some Indians, the piece was of little real military value. Despite this, for some reason Ugartechea decided that he should seize the Gonzales cannon.

Late in September, Ugartechea dispatched a detachment of about 80 cavalrymen under Capt. Francisco Castañeda from San Antonio with the object of repossessing the Gonzales cannon. Word of the approaching column somehow reached Gonzales. As a result, the *alcalde*, Andrew Ponton, was able to send for help, while dispatching the women and children into hiding, mobilizing the available men, all 18 of them, and burying the gun. When Castañeda arrived on 30 September, he found Ponton's men strongly positioned at the only practicable ford across the Rio Guadalupe. Castañeda sent a patrol to essay a crossing of the ford. The Texians opened fire and a bloodless skirmish ensued. The Mexicans hastily withdrew. Castañeda called off his column, camping nearby for the night.

Alerted by Ponton's messenger, men from the surrounding countryside reached Gonzales, so that by the afternoon of 1 October Texian strength had risen to about 150, including William B. Travis and James W. Fannin, a West Point drop out. The group was armed with a hodge podge of small arms, mostly hunting muskets, buffalo guns, shot guns, and fowling pieces, with a few old military muskets and even a couple of rifles; there was not a bayonet in the bunch, but most of the men carried a hunting knife, often a large bowie. The men elected officers, choosing as their colonel John W. Moore, who had come to Texas in 1821 as one of Austin's original 300 settlers, and making Fannin a lieutenant. Then they decided to carry the war to the enemy. The little cannon was dug up, crudely mounted on some wheels made from a couple of slices of tree trunk, and entrusted to Almeron Dickinson, a blacksmith and former artilleryman in the U.S. Army. Meanwhile, Castañeda essayed a reconnaissance from the southwestern side of the Guadalupe. Observing the Texians gathering at Gonzales in some strength, he pulled his troopers back to a position at another ford some seven miles to the north, to await developments and a reply to a message which he had dispatched to San Antonio. Castañeda's brief appearance sparked the settlers to action. Towards evening the little army marched off, with a couple of yoke of oxen struggling to drag the Gonzales gun. Years later Creed Taylor, one of the men who marched that day, would recall, "...Our little army was organized for fighting, but nothing else. We had no commissary, no quartermaster, no medical corps,...no baggage train and not even a flag." This last was soon corrected by two local women, Sarah Seeley and Evaline DeWitt, who made one out of a piece of white cloth allegedly cut from the latter's wedding dress, on which they painted a crude cannon under a single star, with the words "Come and Take It."

The settlers marched for several hours through the night. Before dawn on 2 October they had located the Mexican camp, aided by the fact that Castañeda had neglected to establish a picket line. Although some men demanded an immediate attack, cooler heads prevailed and it was decided to wait until dawn. Sunrise brought a thick fog rising from the river. Despite this, it was possible to observe the Mexican positions. Moore deployed his men on a rough line on both sides of the "Come and Take It" flag and the little gun itself. Once everyone was in position, an advance was ordered. The little army moved clumsily forward through the fog until about 350 yards from the Mexican camp and halted. Dickinson then fired the cannon. Thus rather rudely alerted to the presence of the American settlers, Castañeda immediately put his men into defensive positions and called for a parley.

Castañeda and Moore conferred on horseback in a convenient field. In the elaborately polite style of the day, the Mexican officer inquired as to why the settlers were poised to attack him, receiving in return a rambling address about human rights and the Constitution of 1824, and an invitation to join in the rebellion against Santa Anna's tyranny. Brave enough, though an inept commander, Castañeda spurned the invitation, observing that he had orders to confiscate the cannon and if unable to do so to await further instructions. The Texian countered that Castañeda had but two options, to surrender immediately or to fight, to which the latter once again replied that he had his orders. The two then parted.

As he reached his own lines, Col. Moore waved his hat and cried, "Charge 'em, boys, and give 'em hell." As Dickinson loosed a round at the Mexicans, traditionally "The First Shot of the Texas Revolution," the Texian infantry sprang forward. One or two artillery rounds more followed, as the infantry raced across the intervening ground, most halting once or twice to fire their muskets. The battle was over almost as soon as it began. In less than five minutes, even before the charging Texians had reached their line, the Mexicans, having gotten off a few rounds for honor's sake, fled after taking several casualties, including one or two dead. Deciding that discretion was the better part of valor, Castañeda joined his men in flight, leaving the field to the victorious Texians, who had suffered one man slightly injured. Gathering up considerable booty, for the Mexican troops had abandoned virtually all of their baggage and camp gear, the Texians marched back to Gonzales, reaching it by noon. As Castañeda rallied his men some miles to the west and set out for San Antonio, the victorious Texians held an enormous party at Gonzales, which lasted well into the night. It seemed an auspicious beginning for the Texas Revolution.

Over the next few days several hundred more settlers gathered at Gonzales. Shortly a column of about 50 Texians under

Capt. James Collingsworth marched on Goliad, some 60 miles to the south, the "Come and Take It Gun" in tow. After a brief skirmish on 9 October, the Texians accepted the surrender of the 40 man garrison under Francisco Sandoval, a captain who had been given the temporary rank of lieutenant colonel so that he could command the post. While the captive Mexican troops were paroled and sent on their way to San Antonio, the Texians contemplated their booty: several hundred stand of arms, several dozen lances, about 100 cannon balls for a 4-pounder, though no guns, a considerable store of powder, and some horse furniture, a haul estimated to be worth about $10,000. Coming as it did within days of the news of the Texian victory over Castañeda's cavalrymen, word of the fall of Goliad gave the revolution an enormous boost, and still more volunteers poured in, so that shortly there were in excess of 500 men concentrated at Goliad. Austin arrived and was elected "General of the Army of the People" on 11 October, while James Bowie was made a lieutenant colonel. Almost immediately the overconfident horde demanded to be led into action against the stronghold of Mexican power in Mexico, San Antonio, nearly 100 miles to the northwest. And on 13 October, to cries of "On to San Antonio!" Austin put his army on the march.

The untrained army had no discipline, little organization, and no logistical arrangements. Men came and went as they pleased, wandering off when hungry or bored, drifting back when inclined. There were perhaps 1000 Mexican troops in the vicinity of San Antonio, mostly presidiales plus one good regular battalion, the *Matamoros*, newly arrived with Juan Perfecto Cos. Had Cos acted decisively, marching out to meet the Texians, he would almost certainly have swept them from the field with his battle tested, well-trained men, particularly his cavalry. But Cos' military talents were limited to the fact that he was political boss of Tehuantepec and Santa Anna's brother-in-law. So he did little other than to send out occasional patrols.

On the misty morning of 28 October, the Texian advanced

guard, some 90 mounted men under Lt. Col. James Bowie, ran into one of Cos' patrols not two miles from San Antonio near Mission Concepcion. A hot, running fight ensued as the Texians fell back, pursued by the stronger Mexican force, by some estimates as many as 400 men but actually only about 230. Taking advantage of a steeply banked gully, Bowie dismounted his men and deployed then under cover. Supported by the fire of a light cannon, the Mexican cavalry made three charges, each time being beaten off with some loss. Displaying considerable skill for an amateur soldier, Bowie kept his men well in hand, ordering them to maintain their cover and conserve ammunition. Finally, after about 30 minutes, with many men dead or wounded, the Mexican commander decided that he'd had enough. As the Mexican cavalrymen drew off, Bowie hastily mounted his men and led them in pursuit. Harrying the flying enemy closely, the Texians were able to overrun the Mexican cannon. As someone pressed the captured gun into use against its erstwhile owners, the balance of Bowie's command pursued the retiring Mexicans right up to the town before drawing off. The battle had been a one-sided Texian victory, perhaps 50 or 60 Mexicans had been killed or mortally wounded, against only one man dead and a handful wounded on the Texian side. As the Texians tended the wounded, they learned that the injured Mexicans assumed they would be slaughtered, as was the custom in Mexico's internal conflicts. Assuring their prisoners otherwise, the Texians rendered what aid they could and eventually sent the survivors back to their own lines.

On 1 November the balance of the Texian army arrived before San Antonio de Bexar, a "compact little town dominated by a church dome, lying in a fertile valley watered by ever-flowing springs." Over the next few days Austin imposed a blockade on San Antonio and the Alamo, to its north. Given the small numbers and lack of discipline of his men, the investment was by no means a tight one. As a result, Cos was reinforced by various contingents which managed to pass through the Texian lines, including a column of con-

James Bowie

Even in life, Jim Bowie (1786-1836) was one of the legendary characters of the American frontier. Born in Georgia, he was only six when his formidable parents—his father was once jailed for killing a man and his mother promptly broke him out of jail with the help of a slave—removed to Louisiana, then still in French hands. A wild, untutored youth gained him an early reputation and, somehow, a rather eclectic education. With his brothers, Rezin, alleged designer of the knife which he was to make famous, and John, Bowie made a fortune as a slave smuggler, land swindler, and fence for the notorious pirate—and hero of the Battle of New Orleans—Jean Lafitte, while finding time to take part in James Long's quasi-republican filibustering expedition in eastern Mexico in 1821. Then, in 1828, broke and having found his former stomping grounds grown too hot for him, he moved to Texas, settling in San Antonio.

The apparently rich and gentlemanly American was soon mixing with the elite of *Tejano* society. Converting to Catholicism, in 1831 Bowie married Ursula de Veramendi, a daughter of the lieutenant governor of Texas. Acquiring Mexican citizenship, Bowie shortly gained control of some 750,000 acres, through land grants and purchases. For the next few years Bowie was more or less a model citizen, involved in prospecting and land development schemes, none of which bore much fruit. Then, in 1833 his wife and his in-laws, and, if legend contains truth, his two children, died suddenly, during a cholera epidemic. Despite a hostile tradition to the contrary, this turn of events seems to have greatly disturbed Bowie, although it did not prevent him from becoming involved in a dispute with some of his Veramendi relatives, a dispute which does not seem to have disrupted his relationship with most of his former wife's surviving kin. When the Mexican Army marched up to San Antonio Bowie made sure his two sisters-in-law were safely ensconced in the Alamo.

As tensions rose between the American settlers and the Mexican government, Bowie quite naturally took the side of the former, and was commissioned a colonel at the outbreak of the Texas Revolution. At the Alamo, Bowie at first disputed command with Travis, but soon became too ill to do more than keep to his bed, where he met his end.

scripts, who arrived on the 6th under Col. Domingo Ugartechea, bringing his total strength up to perhaps 1400 or 1500 men. Despite his superior resources, including fairly well stocked magazines and between 50 percent and 100 percent more troops than his investors, Cos maintained a strictly defensive posture, thereby forfeiting the initiative and making his eventual surrender a certainty. Both armies settled down and, aside from an occasional exchange of fire resulting in some casualties to each side, did nothing. Boredom became the principal enemy. Days turned into weeks. Desertion became a problem in the Texian ranks. Meanwhile the Texians began putting together some political machinery to supervise their activities.

On 3 November, the Consultation which had been in the works since early September was finally held at San Felipe de Austin. Some radicals demanded an immediate declaration of independence, but clearer heads prevailed. Stephen Austin and Sam Houston, the most prominent men in Texas, both pointed out that such a course would alienate liberal Mexico and the many *Tejanos* who had joined the rebellion. In the end, citing their loyalty to the Mexican Constitution of 1824 the delegates to the Consultation established a provisional government for a proposed state of Texas within the Mexican Republic. A prominent settler, Henry Smith, was elected as provisional Governor and a council was created to serve as a legislature. Steps were taken to create a regular army, Houston being designated commander. A navy was established, a bond issue authorized, and appeals were made for volunteers, with generous land grants as a reward for service. Most importantly, diplomatic missions were undertaken to the United States. With its work done, the Consultation adjourned on 14 November, intending to reconvene at Washington-on-the-Brazos on 1 March. Although a remarkable amount had been accomplished in short time, the work of the Consultation was seriously flawed: the powers, responsibilities, and interrelationship between the governor and the Council were not properly defined. Consequently, a great deal of confusion resulted, some of it with tragic results.

While the delegates at San Felipe politicked, the blockade of San Antonio continued. Men grew restless. Some drifted off for home, while others took their places. On the 25th, Col. Edward Burleson, a land speculator, was elected to assume command since Austin had been asked by the Consultation to undertake a diplomatic mission to the United States, with Col. Francis Johnson, another land speculator, as his second-in-command. The tedium of the blockade was from time to time broken by some skirmishing, as Texian or Mexican sentries, spooked or merely bored, cut loose with a few rounds, setting off brief, but mostly bloodless firefights. Then too, there were regular artillery duels, also without much bloodshed on either side. On one occasion there occurred a famous feat of marksmanship. When the "1st Company of New Orleans Greys" arrived on 21 November, they entered into a friendly contest with their comrades of "2nd Company of New Orleans Greys," who had arrived about a fortnight earlier, vying to see who were the better marksmen with a couple of 4-pounders, with a good deal of money and other items being wagered. One man lost 100 ready-made rounds of ammunition, representing a considerable investment in time. When another man lost a brace of excellent pistols to him, the famed scout Erastus "Deaf" Smith made the sporting reply, "I will take shot also," pledging to return the pistols if he missed. Smith's round scored square.

On another occasion a contingent of these same New Orleans Greys found themselves engaged in a fire fight with some Mexican outposts on the fringes of the town. Several of the more intrepid volunteers pressed forward, to find that the Mexican pickets fell back. So they pressed on, followed by virtually their entire company. Shortly the Greys found themselves actually inside San Antonio. While the volunteers were having a grand time shooting off their muskets and plundering edibles from nearby houses, Cos got wind of their doings and prepared a response. He ordered his artillery to take the intruders under fire, while collecting some infantry to make a counterattack. As the Greys fled from the town under a shower of cannon balls the Mexican infantry came up behind them. Were it not for some quick thinking by Deaf

Erastus "Deaf" Smith

Erastus "Deaf" Smith (1787-1837) was born in Dutchess County, New York, the son of a Revolutionary War veteran. In 1798 Smith was taken to what would eventually become Mississippi, then largely untamed and unsettled, where he became a skilled frontiersman and scout. Smith settled in San Antonio in 1821, where he married Guadalupe Ruiz de Duran, with whom he had several children, whose descendants still reside in Texas. As a result of his long residence in Texas, Smith proved enormously valuable to the Revolutionary cause, becoming Sam Houston's most trusted scout and a very successful spy. It was to Smith that the former entrusted the difficult and dangerous task of destroying Vince's Bridge on the eve of San Jacinto, in order to prevent the retreat of the Mexican Army. This feat was arguably as important in deciding the outcome of the war as was the Battle of San Jacinto, in which Smith fought, since it prevented Santa Anna from escaping to join the other Mexican forces in the vicinity that were as yet undefeated.

After the war Smith was entrusted with various important duties, his last service to the young Republic of Texas being command of a detachment of rangers which defeated a Mexican incursion at Laredo on 17 February 1837. He died shortly afterwards. When it was determined that Smith had died virtually penniless, the virtually insolvent Republic managed to settle a pension of $500.00 a year on his widow, a considerable sum at the time.

Smith was one of the more remarkable of the many unusual people who took part in the War for Texas. Hard of hearing from childhood—hence his nickname "Deaf," pronounced "deef"—Smith's deafness increased as he grew older and he was eventually unable to carry on anything but a face-to-face conversation. Nevertheless, despite what ought to have been a debilitating handicap, Smith could speak Spanish fluently and was an unusually accomplished scout, even in an age when such skills were relatively common.

Smith the results might have been bad for the Greys. Mounting his horse and taking up a Mexican flag, Smith hastily collected some men and led them to support the fleeing Greys. Seeing these reinforcements, the Mexican infantry fell back into the town.

Those lucky enough to own a horse had somewhat better prospects of avoiding boredom, as the army needed food and foraging expeditions were necessary. During one of these Travis and Deaf Smith managed to round up some 300 horses and mules. The only major engagement took place on 26 November.

Several days earlier, aided by the casualness with which the Texians were maintaining their investment of San Antonio, Cos had managed to send out a column of about 100 cavalry escorting a number of mules, for the purpose of gathering fodder for his increasingly hungry horses. Having completed their mission, the column was returning to San Antonio on the 26th. Patrolling south of San Antonio, Deaf Smith spied the mule train making its way towards the town. Aided by rumors that the mules carried Cos' pay chests, Jim Bowie quickly collected some 60 or so mounted volunteers and rode off to intercept the Mexican pack train, which was escorted by about 100 cavalrymen. Bowie encountered the Mexicans a few miles south of San Antonio. A fast moving, furious running fight resulted. Although the Mexicans succeeded in getting many of their mules into the town, they took enormous losses, perhaps 50 men killed or wounded while inflicting only some minor injuries to two of the Texians. Although the Texians found no gold, their victory— "The Grass Fight"—was nevertheless a cause for joy, bringing a welcome respite from the boredom.

Meanwhile, grumbles about inactivity grew louder. By the end of November many of the Texas men, who had been with the army from the start, including Travis, had gone home for the winter. The army now included a considerable number of newly arrived volunteers, such as the New Orleans Greys. These men had not enlisted for a long war. They wanted glorious action and a quick victory, so that they could take up the land grants promised them upon volunteering. They demanded action. Burleson managed to keep things calm for a while, but something had to be done soon. The problem was to decide upon a proper course of action. Sam Houston, the most experienced soldier among the Texians, urged that the blockade be abandoned and the army pull back to the more heavily Americanized regions of eastern Texas, where it could gather strength while guerrillas sapped that of the Mexican Army. Others, most notably Col. James Grant, a Scot with no ties whatsoever to Texas but extensive holdings in Coahuila, urged that the siege be abandoned in favor of an expedition to capture Matamoros, over 300 miles away across a virtual desert, on the south side of the Rio Grande. Most, however, agreed with Deaf Smith that the best course was an immediate assault on San Antonio. There were a number of reasons to believe that the town might fall quickly. The ease with which the New Orleans Greys had broken into the town some days earlier suggested that Cos was not holding it by strength. Then a Mexican officer-deserter and several Americans managed to slip out of San Antonio, bringing news that the garrison was very demoralized. Considering the alternatives, Burleson decided to attempt an assault on 4 December. However, fearing that the Mexicans had gotten wind of his preparations, at the last minute Burleson changed his mind. Dispirited, Burleson decided that the only thing to do was to order the army to retire to Gonzales. When Burelson informed his principal subordinates, several of them balked. Angrily stepping out of Burelson's tent, Col. Ben Milam, a resident of Texas since 1818, informed the troops of their commander's decision A near-riot broke out.

Clamoring that they had not come to Texas to run away, the army mutinied. Taking a musket, Milam used its butt to draw a line in the sandy soil, waved his hat in the air and called out, "Boys! Who will go with old Ben Milam into San Antonio?" When hundreds of men cried out, "I will!" Milam pointed to his line and said, "If you're going with me, get on this side." An estimated 300 men stepped across the line to stand beside him. Helpless, Burleson was forced to agree to support an attack on San Antonio by Milam's volunteers, and urged those who had not stepped across the line to remain in camp, constituting a reserve under his direct command. Many did so. Meanwhile, Milam, who was supported by Frank Johnson, Burleson's second-in-command, ordered his volunteers to get some rest and be ready for a predawn attack. During the night, which was bitterly cold, some men had second thoughts. As a result, when the men were awakened at 2:00 a.m., there were only about 210 of them. Undaunted, Milam deployed his men for the attack. Most of his men he positioned so that they could directly assault the town. He posted the balance so that they could keep the Alamo under fire, thereby pinning down a sizable proportion of Cos' garrison. It was these men who began the attack at 3:00 a.m. on 5 December, opening up an energetic harassing fire. This drew Cos' attention away from the town proper. As a result, Milam's main body was able to deploy quite close to the Mexican outposts on the fringes of San Antonio, while Cos entertained all and sundry with an enormous expenditure of gunpowder from the Alamo's cannon.

Milam's first assault rapidly scattered Cos' outposts, and his men quickly occupied the outer fringes of the town. Furious house-to-house fighting began. It was a difficult fight, as the troops on both sides worked their way from room to room, the Texians generally advancing and the Mexicans generally retiring. As is the nature of such combat, there were several instances in which men came under "friendly fire." Gradually the Texians forced the defenders back, despite a shortage of drinking water and food. Although untrained, Milam had good soldierly instincts. By rotating tired men into reserve and bringing up fresh ones, he was able to maintain the pressure both day and night, a practice that Cos would have been wise to emulate. Much of the fighting was sniper work, as each side tried to pick off careless men among their foes.

The focus of the Mexican defense was the Church of San Fernando. Its tower, which dominated the town, served as both an observation post and an artillery battery, a couple of small cannon having been painfully hoisted to the top. Mexican officers could thus observe Texian movements for miles around, and direct fire at targets as they presented themselves. Unless the tower was taken, the town could not be secured. But the tower could not be taken unless the Texians gained a foothold on the town's central plaza, which was surrounded by the best houses in San Antonio, the stout residences of the town's wealthiest families. Defended by Mexican troops, these stone buildings were rather impervious to Texian artillery fire. In contrast, the Texians were occupying the less sturdy adobe houses which surrounded those abutting on the plaza. These the Mexican artillery was slowly shooting to pieces.

At about noon on 7 December Henry W. Karnes, a Tennessean and an old scouting partner of Deaf Smith, proposed storming the rear of one of the principal buildings fronting on the plaza. Some men objected, noting that Mexican infantrymen with their muskets—*escopetas*—were sheltered behind every window and behind the parapet of the roof. Karnes replied "Damn the Mexicans and their *escopetas*," and observed that they might as well retreat if they failed to take the house. Then, hefting a crowbar in one hand and his musket in the other, he shouted, "You men do as I tell you," and charged across the street, dodging a rain of Mexican fire to take shelter under the walls, where the Mexican infantrymen could not fire upon him without exposing themselves to fire from the Texians. Using his crowbar, Karnes battered his way into the building, apparently taking advantage of a sealed door, which offered less resistance than did the stone walls. As he did so his comrades charged across the street and followed him into the house. While Karnes and his mates poured into the house, most of the Mexicans holding it were able to bolt out of a rear door. Some, however, were taken. Since there were not enough men to guard the prisoners, and no one had the heart to shoot them out of hand, each man was paroled, under oath to fight no more until formally exchanged; trusting more in the prisoners' faith than in their word, the Texians ensured that the oath sworn was a heavily religious one.

Karnes' innovative use of a crowbar led to the adoption of new tactics by the attacking Texians. Rather than move across streets and through doors, they began to batter their way through walls. Over the next two days the attackers burrowed through dozens of walls. Effecting a breach, they would fire a volley or two through the opening and then, enlarging it, pour into the room. It was a remarkably effective technique. It was slow work, but it proceeded at a steady pace, and was much safer than the alternative, taking to the streets. It was also less dangerous to the numerous civilians, particularly women and children, who were sheltering in many of the houses; none appear to have been deliberately harmed by the attacking Texians, who were more than willing to appropriate whatever food they had before sending them back through the buildings to the rear, along with any prisoners, who were then paroled.

Gradually the Texians bored their way through the finest houses in San Antonio, that of the Navarro family, that of Bowie's in-laws, the Veramendis, which the Mexicans defended with considerable ferocity, and atop which Deaf Smith was wounded.

Mexican morale, already low, began to crack as they were pushed back relentlessly. On 8 December, Ben Milam fell, standing with Frank Johnson and Henry Karnes, in an exposed position near the Veramendi house. Taking advantage of a lull in the fighting , he had been trying to observe the church tower with a field telescope given him by Stephen Austin, when, as Creed Taylor observed, suddenly "a shot rang out and Milam fell, the ball piercing his head." Although they immediately elected his friend Frank Johnson to command them, the loss of Milam resulted in some confusion among the Texians. However, it did little to dampen the pressure which they exerted upon the defenders, their confidence in victory enhanced as prisoners told of the increasingly desperate situation of the Mexican garrison. They somehow managed to drag a 12-pounder through one series of tunneled-through rooms. Using this they fired a few rounds into the church, smashing the roof in. Taking the warning, the Mexicans in the tower quit their harassing fire.

That same day Cos pulled his outposts into the Alamo, abandoning the defense of San Antonio. In the process, 185 men deserted, many led by their officers, the hapless Cos apparently having so lost control of the situation that he was unable to stop them.

Cos' situation steadily deteriorated. As the Texians pressed their attack, he found himself with over 1,100 troops, many of them ill-trained conscripts, as well as hundreds of camp followers penned into the Alamo, an area of about two acres, with food and ammunition supplies dwindling. On the night of the 8th there was a riot by many of the non-combatants, during which Cos himself was manhandled before order could be restored. Deciding that the game was up, at dawn on 9 December Cos ordered a white flag displayed and sent a party of three officers and a bugler to parley with the besiegers. As the guns on both sides fell silent, Johnson met with Mexican *parlementaires* for some tough bargaining. Negotiations dragged on for twenty hours before an agreement was signed. The terms finally agreed upon were simple. Cos would be permitted to withdraw his troops across the Rio Grande upon their pledge to support the Constitution of 1824 and not to bear arms in Texas again. All Mexican troops were permitted to retain their private property, and officers their personal arms as well, but all public property and arms—some 500 muskets and 21 pieces of artillery, plus powder and shot—were to be surrendered save what was deemed necessary to permit the army to retire in safety. Since a number of the men who formed the original garrison of San Antonio were local *Tejanos* with some sympathies for the rebels, the Texians insisted that any of Cos' men who chose to could remain behind, save only those conscripts with prison records. Although the Texians offered to provide supplies to sustain his men through their retreat, Cos replied that "The Mexican Army neither receives nor needs anything provided by its enemies," a haughty response which would cause considerable suffering among his troops during their long march south. On the morning of 11 December Cos surrendered his

James Walker Fannin

James Walker Fannin (1804-1836) was the illegitimate offspring of Dr. Isham Fannin, a Georgia physician and planter, and an erring young woman of "good" family. Raised by his maternal grandfather, who adopted him as "James Fannin Walker," the young man went to West Point in 1819. Apparently finding the academic and military rigors of the academy not to his liking, he ran away in 1821, at a time when he stood 60th in a class of 86. Changing his name to "James Walker Fannin," he settled in Georgia, where he eventually married. With financial help from some friends, in 1834, he took his wife and two infant children to Velasco, Texas. In Texas, Fannin quickly prospered as a land speculator and slave trader. It was said that his slaves all had "Congo" accents, which was a sly way of saying that he was engaged in smuggling slaves from Africa, a practice by then illegal under international, American, and Mexican law. On one voyage from Cuba, Fannin brought in 153 unfortunates. Mean-while, he became prominent among the leaders of the "War Party," and spent part of the winter of 1834-1835 in the United States, drumming up support for an independent Texas.

Fannin took part in several of the earliest actions of the War for Independence, including the skirmish at Gonzales on 2 October 1835, that at Concepcion on the 28th, and the capture of San Antonio in December. After the fall of San Antonio, Fannin, by then a colonel, was placed in command of an "army" massing at Goliad with the object of invading Mexico and occupying Matamoros. This operation proved abortive. However, it was upon Fannin and his army, perhaps 400-450 men at its maximum strength, that Travis relied for relief of the Alamo. Fannin, however, was an indecisive, if brave and even inspiring commander. As a result, not only did the Alamo fall, but Fannin seriously bungled his withdrawal from Goliad, with the result that his entire command was destroyed.

army, reduced to 1,105 men, the balance, some 300-400 men, having deserted or been killed. A few days later the Mexican Army marched south, and the Texians, having already occupied all of San Antonio, moved into the Alamo.

The capture of San Antonio was a major victory for the Texians, and won at relatively little cost, no more than about 20 or 30 men having been killed. It was also a decisive victory, for it marked the final extirpation of Mexican authority in Texas. During the weeks since the Texians had marched up to invest the town, Mexican garrisons all over Texas had surrendered, mostly without a fight, save at Lipantitlan, a small coastal outpost, where there had been a hot little skirmish on 9 November. As a result, Texas was free. In all that vast region, there was not one Mexican soldier under arms. Moreover, with winter coming there would be little to fear from Mexico for many months.

CHAPTER III

Through the Winter

December 1835-February 1836

The fall of San Antonio marked not only the liberation of Texas but also the dissolution of the Texian army. Most native Texians soon drifted off to winter with their families. In a very short time, there were no more than 800 men under arms altogether, most newly arrived volunteers from the United States, garrisoned primarily at San Antonio and Goliad. Texian military power had effectively evaporated. Things were not much more coherent on the political front, either.

The provisional government which had been established at the Consultation in November had initially seemed to be working well. Governor Smith and the Council began conducting business on a regular basis. However, a society of individualists soon found difficult the management of its day-to-day affairs. Early in December the Council was briefed by the distinguished Mexican liberals Lorenzo de Zavala and Brig. Gen. Jose Antonio Mexia on a plan supported by former Acting President Valentin Gomez Farias, then living in New Orleans, for an expedition to Matamoros to raise Northern Mexico against Santa Anna. Impressed, the Council voted to support the undertaking. The very next day Governor Smith vetoed the measure, saying "I consider it a bad policy to trust Mexicans." On the 10th the Council overrode Smith's veto, authorizing the expedition and instructing Mexia to go to San Antonio. This, of course, exacerbated relations between the Council and Governor. Then Mexia decided to withdraw from the venture. Undaunted, and with news of the fall of San Antonio freshly arrived, the Council decided to proceed with the expedition anyway, and issued instructions to this effect to Sam Houston, commander-in-chief of the Texas Army. Houston had other ideas about how the war should be run. He believed that the best course was for the Texians to withdraw eastwards, into the more densely populated areas of Texas, and conduct a guerrilla campaign. So although on 17 December he ordered Col. James Bowie to organize an expedition to Matamoros, he expressed no urgency over the matter. This quickly came to the attention of the Council, and on Christmas Day it asked Governor Smith to press Houston to expedite the venture. As Smith was opposed to the undertaking, he refused to do so. So on 6 January the Council went over both Smith and Houston and ordered Col. Frank Johnson, commanding the Volunteer Army at San Antonio, to concentrate an army at Goliad and march on Matamoros. However, on the 7th Governor Smith managed to convince Johnson that the expedition was a bad idea, so the Council stripped him of his command and named Col. James W. Fannin to command the expedition. The next day Johnson once again changed his mind, so the Council restored him to command, neglecting to remove Fannin in the process.

When Smith protested the Council's continuing interference in his prerogatives as chief executive, he was promptly impeached and removed from office, although there was no provision for such an action in the articles establishing the Council. Nevertheless, Lieutenant-Governor James Robinson was authorized to assume the governorship. However, it soon became evident that Smith was not inclined to give up the job. He refused to surrender various documents and the newly carved official seal which had been entrusted to him, threatened to "shoot any son of a bitch" who tried to take them from him, and dissolved the "damned corrupt Council." An armed clash might well have developed over the matter were it not for the fact that, upon voting to unseat Smith, the Council had gone home, there being no sittings after 16 January. So Smith continued in office, and some rare people even obeyed his instructions, such as Lt. Col. William Barrett Travis, whom he sent to command San Antonio.

Aside from the political chaos which all of this back-biting produced, the military effects were disastrous. The army was virtually in dissolution, with little more than 100 men at San Antonio, and another 500 or so—the Matamoros Expeditionary Force—at Goliad, plus some odd lots of volunteers scattered all the way back to the Sabine River, marking the border with the United States. Worse, Revolutionary forces now had four separate military commanders, each of whom had no authority over any of the others. Sam Houston, who as Major General was technically commander-in-chief, could find no one to obey him. Meanwhile, Colonels Fannin and Johnson, were both officially in command of the Matamoros expedition. Further complicating matters was the presence of Col. James Grant, a physician and land speculator from Coahuila who had recently eluded what was probably a legitimate arrest by the Mexican authorities. By going directly to the Council, Grant had managed to get himself designated the "Commander-in-Chief of Volunteers," with the authority to undertake an expedition against Matamoros. Using this, he had stripped the San Antonio area of volunteers and equipment and descended upon Goliad, from which he shortly managed to convince all of those interested in the Matamoros expedition to de camp to Refugio, where Johnson and Fannin also went, since that was where their men had gone. Although Houston managed to convince many of the men to abandon the Matamoros undertaking, it was clear that he had little influence over more recently arrived volunteers. With the situation deteriorating on an almost daily basis, Houston sent Bowie off to the Alamo with instructions to survey the situation and if he deemed it necessary, to evacuate the de-

Samuel P. Houston

Samuel P. Houston (1793-1863) was born in Virginia. In 1807, his father having died, Houston's mother took her nine children to Tennessee. Soon afterwards, young Houston ran off to join the Indians, living with the Cherokee, who called him "The Raven," for three years and who imparted to him a healthy respect for their culture and skills. Surprisingly, while among them he found the time to read widely, and was ever afterwards able to quote portions of Pope's *Iliad*. In 1812 Houston ran a school for a time, a common occupation for even mildly literate persons on the frontier. However, the following year he volunteered for service in the war with Britain, enlisting in the 7th Infantry. Houston's war experiences were entirely in what was then the southwest, Mississippi, Alabama, and West Florida, against the Creek Indians. During his five years in the army (1813-1818), Houston, a man of reckless courage and sound tactical instincts, was several times wounded, once so severely that it troubled him for the rest of his life, and was later promoted to first lieutenant, while forming lifetime friendships with Davy Crockett, already a celebrated frontiersman, and Andrew Jackson, the nation's most famous soldier. In 1818 Houston resigned his commission in the 39th Infantry rather than take part in Indian removal, a matter which does not seem to have affected his friendship with Jackson, one of the chief promoters of the policy.

Houston soon afterwards became an Indian agent among the Cherokee, while reading law. Admitted to the bar in Tennessee, he rose rapidly, not in the least due to the sponsorship of Andrew Jackson, the state's most famous son. Houston soon acquired a considerable reputation, became a major general of militia, and was elected to Congress in 1823 and again in 1825. In 1827 he was elected governor of Tennessee. Then, in January of 1829 he married the rich, attractive Eliza Allen, who was still in her teens. By the age of 34 Houston's career had been remarkable, and even greater things might well have been expected of him, for there was already talk of the presidency. But it was not to be.

After less than four months of marriage, young Eliza left the governor's mansion for her father's house. Scandal-mongers had a field day, with tales that she had a secret lover or that Houston was an abusive husband. The truth of the matter was never revealed, by either party. In the end, opinion seemed to come down on Eliza's side, and Houston was subjected to considerable abuse. He soon afterwards resigned his governorship and headed west.

Houston settled among the Cherokee in Arkansas, where they had recently been "removed." Despondent, he took to drink for a time, earning the name "Big Drunk." But then Houston "married" Tiana Rogers, a Cherokee woman—a collateral ancestor of Will Rogers—and under her influence gave up drink. Meanwhile, the pressures for Indian "removal" were again at work and in 1832 Houston went to Washington to see what his old friend Andrew Jackson, now President, could do to protect the Cherokee. In Washington he got nowhere, since Jackson was a strong backer of Indian removal. Worse, he had a violent encounter with an anti-Indian member of the House and was sentenced to a public condemnation for contempt of Congress: As the Speaker was a Jackson man, Houston's condemnation sounded more like a commendation. While Jackson was unwilling to do anything for the Cherokee, he suggested that Houston go to Texas to negotiate with various Indians who were raiding into the United States. Houston, who had recently made several trips to Texas, and had even attempted to secure funding for a venture there, took up the assignment and headed west. For the rest of his life he was closely identified with Texas.

Houston was made a major general and commander of the revolutionary army in 1835. Shortly after Texas declared its independence from Mexico—on 2 March 1836, his birthday—Houston led the revolutionary army to victory at San Jacinto (21 April 1836). Three months later he was elected President of the Republic of Texas. Houston served two terms as President of Texas (1836-1838 and 1842-1844). When Texas was admitted

to the Union—a matter which was long delayed because of its slave-holding status—Houston was elected to the United States Senate, serving until 1859, when he was elected governor of Texas, becoming the only man in American history to have been the governor of two states. But Texas had changed, and Houston had not. Over the years the original small population had been swamped by outsiders, mostly from the South. The political status of the Mexican-Texans had deteriorated tremendously, while the Old Americo-Texans had lost power to the newcomers. A strong Union man, Houston found that Texas was heavily secessionist.

Houston's years in office were difficult ones. He openly opposed secession, believing it would be a disaster for the South, and remained staunchly Unionist to the end. When, in March of 1861, he refused to endorse the Ordinance of Secession and would not take the oath of allegiance to the Confederacy, he was removed from office by means of an illegal proceeding.

Houston, a solidly built man, who stood at least 6'2", was a spectacular dresser, often appearing in gaudy, outlandish outfits, mixing Cherokee, Mexican, Arab, and European styles at a whim. A veritable lion in battle, he was also an able and astute politician and diplomat. But when he died, in 1863, he was a lonely, broken man, denied even by his sons, who were enthusiastic Confederates. Among his last words was "Texas." Houston was one of the genuine giants of American history.

fenders, artillery, and stores to Goliad and Copano, and then blow up the place. He then wisely decided to go off and negotiate a treaty with his friends the Cherokees, a task which had the dual advantages of being useful work and keeping him out of the disastrous political skirmishing which was rapidly destroying what unity Texas had.

So by the end of January of 1836, not only did Texas have no effective government, it also had no real military command. And it was shortly to face the severest possible test of its ability to survive. While the Texians were busily mismanaging their affairs, Santa Anna had been putting his in order.

Antonio Lopez de Santa Anna could never be accused of predictability. As early as September of 1835, long before Cos had begun to run into difficulties in Texas, his master had begun to consider ways to bring about the swift suppression of the insurrection in Texas. By the time his unfortunate brother-in-law had surrendered, Santa Anna's plans were fully matured. There were essentially two ways to dispatch a punitive expedition into Texas. One could go by sea, running up to one of the tiny ports along the Texas coast, or one could march overland, crossing the considerable deserts on either side of the Rio Grande and striking directly into the interior.

As many senior officers, including Minister of War and Marine Jose Maria Tornel and Maj. Gen. Vicente Filisola, pointed out, the seaborne route was the traditional and best way to send large forces into Texas. It had been used by several Spanish expeditions into Texas, the most recent in 1814, when a portion of the forces taking part in the bloody Arredondo Expedition had arrived in Texas by sea, and Cos himself had used it when he brought his reinforcements into Texas in September of 1835. This route put a minimal strain on the well-being of the army, while having the added advantage of denying use of the coast to the enemy. However, a sea-borne expedition would require time. A fleet would have to be outfitted. Moreover, such an expedition could not be undertaken in the depths of winter. Time was a commodity which Santa Anna understood perfectly. Any uprising against the central authority had to be put down quickly lest it inspire others, and the situation in Texas required particularly swift attention, before it could draw strength from the United States. So Santa Anna opted for an overland expedition.

Orders went out on 31 October for the concentration of a considerable portion of the regular army and some militia at San Luis Potosi, about a third of the way from Mexico City to the Rio Grande. But before the army could be concentrated, it had to be created and supplied. To do that required money, lots of money. And Mexico was bankrupt. Santa Anna, however, was a master at raising funds. Towns were pressed for contributions, the Church was pressured to make donations, loans were subscribed at ruinous rates of interest, 48 percent a year not being unheard of, and Santa Anna even hocked some of his own estates. Then manpower had to be secured to fill out the many units which existed in cadre, having full complements of officers and noncommissioned officers but relatively few privates. Since no one in his right mind ever volunteered, the method of recruitment was the time honored one of the press. Recruiters snatched up whomever they could find, any time and any place they could find them, swept them up in raids on the jails, cantinas, fiestas, and even churches. About 20 percent of the army, about 1100 men, came in this way. However, the balance of the army was composed of seasoned men, whether regulars, *permanentes*, or state troops, *activos*, who had been under arms for some time, and in many cases men with one or more campaigns under their belts. Gradually the army began to concentrate. By the time Cos surrendered at San Antonio, 11 December 1836, Santa Anna had some 5,300 men and 20 cannon, plus sundry camp followers, at San Luis Potosi or further north at Leona Vicario (Saltillo), as well as an additional 350 men and one cannon which were en route to Matamoros. It was a formidable feat of organizational improvisation. But it was a flawed effort. Logistical arrangements were weak, there only being sufficient rations for the troops to last about a month, while no provisions were made for officers, who were supposed to provide their own rations. Worse, although Santa Anna had

---

Vicente Filisola

Vicente Filisola (1789-1850). One of the ablest commanders in the Mexican Army, Filisola was born in Ravello, on the Amalfi coast in Italy. In 1804 he went to Spain, where he enlisted in the army, rising to sergeant by 1808, on the eve of the Napoleonic invasion. Filisola served ably and successfully, and in 1810 was made a second lieutenant, having "conducted himself with valor in more than twenty battles" in little more than two years. In 1811 he was shipped to Mexico to help put down the revolution which had broken out there in 1810. Landing in Mexico in November, Filisola's skills were quickly recognized and rewarded: he was promoted first lieutenant of light infantry in January of 1812, captain of artillery in June of 1813, and captain of grenadiers in May of 1814. Attached to Agustin Iturbide's command from early 1814, by 1821 Filisola was a lieutenant colonel commanding fully 4,000 men, the largest contingent of Royalist forces in Mexico. When Iturbide made himself Emperor in late 1821, he made Filisola a brigadier general and a knight of the *Orden de Guadalupe*, and sent him to "liberate" Central America, in the process annexing it to Mexico. By late 1822 Filisola had essentially accom-

plished his goal, with only El Salvador, which preferred being annexed by the United States than Mexico, dissenting, a matter which Filisola was well on the way to resolving by early 1823, about the time that Iturbide's future as Emperor of Mexico became uncertain.

With the fall of Iturbide inevitable, in February of 1823, Filisola convened a convention of representatives of the Central American provinces in Guatemala City, at which he promoted the independence and union of the Central American provinces.

Soon afterwards returning to Mexico, Filisola was given various important assignments, helping to consolidate the infant republican regime. During a Spanish attempt to reassert control in 1829 he was promoted to major general. In 1830 Filisola was made President of the Supreme War Council and a justice of the military appeals branch of the Supreme Court, which posts he held until January of 1833, when he was made commanding general of the eastern regions of Mexico. He shortly afterwards became ill, and retired from active service

Recalled to duty by Santa Anna in November of 1835, Filisola was Santa Anna's second-in-command during the Texas campaign. After included a field hospital in his plans, none was actually provided. Nor was the army accompanied by a single priest. Despite this, by mid-December Santa Anna, who had organ-

---

San Jacinto Filisola assumed command of the army, and obeyed his imprisoned commander's orders to withdraw from Texas, a duty which he performed correctly, but which brought him under the severest displeasure of Santa Anna and he was bitterly attacked by other officers as well, most notably the very able Brig. Gen. Jose Urrea. The principal charge was that Filisola should have disobeyed Santa Anna's orders, as being illegal because they were issued by an officer who was a prisoner-of-war. Although the legal question is rather cloudy, Filisola probably failed in his duty in this matter. One consequence of these charges was that Filisola tended towards the more liberal side of Mexican politics thereafter.

Named commanding general of Tampico and Nueva Leon, in 1837 Filisola enthusiastically opposed a coup by Urrea. In the following year he took part in repelling the French incursion in the "Pastry War," for which he was rewarded with the post of Commanding General of the Mexican Army early in 1839. In mid-1840 Filisola was forced to leave this post when he was imprisoned and subjected to a court martial concerning his activities after San Jacinto. Although the proceedings were prolonged, Filisola secured an acquittal in 1841, whereupon he retired. Recalled to

duty during the Mexican-American War, in late 1847 Filisola commanded a division with some distinction in Chihuahua. The following year he was once again named to head the Supreme War Council, in which post he died of cholera in July of 1853.

An able soldier, Filisola was one of the few honest generals in the Mexican Army, leaving a relatively modest estate upon his death. Interested in the scientific improvement of agriculture, in 1831 he secured a considerable grant in Texas, but never made any serious attempts to exploit it.

Filisola's Italian background militated against taking a serious interest in politics, and, an unsuccessful 1843 run for the Senate aside, he was one of the few apolitical officers in the Mexican Army. Filisola was probably the most professionally capable of the Mexican generals, and the campaign in Texas in 1836 might well have turned out quite differently had he been in command. A dour, unemotional man, "the least Italian of Italians," as one observer put it, Filisola was a relatively prolific author, producing an excellent two volume memoir of his role in the struggle for independence in Central America, plus a four volume work dealing with the war in Texas.

---

ized the army into two infantry divisions plus a separate cavalry brigade decided that all was in readiness and gave the order to march.

The march from San Luis Potosi to Leona Vicario, to Monclova, and then on to Laredo and the Presidio of the Rio Grande was a difficult one, nearly 500 miles across the cold desert, with chilling winds blowing down from the north. People and animals suffered terribly, particularly the women and children among the camp followers. Scores dropped out to die, but the army made remarkably good time, averaging 15 to 20 miles a day. The *First Division* moved out on 10 December, reaching Laredo on the 26th, where it effected a juncture with the remnants of Cos' command, about 500 men, who had arrived on Christmas Day. The *First Brigade* of the *Second Division* marched north on the 22nd, followed two days later by its *Second Brigade* and four days after that by the *Cavalry Brigade*. On 5 January, the *First Division* was concentrated at Laredo and the *Second Division* and the *Cavalry Brigade* at Leona Vicario. There the "Napoleon of the West" rested and resupplied his troops. Having learned of the Texian proposal to occupy Matamoros, Santa Anna decided to modify his organization. He sent the *Cuautla Permanente Cavalry Regiment* plus the *San Luis Potosi Auxiliary Cavalry Troop* and the *Bajio Auxiliary Cavalry Troop*, about 250 men, eastwards to Matamoros under the command of Col. Jose Urrea, to whom he gave a brigadier general's brevet and orders to march northwards into Texas after effecting a juncture with the *Yucatan Activo Battalion* which was then also en route to Matamoros. He then reorganized the entire army, so that the former *First Division* became the *Vanguard Brigade*, while dissolving the *Second Division*, so that the main body, the *Army of Operations Against Texas*, comprised three infantry divisions and one of cavalry, while Urrea's column was designated the *Independent Division*. Including this column, the invading force totaled perhaps 6,100 men with 21 pieces of artillery. Meanwhile, Santa Anna decided to rest his army at Leona Vicario for a few days, to prepare it for the difficult tasks ahead, the actual invasion of Texas, with its promise of hard fighting.

Amazingly, Santa Anna's energetic preparations and remarkably rapid concentration had gone completely unnoticed by the Texians, despite often highly accurate information supplied by a number of scouts. Through a combination of over confidence, contempt for their foes, a lack of trust in *Tejanos*, and simple carelessness, no real preparations whatsoever had been made for receiving an enemy offensive. To be sure, Texian representatives had been active in the United States, raising funds, encouraging volunteers, and lobbying for diplomatic assistance. By offering generous land grants to volunteers, the army had begun to grow again. At the end of January there were perhaps 1,000 men under arms, but 450-500 of them were involved in the Matamoros expedition.

The Matamoros expedition was consuming most of the slender military resources of Texas. Approximately 500-600 men were concentrated about Goliad by late January, and shortly afterwards moved southwards to Refugio. Before he departed for Cherokee country, Sam Houston had made a personal appeal to the volunteers at Refugio to abandon the ill-advised undertaking. He had some success in this endeavor, but not everyone agreed. By this time most of the men serving with the army were newcomers to Texas, many far less interested in the cause for which most Texans, both American and Mexican, had taken up arms than in the prospects of loot. Like the Alamo cursed with three commanders, Fannin, Grant, and Johnson, this expedition made little progress. Finally, after a couple of weeks during which the leaders of the expedition bickered among themselves while freezing out on the prairie, Fannin decided he'd had enough. Perhaps because of his abortive West Point career, Fannin decided that the expedition was a bad idea and decided to fall back on Goliad, which he reached on 12 February. Once ensconced at Goliad, which, between the troops he brought with him and those who had never left, was now held by some 400-450 men, Fannin resisted orders from the Council and *its* governor, Robinson, to resume movement south. Of course, there was still a Matamoros Expedition, or rather two, as colonels James Grant and Frank Johnson were still at Refugio, with about 100-150 men and delusions of grandeur between them, and they were preparing to advance towards the Rio Grande.

Meanwhile, of course, there was the Alamo. Jim Bowie and his company of 20-30 men had arrived at the Alamo in late January. The commanding officer, Lt. Col. James C. Neill, a good man, briefed him on the condition of the post, which was poor. Preparations for the Matamoros expedition had stripped the Alamo of much useful equipment. There was relatively little ammunition and including Bowie's company there were only about 115-120 men available, perhaps a sixth of the number necessary to hold the place. Worse, the walls were in terrible shape after the battering which they had received during the fight for San Antonio in December, and little had been done to repair them or to extend the works so that the mission could be converted into something more like a proper fortress. Despite this, Neill stated that he believed holding the Alamo was vital to the defense of Texas, since it covered the main overland invasion route from Mexico, and, not unimportantly, was the only settlement of consequence in the whole southern part of Texas. Neill won Bowie over to his point of view, and in a letter of 2 February explained to Governor Smith his reasons for deciding not to blow up the post, as was within his authority. He concluded by noting "The salvation of Texas depends in great measure in keeping Bejar out of the hands of the enemy," and added an appeal for more men and supplies, to bolster the defense. The very next day, Lt. Col. William B. Travis arrived, with his company of 30 cavalrymen and orders from Smith to take command of the Alamo. Travis too concurred that the Alamo must be held. But his presence created a problem; officially both he and Neill were in command, Smith having neglected to relieve the latter upon appointing Travis, but Bowie outranked them both. This awkward situation was partially relieved when Neill departed for a 25-day furlough on 13 February. Difficulties soon arose between Bowie and Travis, and between Travis and the men of the garrison, most of whom wanted no part of his notions about imposing regular discipline on them. In an election called by Travis, Bowie was overwhelmingly chosen as commander by the volunteers, leaving Travis with only his 30 or so regulars under command. In the end, the two men decided to compromise: Travis would command the cavalry, both regular and volunteer, while Bowie commanded the fortress itself, and Neill, when he returned, would be superior to both. It was a compromise that resolved little. But at least both men agreed on the need for more troops and more supplies, and both signed numerous requests for such to Governor Smith. But little was forthcoming. To be sure, even though on 8 February the 14 men of the Tennessee Mounted Rifles had turned up, led by the famous, though now 50-ish frontiersman, politician, and tall-tale teller David Crockett, the Alamo would need far more men and much more ammunition in order to attain a reasonable state of readiness, particularly as it was beginning to become clear that Santa Anna was likely to be upon them far sooner than anyone had dreamed possible.

Word of Santa Anna's movements south of the Rio Grande had begun to reach San Antonio by 11 February. That very night, at a dance held to celebrate Crockett's arrival, a message had arrived indicating that Santa Anna was approaching the Rio Grande with 13,000 troops. Travis and Bowie were both convinced of its authenticity, and concluded that it would take Santa Anna about ten days to reach San Antonio. Then, on the morning of 20 February, Blas Herrera, a cousin of Juan Seguin, one of the most prominent *Tejano* supporters of the uprising, rode up. Herrera and some other *Tejanos* had been active for some time south of San Antonio, looking out for signs of enemy activity and rendering other useful services, such as burning a bridge over the Nueces River, which delayed the Mexican advance by about two days. He now brought in some surprisingly accurate information. He had observed the Mexican Army as it crossed the Rio Grande some days earlier, and even spoken with some of the men. Herrera noted the strength of the enemy at some 5,000 men. Though some of the officers in the Alamo doubted the report, Travis was inclined to believe it, but it appears to have done little in the way of preparing for the imminent arrival of the Mexican Army beyond posting a lookout in the tower of the Church of San Fernando, and sending some more dispatches to Governor Smith. Of course, there was not much more that could be done, but he could have at least called into the

Blue Norther

In its march from Monclova to San Antonio, the Mexican Army was buffeted by two Blue Northers. Blue Norther is the name given to a very unusual weather phenomenon characteristic of the Texas plains. It is caused by an extremely strong cold front ripping southwards from Canada across the plains into Texas. Since there are no mountain ranges to moderate the winds, they tend to build up considerable velocity. The effect of the wind chill can drop the temperature 20-30 degrees in a very short time. A Blue Norther is often preceded by rain and is followed by sleet or freezing rain. When the cold air mass moving south meets moist air moving in from the Gulf, snow results, as far south as San Antonio and even on into northern Mexico, as occurred twice during the advance of the Mexican Army, once as they crossed the mountains in Coahuila and again as they crossed the Rio Grande. The temperatures can re-main low, down into the 20s Fahrenheit, for as long as two weeks, a particularly devastating situation when one considers that the temperature before the Blue Norther may well have been in the 70s or even 80s.

In his diary, William Fairfax Gray, a Virginian who went to Texas during the Revolution, wrote that a Blue Norther "...generally lasts for two or three days, and is sometimes so excessively cold that persons have been known to freeze to death in crossing the plains."

A true Blue Norther is accompanied by two unusual atmospheric phenomena. As the cold front is approaching, it is possible to observe a distinct blue line, darker than the normal color of the sky, marking the advancing edge of the cold front. In addition, the temperature drop is so drastic, that one can actually feel the foreward edge of the front passing over.

Alamo those of his troops who were housed in San Antonio, and arranged for all possible supplies to be brought into the mission/fortress as well. By this time Santa Anna's army was only about two days' march to the southwest.

After pausing for several days at Leona Vicario, on 26 January Santa Anna resumed the advance. The weather grew uglier. For the first few days, the army managed a good 15 miles daily, but troops, camp followers, and animals fell out in considerable numbers. The march was broken at Monclova, then resumed in increasingly inclement weather. A particularly fierce "Blue Norther" on 13 February deposited nearly two feet of snow. Many fell by the wayside to die unnoticed and morale sagged. But the march continued. On 15 February Brig. Gen. Joaquin Ramirez y Sesma's *Vanguard Brigade* began crossing the Rio Grande at the Presidio, an old frontier outpost. The *First Brigade* crossed on the 17th, and the *Vanguard Brigade*, having been given two days rest, was put on the road to San Antonio, 120 miles to the northeast. He planned to cover the distance in seven days, a respectable pace of somewhat more than 17 miles per day, to surprise the Texians on the morning of 22 February. Due to heavy rains and great cold he was delayed by one day, the army covering the 120 miles in a still impressive eight days, to arrive at dawn on 23 February before San Antonio de Bexar, with its garrison of some 150 or so Texians. Santa Anna had achieved almost complete surprise.

CHAPTER IV

The Defense of the Alamo

23 February-5 March 1836

Santa Anna's arrival at San Antonio on the morning of 23 February came as a virtual complete surprise to the tiny Texian garrison. Despite the fact that for some time reports had been arriving to the effect that Santa Anna was on the march, no one in Texas expected Santa Anna to campaign in the winter. As a result, the garrison was ill-prepared. Not that there was much that could be done to put the town in a state of readiness for defense. Given that there were fewer than 200 men available, any attempt to have defended San Antonio would have been foolhardy. The key to holding the town was to hold the old mission just to its north, the Alamo. Yet despite having served as a military post for some 40 years, the Alamo could hardly be called a fort. It lacked proper parapets to shelter the troops holding the walls, had no bastions to permit flanking fire to enfilade attacking enemy troops, and had a wholly impossible trace, the outer perimeter actually being much too long not only for the number of men available, but also given the amount of space which it enclosed. Under the direction of its various commanders, James C. Neill, James Bowie, and William B. Travis, a great deal of work had been accomplished by Maj. Green B. Jameson, the Chief Engineer of the Alamo, who seems to have believed that the place should have been abandoned and destroyed and a proper fort constructed, an impossible task, given the resources and time available. Despite this, considering what he had to work with, Jameson did about all that could have been done.

Where possible, rough parapets had been raised to offer some protection to men manning the walls. A log and earth palisade had been erected to close a gap in the wall on the south side of the old cemetery in front of the chapel, and a gap which had been made in the northern wall when the Texians besieged the place in December was crudely repaired. Earthen ramps were built to provide gun emplacements, so that by late February some 18 to 21 guns had been mounted, mostly along the walls, but with two mounted in the interior facing the main gate. Also inside the enclosure itself, some field works had been erected, and the interior walls of many of the bui'.:ings had been pierced, to provide passage from room to room if the main plaza was lost. To improve the water supply an old well had been reopened.

There were some problems with the arms available to the defenders. In addition to the 18-21 pieces of artillery which were actually mounted, there were several other pieces available which could not be used because they lacked proper carriage. Although there was plenty of gun powder available, albeit much of it was poor quality Mexican Army surplus, ammunition was in short supply. The garrison was to some extent able to improvise in this regard. Musket balls were made from the leading of the windows of the Alamo and some other buildings in San Antonio. Lacking a supply of canister or grape shot for the artillery, the gunners improvised anti-personnel ammunition by using pieces of scrap metal, bits of chain, and chopped up horseshoes.

While this work proceeded, the tiny garrison gradually grew. At the end of January there were only about 115 to 120 men in the Alamo. Travis' arrival on 3 February brought the total up to about 145 to 150 men. Over the next three weeks the number rose as more men arrived, including David Crockett

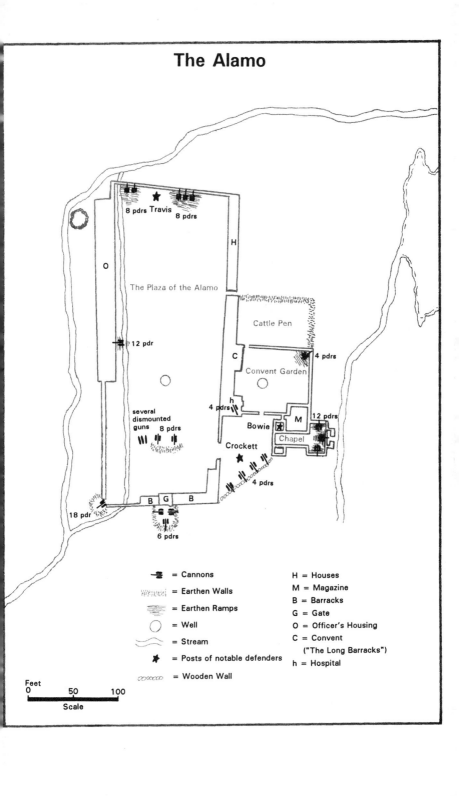

The Alamo

8 pdrs Travis 8 pdrs

H

O

The Plaza of the Alamo

Cattle Pen

12 pdr

C

Convent Garden

4 pdrs

h

4 pdrs

M

Bowie

12 pdr

Chapel

several dismounted guns 8 pdrs

Crockett

4 pdrs

B G B

18 pdr

6 pdrs

⊶ = Cannons

🌿 = Earthen Walls

= Earthen Ramps

◯ = Well

≋ = Stream

✹ = Posts of notable defenders

ᴐᴐᴐᴐ = Wooden Wall

H = Houses

M = Magazine

B = Barracks

G = Gate

O = Officer's Housing

C = Convent
("The Long Barracks")

h = Hospital

Feet
0   50   100
Scale

with his famed musket "Old Betsy," his fiddle, and his 14-man Tennessee Mounted Rifles, so that by the time Santa Anna arrived there were apparently some 150 or so men available. Of course, the garrison was hardly what one would called well disciplined or well trained. And getting the men into shape was complicated by the serious command problem

The Alamo

The Alamo was originally built as a mission, the *Mision San Antonio de Valero*, a link in the historic chain of missions with which Spain gradually pushed her authority further and further into North America, while simultaneously getting in well with the Lord by converting the Indians. The first mission in the area was a small affair erected in 1718 by Father Antonio Olivares. This was soon abandoned and a larger structure was put up at the present site. The new building was destroyed in a hurricane in 1724. Construction of a proper stone mission was immediately taken in hand, and in 1727 what is now known as the Long Barracks was completed, as the principal residential facility of the mission. A stone church was completed in 1744, but collapsed in 1756. Two years later the present church was begun, but it was destined never to be completed as a church. During the latter portion of the eighteenth century, Texas was swept by a series of epidemics, which led to the abandonment of missionary activity. In 1793 the mission was secularized and turned over to the Spanish frontier guard. Over the years the structure grew, as additional buildings and walls were added. At no time was it converted into a proper fortress. However, with a sufficient garrison, the place was sturdy enough to hold off an Indian raid.

By the time of the Texas War for Independence, the structure had evolved into that which is more or less familiar from various films and illustrations. The "more or less" is dictated by the fact that the precise dimensions and plan of the Alamo in 1835-1836 are not known with any certainty. No two plans or sketches of the place known from contemporary sources are in more than general agreement. One version, for example, has the cattle pen on the northeastern side of the structure extend full to the north wall, while another shows the earthen redoubt which covered the main gate as a large semi-circular structure providing cover for the entire southern wall. Further complicating matters is the fact that not much of the original structure survives.

The buildings that are preserved in downtown San Antonio are the church, which at the time of the which resulted from the fact that the Alamo had three separate commanders, Neill, Bowie, and Travis. The departure of Neill on furlough on 13 February actually made the matter worse, as most of the men in the Alamo had originally been under his command. Since Travis had delusions of turning the men into regulars, they much preferred the more easy-go-

---

siege was a very minor part of the Alamo, and the Long Barracks. Roughly speaking, the dimensions of the large square in front of the church and the Long Barracks, the Alamo Plaza with its Cenotaph, define in shaky outline the dimensions of the enclosure that existed in 1836. The total area contained within the walls was apparently about two acres.

The original walls were mostly torn down by the Mexican Army after the successful assault, to insure that the place could not again be used as a strongpoint. Archaeological activity has helped to establish the original dimensions with some degree of certainty, so that the actual trace of the log and earth palisade which ran southwesterly from the chapel to the southern wall is now known.

Much of the area on the western side of the plaza which was formerly occupied by barracks is now under various buildings. The northern portion of the wall is now beneath the post office. The site where Travis fell is approximately under the main steps.

The Long Barracks which consituted the eastern side of the enclosure originally had two storys, but the upper floors were torn down in the 1890s.

At the time of the siege, the church was only one story high, and there was no roof over the central portion, it having been torn down by Brig. Gen. Martin Cos when he prepared the Alamo for defense in late 1835: The rubble from the roof was packed against the eastern wall and covered with earth to form the ramp leading up to the 12-pounders sited above the apse. The facade of the building also lacked the distinctive "hump" and upper row of windows, which, along with a roof, were installed after the U.S. Army took over the site for use as a Quartermaster depot during the Mexican-American War.

The U.S. Army moved out in 1873, and over the next 20 years the remaining structures underwent numerous changes. At various times the portions that remained were occupied by a saloon and what may charitably be termed a "short-stay" hotel, which was installed in the Long Barracks. During the 1890s various "improvements" were made to the structure, such as the demolition of the upper floors of the Long Barracks. Since 1905 the structure has been in the hands of the Daughters of the Republic of Texas, who have endeavored to keep the remaining structure from further harm.

How Many Guns Were in the Alamo?

The number of cannon at the Alamo is a matter over which there is some historical debate. The dimensions of the question may be summarized by comparing the figures for the number of guns on hand as given by various historians of the Alamo.

The letters across the top of the table indicate the sources as shown below:

A. Francisco Bulnes, *Las grandes mentiras de nuestra historia* (Mexico: 1904).
B. Green B. Jameson, letters to Sam Houston and James Robinson, *Papers of the Texas Revolution* (Austin: 1973), items 1831 and 2110.
C. Walter Lord, *A Time to Stand* (New York, 1963)
D. Maury Maverick, "The Alamo," *Southwestern Historical Quarterly*, Vol. 44.
E. David Nevin, *The Texans* (New York, 1975).
F. Reuben Marmaduke Potter, "The Fall

of the Alamo," *The Magazine of American History*, 1878.
G. Miguel A. Sanchez Lamego, *The Siege and Taking of the Alamo*, translated by Consuelo Velasco (Santa Fe, 1968)
H. Carlos Sanchez Navarro, *La Guerra de Tejas: Memorias de un Soldato* (Mexico: 1966)
I. Richard G. Santos, *Santa Anna's Campaign Against Texas, 1835-1836* (Waco: 1968)
J. The figures used in the present account.

This table by no means provides an exhaustive survey of the literature relating to the number of cannon at the Alamo. It is merely intended to provide some idea as to the range of opinion, and as such combines essentially primary materials with secondary ones. Thus, the accounts by Lord and Nevin are popular treatments, while those of Maverick, Sanchez

Artillery Pieces at the Alamo

Source	A	B	C	D	E	F	G	H	I	J
4-pdr				4	6?	4				4-6
6-pdr	1			2	2	2				5
8-pdr	2			3	6	3				5
12-pdr	4			4	4	4				3-4
18-pdr				1	1					1
24-pdr	5									
36-pdr	2									
Total	14	20	14	14	19	13	14	18	20	18-21
Dismounted		3			3			3	3	3

Lamego, and Santos are more scholarly. Bulnes is a highly pro-Mexican treatment which frequently treads on the truth. While Potter based his account on interviews with Juan Seguin and others who had been in the Alamo before it fell, any treatment which omits mention of the 18-pounder mounted at the southwest corner of the mission is seriously flawed. The critically important sources are those of Major Green B. Jameson, the chief engineer of the Alamo, and of Sanchez Navarro, who was present during the assault as a member of Santa Anna's staff, and surveyed the post afterwards. So, although neither of these men provided details, it seems reasonable to conclude that there were some 18-20 serviceable cannon in the Alamo. It is interesting to note that the various estimates fall roughly into two groups, those indicating that there were only 13-14 guns (Bulnes, Lord, Maverick, Potter, and Sanchez Lamego), and those who argue for 18-20 guns (Jameson, the most authentic source, plus Nevin, Sanchez Navarro, and Santos).

The figures used in this account, 18 to 21, are based on several problems concerning the exact number of guns of each caliber and their dispositions about the fortress, as can be seen in the accompanying survey.

4-pdrs: four along the palisade in front of the Chapel, plus one possibly on the roof of the hospital and one possibly at the northeastern corner of the convent garden.

6-pdrs: two on an earth mound in the plaza about 50 feet behind the main gate, plus three, but possibly only two, in the circular earthen rampart built to cover the gate.

8-pdrs: these definitely were all disposed on platforms along the northern wall, two at its western, and three roughly to the right of the center of the wall

12-pdrs: one was certainly mounted atop the barracks along the center of the western wall, with the other three, but possibly only two, mounted on an earthen platform in the apse of the chapel.

18-pdr: this was unquestionably disposed in the southwestern corner of the walls.

In addition, excavations in the vicinity of the Alamo have turned up a carronade, a type of short barrelled heavy caliber cannon normally used on shipboard. Since this was deliberately damaged, by the smashing of one trunnion—the stubby axle-like protrusions which serve to fasten the piece to its carriage while still permitting elevation—it seems clear that the piece was one of those rendered unserviceable by Brig. Gen. Juan Andrade, it must certainly have formed part of the artillery complement of the Alamo. Yet there is no record of the presence of this piece, unless it was one of those for which the defenders had no carriage, of which there were at least three.

Thus, it would be unreasonable to attempt to be any more precise than to say that there were some serviceable 18-21 cannon in the Alamo at the time it was stormed by the Mexican Army.

David Crockett

David Crockett (1786-1836), among the greatest of the frontiersmen, was born in rural Tennessee, the son of a Revolutionary War veteran who had fought at King's Mountain. He worked on the family farm until the age of 13, when he ran away to Baltimore to avoid being punished for some transgression. His life in Baltimore is rather obscure. At 16 he returned home and spent a year working off some debts which his father had incurred. Although well-schooled in the ways of the woods, he had little formal education, but he spent about six months in school in order to impress a young lady in whom he was interested. He left school when she jilted him. Apparently not particularly broken hearted, Crockett soon afterwards married another, with whom he had three children, and took up farming.

He volunteered for the Creek War of 1813-1814, serving under Andrew Jackson, but left the army in disgust over atrocities inflicted upon the Indians, providing a substitute to finish out his enlistment. His wife died in 1815, he soon married a young widow, acquiring two additional children in the process.

Although not a success as a farmer, nor as a businessman, losing his shirt in several ventures, Crockett made something of a mark in local politics and was elected to a magistracy. He would ever afterwards boast that although he had no legal education whatsoever, not a single one of his decisions was ever overturned by a higher court. He was also elected a colonel in the militia, and served in the state legislature (1821-1825) from two different constituencies. In addition to all of this activity, he found time to disappear into the woods for extended periods, while penning fanciful tales about his adventures. Although admittedly a mighty hunter, his claim to have accounted for 108 bears in one period of eight months may perhaps have been a bit exaggerated. A bitter opponent of Andrew Jackson, with whom he quarreled on a variety of issues, including Indian removal, Crockett served several terms in Congress, 1827-1831 and 1833-1835. In 1835 he made a triumphal tour of the major cities of the east, where he was well known from his writings and those of others who had written about him. When defeated at the hands of a Jacksonian cabal, Crockett is alleged to have informed his constitutents, "I'm going to Texas and you can go to hell," and headed west. He brought a dozen followers and his fiddle to Texas and ended up in the Alamo.

ing Bowie. Since Bowie technically outranked Travis and, moreover, had been elected commander in vote called for by

Travis, this led to several clashes between the two men until they worked out a modus vivendi in which they agreed to "share" command. Crockett's arrival helped Travis' control, since he deferred to the younger man, refusing even a command, asking only to be treated as a "sort of high private."

Perhaps because of their constant bickering, Travis and Bowie made several serious errors in preparing the Alamo for defense. Despite having available Capt. Juan Seguin's mounted company of locally recruited *Tejanos*, they did not institute any systematic program of routine reconnaissance, thereby frittering away an immensely valuable asset. As shown by the success of Blas Herrera's activities, familiar with the countryside for hundreds of miles around, these men could easily have conducted patrols well south of the Rio Grande, providing timely information as to Santa Anna's activities. In addition, Travis and Bowie neglected to bring adequate stocks of food and firewood into the Alamo, a matter which ought to have been relatively simple, given that there were more than sufficient supplies available in the neighborhood of San Antonio. Equally serious was their failure to clear buildings, brush, and trees from the vicinity of the Alamo, objects which could provide cover for anyone attempting to attack the place. It is also unclear as to whether the garrison's gunners, Almeron Dickinson among them, attempted to pre-determine the ranges to various prominent features, so as to be able to bring targets under fire without the necessity for ranging shots.

Despite Travis' strenuous efforts, the daily routine for most of the garrison was hardly military. Many of the officers and men, apparently as many as half of them, had quarters in San Antonio itself, rather than at the Alamo. The dozen or so *Tejanos* in the garrision had wives and families in the town, as did a number of the other men as well, such as Almeron Dickinson, who lived in town with his wife Susanna and infant daughter Angelina, and Jim Bowie himself, who had two sisters-in-law living in San Antonio. On balance, it must be said that despite the state of war, in late February of 1836 the officers and men of the Alamo were essentially living to the rhythms of peace rather than war.

On the evening of 22 February, with Santa Anna camped on the Medina River, only some 18 miles to the southwest, and the pickets of the *Dolores Cavalry* not eight miles from the town, virtually the entire garrison of San Antonio, as well as most of the 2,000 or so inhabitants of the town, turned out for a fiesta in honor of George Washington's birthday; only about ten men were left on duty at the Alamo. It was a splendid party, the second in two nights, with much food, dancing, oratory, and drink. The affair broke up around midnight, and everyone went home cheered, and not a few drunk. But during the wee hours of the morning, word of Santa Anna's imminent arrival began to reach the Mexican community. People began packing up their valuables and leaving town. The unusual pre-dawn movement of wagons and ox carts awoke Travis. Realizing the implications, he questioned some of the fleeing residents, whose answers made him even more certain that Santa Anna was on the march. But he had to be sure. He gave orders for the flight to halt, and then ascended to the top of the tower of the Church of San Fernando with Dr. James Sutherland and another man. A hasty survey of the horizon in the inadequate predawn light proved useless, and Travis returned to the ground with Sutherland, leaving the unnamed soldier on watch in the gathering dawn.

Travis had barely returned to his quarters when the church bell began to ring. Racing out into the Plaza, Travis and Sutherland scrambled once more up to the tower. The young man ceased ringing the bell and reported seeing flashes in the distance, much like sunlight glinting off lanceheads. But when he looked, Travis could see nothing. Uncertain, he dispatched Sutherland and red-haired John W. Smith, an American carpenter who had married a local girl and settled down in San Antonio several years earlier, to reconnoiter on horseback. The two men managed to get no more than about a mile and a half south of the town when, cresting a hill, they beheld before them the troopers of the *Dolores Cavalry Regi-*

ment, drawn up in line-of-battle. Wheeling about, the two raced back to San Antonio to alert Travis, fortunately unpursued by the Mexican cavalry. As they ran, Sutherland's horse stumbled, spilling him to the ground and then rolling over his legs, breaking one of his knees. In great pain, Sutherland remounted and rode on. The lookout in the belfry spied the two riding back and began ringing the church bell in alarm. Santa Anna was at hand!

San Antonio soon swarmed with people, as all anticipated the imminent arrival of the Mexican Army. While residents fled in all directions, the men of the garrison gathered their equipment and hastened off to the security of the Alamo. Grabbing his infant in his arms and with his wife behind him, Almeron Dickinson rode for the Alamo, while Bowie roused himself from his sick bed to see to the safety of his two young sisters-in-law and little nephew, and Gregorio Esparza, whose brother rode with the Mexican Cavalry, hurried his wife and children along. Someone intelligently, if belatedly, drove a herd of about two dozen cattle before him. All sought the safety of the Alamo. Their haste was understandable, but in fact, Santa Anna's troopers approached cautiously. Although some Mexican cavalrymen entered the town, at times forcing those fleeing to the safety of the Alamo to take alternative routes, it was more than an hour before they were present in strength. By then, San Antonio was quiet again, as everyone sought what safety they could, some—apparently including a few men belonging to the garrison—fleeing the town, others sheltering in their homes, and still others ensconced within the Alamo.

It had been a near thing. If the *Dolores Cavalry Regiment* had pursued Sutherland and Smith closely, they would have caught many of the garrison still running through the streets. Indeed, Santa Anna would later say that had his cavalrymen not dawdled on that morning, breaking camp and moving out later than he had ordered, he would have taken the Alamo without a fight; he may well have been right. But now, by Travis' own count, there were 146 fighting men in the Alamo, plus about three dozen noncombatants, and he had a fight on his hands.

As the Mexican cavalrymen filed into San Antonio, Travis conferred with his officers. He dispatched a young man named Johnson with a message to Fannin, nearly 100 miles to the southeast at Goliad, asking for immediate reinforcements, concluding "For God's sake and the sake of our country, send us reinforcements." At about 3:00 p.m. he sent Smith and the seriously injured but still game Sutherland to Gonzales, some 70 miles away, with an additional appeal for assistance. As Travis' couriers headed out of the Alamo, they encountered an earlier messenger, James Bonham, who was returning. Several days earlier Travis had dispatched Bonham to Fannin with an appeal for aid, and the young South Carolinian was returning with the latter's excuses for failing to come up.

Meanwhile, by late afternoon the bulk of Santa Anna's *Brigada Avanguardia* and cavalry had come up, and San Antonio was completely occupied by Santa Anna's troops. Ominously, above the Church of San Fernando, Santa Anna had a blood red flag raised, symbolizing "No quarter." But he also ordered a bugler to sound the call for a parley.

Perhaps unfamiliar with Mexican Army bugle calls, Travis boldly gave answer with a round from the Alamo's biggest gun, an 18-pounder. This gesture annoyed Bowie enormously. More level-headed than his younger co-commander, Bowie was inclined to treat Santa Anna's red flag as a warning, rather than a statement, and to assume that the call for a parley was the message that the general really intended to deliver. By firing, Travis indicated a willingness to fight it out without negotiation, which seemed foolhardy given the condition of the Alamo and size of its garrison. Of course, Santa Anna had to respond to Travis' challenge, and his artillery opened upon in response, firing four 7-inch howitzer bombs into the interior of the Alamo, all of which exploded harmlessly in the middle of the Plaza. Acting quickly, Bowie dispatched Green Jameson under a flag of truce with a message to the enemy. In his message, which he penned in his excellent Spanish, Bowie explained that the round from the Alamo had been fired before the call for a parley had been heard, and inquired, "I wish, Sir, to ascertain, if it be true that a parley was called...?" While Santa Anna and his staff formally considered a reply to Bowie's message, Jameson conveyed the gist of Bowie's intentions informally to Juan Almonte, Santa Anna's American-educated aide. Whatever hopes Bowie had that some sort of reasonable terms might be arranged were dashed by Santa Anna's reply, delivered by one of his aides, Col. Jose Batres. Formalities aside, Santa Anna stated that he would accept nothing less than surrender at discretion, meaning that the garrison could expect no terms, but must surren-

---

Juan Nepomuceno Almonte

Juan Nepomuceno Almonte (1803-1869), the illegitimate son of the Mexican revolutionary hero Father Jose Morelos, was no stranger to the war, his first taste of battle coming when he was still a child. Sent to New Orleans to be educated in a Catholic school, Almonte became fluent in English. With the establishment of an independent Mexico he returned to his homeland and embarked upon a long and rather successful career as a soldier, diplomat, and politician. During the Texas Campaign Almonte served as an aide to Santa Anna, falling prisoner at San Jacinto. His memoirs of the campaign are among the most valuable sources of information on the operations of the Mexican Army.

In the mid-1840s Almonte served as Mexican Minister in Washington, and it fell to him to break off diplomatic relations between the two countries when the U.S. annexed Texas in 1845. He held no important command during the Mexican-American War, after which he returned to politics. Although for most of his life he had been an extreme liberal, for various reasons, partially political and personal, but also because of the increasing anticlericalism of the *juarista* faction of Mexican liberalism, he began to move to the right. Following the conservative *coup d'etat* which ousted Benito Juarez, Almonte was President of Mexico from April through September of 1862. He welcomed, indeed helped engineer, the French intervention and subsequently served the *soi disant* Emperor Maximilian faithfully, rising to Lieutenant General of the Realm. He died in exile in Paris.

---

der to his mercy. Jameson returned to the Alamo with Santa Anna's response.

Santa Anna's terms created a bit of a stir in the garrison. But that was nothing compared to the storm which resulted between the two commanders. Travis had fired the cannon without Bowie's knowledge or consent, and now Bowie had attempted to negotiate with the enemy without Travis' knowledge or consent. To assert his authority, Travis sent his own *parlementaire* to Santa Anna, with an oral message. Albert Martin, a young clerk from New Orleans, never got past Almonte. But Bowie's attempt to negotiate with Santa Anna was his last hurrah. Worn out by his illness and drink, he took to his bed and played little role in the events which were to follow. This left Travis in undisputed command of the Alamo. His instructions had been to hold the Alamo and he intended to do so or to die in the attempt. The ardent young man had many things to do. Among them was to request immediate assistance.

Even as he arranged guard routines and assigned defense sectors to the various companies comprising the garrison, matters which ought to have been arranged days, if not weeks, earlier, Travis gave some thought to the shortage of provisions, in a belated attempt to compensate for his failure to adequately stock the Alamo's larder over the previous weeks. That same evening, a party of men was dispatched to La Villita, a settlement of *jacales*, daub-and-wattle huts inhabited by some of San Antonio's humblest residents, just southwest of the Alamo. Unhampered by the Mexican Army, which had yet to advance its outposts to the area, the foragers came back with some 80 bushels of dried corn, an indeterminate amount of beans, and about 30 head of cattle.

Santa Anna, who was ailing, was also busy that evening. There was much to do, and few resources with which to do it. On that very first day only a small part of his army had managed to come up, some 1,500 men with only a couple of pieces of artillery. He spent most of that day inspecting the defenses and dispatching urgent messages to the brigades still en route from the Rio Grande to make haste. This was easier said than done. Not only were some 400-500 men and most of the artillery of his advanced guard mired in the mud some miles south of town, but the *First Brigade*, under Col. Antonio Gaona, was still several days march away. Santa Anna could have attempted an immediate assault, but was uncertain as to the strength of the garrison. As a result, he decided to impose a blockade, while emplacing artillery so that he could begin a more formal investment.

Over the next few days, both sides settled into a sort of easy routine. Still not strong enough to impose a proper siege, Santa Anna made sure troops maintained a voluminous, if relatively ineffective harassing fire, while trying to prevent any possible movement of men or supplies into or out of the Alamo. The Texians, in turn, returned the harassing fire, with equal lack of effect. Meanwhile, Santa Anna spent much of his time carefully reconnoitering the defenses, searching out the best places to site new artillery pieces as the guns came up, while trying to determine the points along the outer perimeter which would be most vulnerable to an infantry assault, which he concluded were the northern and western faces of the defenses.

The first guns were emplaced in two batteries about 1,000 feet from the Alamo on 24 February, each of four guns of mixed calibers. One battery was emplaced along the right bank of the San Antonio River, fronting on the south wall of the Alamo, while the other was more or less directly east of the eastern wall—the front—of the mission. The two batteries together totalled two 8-pounders, two 6-pounders, two 4-pounders, and two 7-inch howitzers. None of the cannon were sufficiently powerful to seriously damage the 30-inch thick stone and adobe walls of the mission quickly. Although the 7-inch howitzers could hurl an explosive bomb over the walls, the interior plaza of the Alamo was rather spacious, and the garrison soon learned to avoid it. Despite the lightness of their cannon, the Mexican artillerymen did manage to damage the Alamo's biggest piece on their first day in action, the 25th, knocking the 18-pounder off its mounting. Although the gun was repaired, it was a clear demonstration that given time the light Mexican guns would have shot the Alamo to pieces. But Santa Anna was not inclined to waste time. What he needed was his 12-pounders. But these were far to the south; they did not even cross the Rio Grande, some 170 miles to the southwest, until the morning of 26 February. So he made do with what he had, as his patience wore thin.

Meanwhile, Travis penned an eloquent appeal for assistance.

Commandacy of the Alamo
Bexar, Feby 24th, 1836

To the People of Texas and All Americans in the World-
Fellow Citizens and Compatriots:

I am besieged with a thousand or more of the Mexicans under Santa Anna. I have sustained a considerable Bombardment and cannonade for 24 hours and have not lost a man. The enemy has demanded surrender at discretion, otherwise the garrison is to be put to the sword, if the fort is taken. I have answered the demand with a cannon shot, and our flag still waves proudly from the wall. I shall never surrender or retreat. Then, I call on you in the name of Liberty, of patriotism, and everything dear to the American character, to come to our aid with all dispatch. The enemy is receiving reinforcements daily and will no doubt increase to three or four thousand in four or five days. If this call is neglected I am determined to sustain myself as long as possible and die like a soldier who never forgets which is due his honor and that of his country.

VICTORY OR DEATH.
William Barrett Travis
LT. COL. Commanding

Travis did not sit passively within the walls during the siege. Over the dozen days which followed Santa Anna's arrival at San Antonio, Travis' men regularly responded to Mexican fire. A few skirmishes occurred.

On the morning of 25 February, Santa Anna essayed a probe of the defenses on the southeastern side of the Alamo.

About 200 infantrymen filtered through the *jacales* of La Villita to emerge only a few dozen yards from the walls. As they charged across that last bit of open ground, the Texians opened a furious fire from their artillery and muskets, beating off the attackers with some loss. This convinced Travis that Santa Anna was planning to site a battery at La Villita, close to the front gate of the Alamo. He decided to make a sortie. Later that night a raiding party poured out of the main gate. Covered by musket and cannon fire from the walls, the troops put much of the shanty-town to the torch. About 300 men of the *Matamoros* and *Jimenez Battalions* attempted to intervene and a heated action developed as the garrison increased its fire to cover the retreat of the raiding party. Things tapered off during the small hours of the morning as a light rain began to fall.

Not knowing that the Texians had opened an old well inside the Alamo, on 27 February some Mexican troops attempted to dam an *acequia*, an irrigation canal, which flowed into the Alamo from the west. Spotted by sentries, the working party was immediately peppered with musket balls. Some Mexican infantry and artillery fire was brought to bear to support the work detail. A hot, but short little skirmish resulted, in which the Mexican troops, working without cover, had the worst of it. After four or five of the party were hit, the rest pulled back. Similar skirmishes occurred several times, helping to break the monotony.

But nothing could drive off the cold. The weather stayed unseasonably cold during those last days of February and the first days of March. Another blue norther blew through the area on the 25th, sending the temperatures plunging to below freezing. Neither side was adequately prepared to deal with such temperatures, the Texians not having a sufficient supply of firewood and most of the Mexicans not used to such cold.

There were other ways to keep warm besides making fires, and to keep up morale as well. On several nights Santa Anna ordered his regimental bands to serenade his troops and incidentally the men in the Alamo as well. For their part, the defenders also took a musical turn on many a night. On one occasion Davy Crockett challenged John McGregor to a musical "duel," he on his famous fiddle and the expatriate Scot on his bagpipes. It may not have been good, but it was loud and entertaining, and the eerie sounds emanating from the blockaded mission must have mystified the troops outside.

Of course the Alamo, though tightly blockaded, was not completely sealed off by the Mexican Army. Non-combatants occasionally flitted back and forth during the night. One or two men who had left their wives or sweethearts in town managed to pay them surreptitious visits. A number of the defenders decided to choose the better part of valor and slipped over the walls in the chilly dark, to disappear forever. And Travis several times was able to dispatch couriers in various directions appealing for reinforcements. Altogether he appears to have sent out at least 16 couriers. Some of these men had impressive adventures, such as Capt. Juan Seguin, the scion of one of the most distinguished families in Texas. On the night of 25-26 February Travis ordered Seguin to carry an appeal for reinforcements to Houston, whom he believed was gathering an army at Gonzales. Since his own horse was lame, Seguin went to Bowie to borrow his mount. Bowie was seriously ill, and barely recognized his old friend, but did manage to give his assent. It was a good night to make an attempt to slip out of the Alamo, for the raid on La Villita would offer cover, and the light rain still more. As a result, Seguin, who was accompanied by an aide, Antonio Cruz, had little difficulty in slipping through Mexican lines. Once clear, Seguin and Cruz headed up the Gonzales road at a steady pace. Some miles on they chanced upon a Mexican outpost. It consisted of a few dismounted cavalrymen, who had drawn some brush across the road as it passed through a defile. The two riders came up easily, almost casually. A lookout spotted them and raised a challenge. As several of the troopers sprang to arms, Seguin showed no alarm. He called out reassurances in good educated Spanish. The cavalrymen relaxed, thinking an officer was approaching. When almost

Juan Nepomuceno Seguin

Juan Nepomuceno Seguin (1806-1890) came from a wealthy and influential family, originally French, which had settled at San Antonio from the Canary Islands in 1731. His father, Erasmo Seguin, had been several times *alcalde* of San Antonio, and, as a delegate to the Mexican Congress had helped draft the liberal Constitution of 1824. Like his father, the political boss of south Texas, the younger Seguin had several times served as *alcalde* of San Antonio, the first when he was only 18, and he had served in the Coahuila-Texas state legislature and the Mexican Congress. A friend of American settlers in Texas, Seguin was active in the movement to make the area a separate state, and later joined the independence movement.

On the outbreak of the Revolution, Seguin recruited a company from among the local Mexican population. Although present in the Alamo when the Mexican Army began its investment, Seguin was one of the couriers whom Travis sent to seek assistance, escaping with the help of an aide on the night of 25-26 February. Joining Houston, Seguin commanded a company at San Jacinto, and was shortly promoted to colonel. He was assigned command of the San Antonio area, but soon found himself at odds with the flood of newly arrived settlers from the United States, who disputed his authority and generally abused the *Tejanos*.

Elected to the Texas Senate in 1838, he resigned in 1840 when he was elected mayor of San Antonio. His defense of *Tejano* rights led to scurrilous charges being brought by newly arrived American settlers that he was in treasonous correspondence with the Mexican Army, having betrayed the Texas expedition to Santa Fe in 1841 and collaborated in Mexican raids across the border. In 1842 Seguin was forced from office. Fearing for his safety, he took his family and fled to Mexico, where he was promptly arrested. Shortly afterwards impressed into the Mexican Army, Seguin served as an officer against Texas during the continuing border troubles and later against the United States during the Mexican-American War.

After the U.S.-Mexican peace settlement in 1848, Seguin petitioned for and received permission to return to the United States. He lived quietly thereafter as a rancher, until 1867, when he settled on some lands he owned in Mexico, where he stayed for the rest of his life. The unfortunate fate of Seguin was shared by many *Tejanos* who had supported the independence movement in Texas. Although the original American settlers got along quite well with the *Tejanos*, those who came later were contemptuous of them. Indeed, it seems that the later a person arrived in Texas the more hostile he was likely to be towards the *Tejanos*.

upon the simple obstacle, Seguin and his man put spurs to horse and were off. The horses easily cleared the loosely piled brush, and raced past the startled cavalrymen, and on into the darkness as a few ragged shots rang out, whistling wide of their marks. The troopers sprang to horse and were up and away almost immediately, but by then it was too late, their quarry had flown, taking advantage of terrain which they knew intimately. A day or so later Houston was reading Travis' latest dispatches.

Traffic through the blockade was not all one way either. At about 1:00 a.m. on 1 March, 32 men under Capt. George Kimbell, a former hatter from New York, and John W. Smith, the red-haired carpenter from San Antonio who had ridden out of the Alamo with Sutherland on 23 February, approached the Alamo in single file. Most of the men were from Gonzales, but there were two others who had recently left the Alamo as couriers, Albert Martin and Charles Despalier. The column passed unchallenged through the Mexican lines, which were quite thin to the north of the mission. Smith sent a messenger ahead but somehow not all of the sentries in the Alamo were properly alerted. As the column neared the walls, one of the sentries loosed a round, striking one of the approaching men in the foot. He cut loose with a loud, foul oath, which convinced the sentry that the stealthily approaching men were fellow Texians and the Gonzales Mounted Volunteers were welcomed with open arms. The arrival of the men from Gonzales helped strengthen the garrison, bringing it up to some 180-190 men. But it would take still more men before the Alamo could be considered secure. On the night of 3-4 March, Travis dispatched John W. Smith once more through the enemy lines, the doughty scout's third trip, with yet another appeal for aid.

Travis wasn't the only commander to receive reinforcements during the siege. On the morning of 4 March the advance elements of the *First Brigade* began arriving under Col. Francisco Duque, altogether some 980 men of the *Toluca* and *Aldama Battalions*, plus the elite *Zapadores* and one 7-inch howitzer. This was good news, as Santa Anna's patience was wearing thin. As soon as these men were rested from their long march, their general intended to put them to good use.

Travis had infinite patience, but realized that he was running out of time, not to mention supplies. He knew well the weakness of his position. He also knew that many good men were at Goliad under Col. Fannin, reputedly an able, decisive man. He had sent several couriers to Fannin already, asking for aid. He could do little more than await Fannin's arrival.

CHAPTER V

Military Operations

23 February-6 March 1836

Col. James W. Fannin commanded the largest single body of Texian troops, on paper over 450 men. They were at Goliad, not 100 miles southeast of the Alamo. Fannin learned that the Mexican Army had arrived at San Antonio early on 25 February, when young Johnson, Travis' first courier, reached him. Travis' communique was short, but to the point: "We have removed all our men into the Alamo, where we will make such resistance as is due our honour, and that of the country, until we can get assistance from you, which we expect you to forward immediately. In this extremity, you can send us all the men you can spare promptly." Having only a few days earlier sent James Bonham back to Travis with various excuses as to why he couldn't come up to reinforce the San Antonio garrison immediately, Fannin now suddenly began to act. He ordered the army to prepare to march. After allowing for a garrison to remain at Goliad, he had available 320 men, with two 6-pounders and two 4-pounders plus a few wagons loaded with supplies, but not much of the latter, as he was short of everything, including even coffee and salt. The men were mostly well armed, with captured Mexican muskets, complete with bayonets. But ammunition was short, there being only a dozen rounds per man available. He also had almost no horses, and had to use oxen to pull not only his supply wagons but also his artillery, which made it impossible for him to move quickly. The men were also poorly clothed and lacked adequate footwear. Fannin was aware of the limitations of his resources. However, commenting that, "The appeal of Cols. Travis & Bowie cannot however pass unnoticed...," he observed that honor required that "Much must be risked to relieve the besieged." Had it not been for the foolhardy effort of the Council to undertake an expedition

Juan Jose Urrea

Juan Jose Urrea (1795-1849) was born in Tuscon, in what is now Arizona, though his family apparently had strong roots in Durango. Although he passed himself off as a *criollo*, he was apparently of *mestizo* background. He entered the Royal Army as a cadet at the age of 12. His early military career was largely spent in suppressing revolutionary outbreaks in Sinaloa, Nayarit, and Michoacan. By the time Mexico attained its independence, Urrea was a captain, serving with the forces which blockaded the island fortress of San Juan de Ulua, Spain's last bastion in Mexico. Soon after the Spanish departed he left the army to return to the family estates in Durango. However, he returned to duty as a major in 1829, after the Spanish seized Tampico. Promoted lieutenant colonel in 1832, he raised Durango for the then still-liberal Santa Anna, who promoted Urrea to colonel upon assuming the presidency. Between tours of duty with the

troops Urrea served for a time as Mexican minister to Colombia, in which post he became friendly with William Henry Harrison, the U.S. minister in Bogota and Dr. Benjamin Harrison, father of the later President of the same name, whom he rescued from probable execution in 1836.

A reluctant participant in the suppression of Zacatecas in 1834, Urrea was promoted to brigadier general in 1835 and sent to Durango to fight Apaches. It was from this post that Santa Anna—with whom he was on increasingly unfriendly terms due to the latter's abandonment of federalist principles—called him to duty in Texas. Urrea commanded the independent division which operated along the Texas coast with considerable skill, certainly more than was displayed by Santa Anna himself. He was responsible for the series of defeats sustained by the Texas forces at San Patricio, Refugio, Goliad, and Coltelo Creek, culminating in the against Matamoros, Fannin might have had a considerably stronger and better prepared force with which to work. Some 500-600 men and most of the stores and ammunition from the Alamo and Goliad had been committed to the Matamoros expedition, which was concentrating at Refugio by mid-January. At that time Houston had succeeded in convincing many of the men to abandon the effort.

Unbeknownst to the Texian forces concentrating at Refugio, the military situation at Matamoros, which had hitherto

---

surrender of Fannin. Among those who objected to Santa Anna's orders to execute all prisoners, Urrea managed to save many of them from that fate. He was one of the officers who urged Filisola to disobey Santa Anna's orders to evacuate Texas after San Jacinto; had the latter listened to him the outcome of the Texas Revolution might readily have been reversed.

After the Texas Campaign, Urrea served as commanding general in Sonora and Sinaloa. Having fallen completely out with Santa Anna, in 1837 he raised his command in the name of a federal constitution, but early the following year was defeated at Mazatlan. Escaping, he attempted a *coup* at Tampico which failed. Imprisoned, he escaped and was recaptured several times. Expelled from the army, Urrea was returned to duty during the "Pastry War." In 1840 he led an uprising against the Bustamante government. Defeated, he fled to Durango, which he rallied to the federalist cause in 1841, helping to put the "born-again" federalist Santa Anna into the presidency

once again. Santa Anna named him governor of Sonora and he held various other civil and military posts thereafter. During the Mexican-American War he ably commanded a cavalry division in northern Mexico, but also took part in the Mexican defeat at Buena Vista. Urrea died of cholera shortly after the war ended.

Extremely influential in his native Durango, which he served as governor and senator at various times, and a staunch federalist, Urrea was one of the ablest politically-connected commanders in the Mexican Army. Perhaps the best testimony to his abilities is the fact that despite Urrea's strong devotion to a federal Mexico, Santa Anna found it necessary to entrust him with command of the independent column advancing up the Texas coast, a command which was subsequently enlarged to the point where it included about 20 percent of Mexican forces in Texas at the time of San Jacinto. Urrea was a thorough professional, from whose advice Santa Anna and Filisola might well have profited.

been guarded only by a handful of *presidiales*, had recently undergone a significant change. The Texians had talked so much and so loudly about the Matamoros operation that Santa Anna could not help but hear of it. As a result, in mid-January the general, then camped with the bulk of his army at Leona Vicario, had dispatched the *Cuautla Permanente Cavalry Regiment* plus two companies of *auxiliares*, some 250 cavalrymen, eastwards to Matamoros under the command of Col. Jose Urrea, while ordering the *Yucatan Activo Battalion* to march northwards from Tampico to Matamoros, dragging a field piece with them. By early February the two columns had linked up at Matamoros. Urrea's instructions were simple: first to ensure the safety of Matamoros and then to carry the war into Texas, advancing northwards along the coast parallel with Santa Anna's own drive from the southwest.

Word of Urrea's arrival at Matamoros reached Refugio around 10 February. This convinced Fannin as to the foolhardiness of the Matamoros expedition, and he had fallen back to Goliad with the men under his command. But this still left 150-200 men and a great deal of supplies at Refugio under the expedition's two other officers designated as Commander-in-Chief, James Grant and Frank Johnson. As they both had equal authority over the same body of men, Grant and Johnson soon began to fall out, since the former pressed for an immediate advance on Matamoros, while the latter stressed the need for additional preparations. The two did manage to agree to advance their little army the 50 miles from Refugio to San Patricio, on the Nueces River, still more than 100 miles short of their objective at Matamoros, but concurred on little else. And they were hardly ready to undertake an offensive. In late February, by which time desertions had reduced the expedition to only about 90-100 men, Grant and Johnson had a falling out over the procurement of horses for the expedition. Grant took off with about half the men, including most of the New Orleans Greys who weren't at the Alamo, and headed west to see what horses he could collect, while Johnson remained behind at San Patricio. However, even as Grant

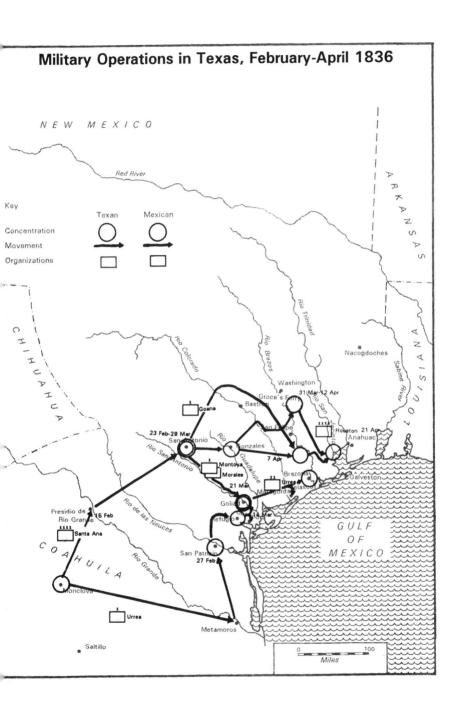

Military Operations in Texas, February-April 1836

NEW MEXICO

Red River

ARKANSAS

Key

Concentration

Movement

Organizations

Texan   Mexican

CHIHUAHUA

Rio Colorado

Rio Brazos

Rio Trinidad

LOUISIANA

Sabine River

Nacogdoches

Washington

Groce's Ferry   31 Mar-12 Apr

Bastrop

Goana

23 Feb-20 Mar
San Antonio

Rio San Antonio

San Felipe

Houston 21 Apr
Anahuac

Rio Guadalupe

Gonzales

7 Apr

Montoya
Morales
21 Mar

Brazoria
Urrea
Velasco
Galveston

Matagorda

Goliad

Presidio de
Rio Grande   15 Feb

Santa Ana

Rio de las Neuces

Refugio   14 Mar

COAHUILA

Rio Grande

San Patricio
27 Feb

GULF
OF
MEXICO

Monclova

Urrea

Metamoros

Saltillo

0   100
Miles

and Johnson were having their final quarrel, Urrea was marching north at the head of some 600 troops.

Around 3:00 a.m. on 27 February, using a driving rain for cover Urrea swept into San Patricio at the head of some 100 cavalry troopers. His attack achieved complete surprise, Johnson not even having had the sense to post sentries. It was over in minutes, the sounds of the hooves, some shouts, a few shots, and then silence. At no loss to his own men, Urrea had killed 16 Texians and captured 24, the rest, including Johnson, having fled into the surrounding wilderness. As the fugitives fled northwards towards Goliad, Urrea shipped his prisoners to Matamoros and then began searching for Grant. On 3 March a patrol ran Grant's column to earth at a place called Agua Dulce, about 20 miles west of San Patricio. The Mexican cavalry surrounded Grant's men, by then reduced to only about 25, and went in with the lance; only three men survived, one of whom later escaped as they were being led south towards Matamoros. The Texian expedition to Matamoros and its glorious vision of empire perished in horror and blood on the cold Texas prairie.

But none of this was known to Fannin, as he prepared to go to the relief of the Alamo. It took him nearly 72 hours to get his little army ready, but finally it marched on the morning of 28 February. The column had scarcely gone 200 yards when a wagon broke down, delaying the advance. A few hundred yards further and two additional wagons broke down, right at the ford across the San Antonio River. Since the river was high, the oxen proved unable to haul the artillery across. As a result, the troops had to manhandle the pieces across, an arduous task which took some time. By the early afternoon the little army had halted on the far side of the river. It had most of its equipment, but no ammunition, the water being too high to allow the ammunition wagons to cross in safety. The army made camp. It had advanced little more than a half mile.

No one having thought to put a guard on the oxen during the night, they wandered off, there being little forage in the immediate area. So when the troops awoke the next morning they were ordered to round up the livestock, a task which took much of the day. Two days on the march and the army was still within a mile of Goliad. Disheartened, Fannin called a council of war. As Fannin and his principal subordinates conferred in the cold, a courier came in with word that a considerable shipment of desperately needed supplies had been landed at Matagorda Bay, where it now lay unguarded. It is the nature of councils of war to make the most conservative decisions. And this one was no different. Concern for the safety of the supplies outweighed the desire to march to the relief of the Alamo. Fannin ordered the army back to Goliad, so that he could organize a column to secure the supplies, after which he would resume the march on San Antonio. However, no sooner were the exhausted men back in Goliad when Col. Frank Johnson rode up with the four other survivors of the battle at San Patricio. The presence of Urrea's troops not 50 miles off was startling enough news, but Johnson also told a wild tale of massacre, asserting that all of the prisoners had been brutally cut down by the Mexicans. All thoughts of relieving the Alamo, or, indeed, of securing the mountain of supplies at Matagorda, were abandoned, as Fannin ordered Goliad readied for defense against what he believed was the imminent assault by at least a thousand Mexican troops. Although Travis would deliver several additional appeals for aid to Fannin, the latter would not make reply.

While Travis, Bowie, Crockett and the others were sitting it out in the Alamo, and Fannin was dithering away any chance of offering them some relief, men were mobilizing across Texas. Altogether there were perhaps 1,800 men under arms in Texas. But few were ready for action. And the men of the Alamo and Goliad represented the two largest concentrations of Texian manpower. Moreover, the one man in Texas with the popular prestige and military skill to accomplish anything was nowhere to be found. Sam Houston had gone off to negotiate with the Cherokee in January, and was still at it through February. So there was not much that could be done to save the Alamo or even to help Fannin. At least nothing military. But there were momentous political events in the offing.

The Consultation or convention of representatives of the people of Texas, which had adjourned in late 1835, resumed its deliberations in Washington-on-Brazos on 1 March. Sitting in an incomplete house, with the paneless windows covered by linen to keep out the cold, the delegates had come with serious purpose. Although more men had been elected, only 59 delegates were able to make the Convention. They were fairly representative of the Texians of the day, most had been born in the United States, and most of them were relatively recent immigrants to Texas. But five had been born

Financing the War for Texas

There was little public money in Texas when fighting broke out with the Mexican authorities in late 1835. As a result, as soon as the representatives of the rebellious Texians met at San Felipe for the Consultation, they began to discuss ways to raise money. As one historian put it, there were six ways for a government to raise money: "taxing, borrowing, begging, selling, and robbing and cheating...and the Texans decided to try all six."

Taxes came from import duties which, although they had objected to them when collected by Mexico, the wily Texians realized were a valuable source of revenue. In addition, many individual Texians contributed funds. Of course, these sources were wholly inadequate to finance a war. As early as December of 1835, representatives of the Texas Consultation were negotiating for loans in New Orleans, using land as collateral. Other representatives were dispatched to sell land outright to speculators. Land was also used to back scrip and to pay the troops. These methods helped ease some of the financial pressure. But since none of them could bring in much cash immediately, representatives of the provisional government were authorized to issue promissory notes in exchange for goods.

Land scrip aside, Texas had no money of its own, and would not issue any until June of 1837. As a result, Mexican and American coins had wide circulation, as did notes issued by banks, particularly those in Louisiana, and U.S. treasury notes.

As of the end of August of 1836

British subjects, and three more in Mexico, two of whom were native *Tejanos*. Of those who couldn't make it, one, a *Tejano*, had died en route, two, another *Tejano* and an Irishman, were too ill to travel, and two were in the field. The delegates did their business quickly. On 2 March—Sam Houston's birthday—a Declaration of Independence was adopted without debate and with only one speech, a rather rambling one by Houston, just back from negotiating with his Cherokee brothers. Quickly upon this resolution, the Convention created a provisional government, electing David Burnet, an *empresario*, as Provisional President of the Republic of Texas, and Lorenzo de Zavala, the *mestizo* liberal from Yucatan, as Provision Vice-President. Houston was confirmed as Commander-in-Chief. So the Texians were no longer fighting for a liberal

---

the war had cost Texas about $1,250,000. About $25,000 was raised through voluntary donations from communities and citizens of Texas, an uncertain larger sum from donations by people in the United States (Mobile, Alabama, for example, kicked in $1,500), and only a pittance procured from import duties; most of this money came from loans or promissory notes. Among those to whom the infant Republic owed money was Travis, due $143 to cover out-of-pocket expenditures contingent upon raising his company of cavalry. Whatever else they were, the Founding Fathers of Texas certainly understood how to wage war without money, a lesson that they had undoubtedly learned from their forebearers in the American Revolution.

These monies were expended in various ways.

Cost of the War

Army	$412,000
Navy	$112,000
Supplies	$450,000
Civil Expenditures	$118,000
Interest	$100,000
Miscellaneous	$ 60,000

Figures for the Army and Navy include salaries and recruiting bonuses, payable in land (volunteers received 320 acres for each three months of service), plus the cost of equipment and ships, but not of foodstuffs, ammunition, and other consumables, which are covered under Supplies. Civil Expenditures included the cost of sending representatives abroad, pay for members of the provisional government, the rental of quarters, and the like. Interest was that due on loans, most of which were eventually paid off in land. Miscellaneous is that wonderful category with which the books can be balanced.

Mexico, but for themselves. But this had little effect on the military situation.

On 29 February Travis' first communique from the besieged Alamo, that carried out by Sutherland and Smith, had reached Washington-on-Brazos. It caused a stir, and Governor Smith ordered copies distributed to all the towns in Texas, to stimulate recruiting. There was little more that could be done until the Convention met to create a sturdier political structure for Texas. What with assembling the delegates and adopting the Declaration of Independence, the matter of the Alamo was forgotten. Then, on 3 March, as the delegates and the townspeople were still celebrating the day's events, Travis' second courier arrived. The message created a storm. One delegate rose to call upon his colleagues to immediately take up arms and ride for the Alamo. A dozen members leaped to their feet to second his proposal. However, Houston took the floor, to urge calm deliberation. Nothing could succeed unless carefully planned. Texas required time to gather its strength. A provisional government was fine, but a proper constitution had to be drawn up before the government could act with determination. It was, he went on, the lack of a properly structured government which lay at the bottom of the present unfavorable military situation; without actually saying so, Houston was alluding to the disastrous situation which had resulted from the clash between Governor Smith and the Council, caused in large measure by a lack of clear definition of the duties, powers, and authority of the provisional government established by the Consultation. Houston's words imposed a more sober tone on the proceedings. There was much work to be done, and the delegates began the drafting of a proper Constitution, which was not completed for nearly a fortnight. Houston's words had brought the delegates to their senses. But implicit in them was an understanding that nothing now could be done to aid Travis and the men of the Alamo.

Travis would receive but one more reinforcement.

On the night of 27 February Travis had once again dispatched James Bonham to Fannin at Goliad with yet another appeal for reinforcements. Riding hard, the tall, dark haired attorney from South Carolina had reached Goliad on 1 March, about the time that Fannin's command was straggling back from its abortive march on San Antonio. Failing to convince Fannin to make another attempt to go to the relief of the Alamo, Bonham announced that he would return himself. Fannin attempted to dissuade him from this course, which would mean certain death. Bonham spat on the ground, said something to the effect that Travis at least deserved a reply, mounted his horse, and headed northwest. Once more riding hard, Bonham reached the Alamo on the morning of 3 March. Approaching from the north, the same route used by the gallant 32 from Gonzales, Bonham slipped easily through the Mexican lines, to enter the Alamo at about 11:00 a.m. Now at last Travis knew that no help was coming.

Weapons of the Texas Revolution

The weapons used in the Texas War were all virtually identical to those used during the Napoleonic Wars, and in many cases the weapons themselves were actual veterans of those wars. That is, they were mostly smoothbore muskets and artillery.

Muskets. Although tradition pits rifle-armed American frontiersmen against musket toting Mexican infantry during the Texas War, in fact both sides were more or less similarly armed, mostly with heavy smoothbore muskets little changed since the beginning of the eighteenth century. These weapons were highly inaccurate, unreliable, and of very short range. To be sure some of the Americo-Texans had rifles of various sorts, but these were hunting weapons, rather than military arms, with an even slower rate of fire than the smoothbore muskets. Moreover, the Mexican Army had its own rifle, the very effective British Baker.

The characteristics of the principal muskets are shown in the chart below.

The Mexican troops in the Texas War were equipped with surplus British firearms which, tradition holds, had been used at Waterloo. Although some ill-educated authors have denigrated the Mexican use of such "antique" weapons, it is worth recalling that in the opening stages of the American Civil War, a quarter of a century later, many troops on both sides went into action with arms of equal vintage.

The British Baker was the first practical military rifle, since it could be fitted with a bayonet and had a rate of fire twice that of contemporary military or hunting rifles. It had rendered excellent service as a light infantry weapon

Infantry Weapons	Cal	WT	RPM	Range
Mex. Baker Rifle, 1800	.64	9.6	1-2	140/275
Mex. "Brown Bess" Musket, 1700	.75	11.0	3	70/140
U.S. Musket, Model 1816	.69	11.0	3	75/150
U.S. Rifle	.59	8.0	1	140/275

Key: *Cal.*, caliber in inches. *Wt.*, weight of the piece, in pounds, without bayonet, which could add about a pound. However, the U.S. rifle could not be tipped with a bayonet. *RPM* is sustainable number of rounds per minute attainable by reasonably well-trained troops.

Under ideal conditions a well-trained man could get off about double this number of rounds for a few minutes. *Range* is in yards, with the practical given first, followed by the maximum distance at which the weapon might be considered effective.

during the Napoleonic Wars. It was with a Baker that the Mexican sharpshooter Felix de la Garza killed Ben Millam at San Antonio in December of 1835.

Although first introduced around the beginning of the eighteenth century, the British "Tower Musket, Mark III" or "Brown Bess"—so named because it had been in service so long it was rumored to have been introduced by Queen Elizabeth—used in the Mexican Army had apparently been manufactured in 1809. A rugged, reliable weapon, it had often proven its worth. Most of the Americo-Texans were actually equipped with the Brown Bess, several hundred stand of them—a "stand of arms" was defined as the musket with bayonet and accoutrements—having been captured at San Antonio and Goliad in December of 1835.

The Brown Bess and the Baker remained in use with the Mexican Army through the Mexican-American War of 1846-1848 and during the early part of the long struggle against the French and Maximilian. Indeed, on 5 May 1862 some 1,500 Mexican troops armed with the Brown Bess and the Baker soundly thrashed some 7,500 rifle-armed Frenchmen at Puebla, thereby keeping Mexico City in *Juarista* hands for another year.

The Texian forces began the war with an extraordinary hodgepodge of weapons. Not only were most of them, whether Texas rebels or American volunteers, not equipped with rifles, but initially many were armed only with shot-guns and fowling pieces. By the end of the war the Texas Army was mostly equipped with captured Mexican weapons, as well as some U.S. arms.

The U.S. 1816 musket was in use until the early 1840s. Aside from being a "French-pattern" weapon, in keeping with all U.S. muskets, in practical terms it differed little from the Brown Bess. The principal difference was that the barrel was fastened to the stock by metal bands, rather than pins. Some of the volunteer companies raised for Texas in the U.S. were apparently equipped with this weapon, as were most of the 200 or so U.S. Army deserters who fought at San Jacinto. In 1839 this weapon was adopted as standard issue by the Texas Army.

There was no standard "U.S. Rifle" at the time of the Texas War, there being as many different models as there were manufacturers. The figures given here are for a "typical" hunting rifle of the period.

In all armies infantry firearms were issued in units called a "stand of arms." This consisted of the musket, a bayonet, belt with ammunition pouches and scabbard, and a small tool kit to clean and service the weapon. The cost at the time of the Texas Revolution appears to have been about $20 for a stand of arms, a considerable sum, equivelent to at least $250-$350 in money of 1991.

Loading these weapons was by no means a simple task. Paper-wrapped cartridges were used. These were about two inches long or a bit less, depending upon the weapon, and weighed upwards of an ounce. Each contained powder and a bullet, the latter being of soft lead and weighing from about a third to two-thirds of an ounce. Although in the Mexican Army, as in all regular armies, cartridges were manufactured centrally, among the Texians most men made their own. Indeed, they even used cartridges as a sort of money. The Mexican Army was sparing of ammunition, and troops were normally issued only two or three rounds: The U.S. Army was issuing about 40 rounds at the time. Most of the Texas volunteers would have carried much more than that; one man actually offered a hundred made-up rounds as the ante for a bet.

Regardless of the type of piece, the loading procedure was essentially the same.

Grounding his weapon, the musketeer held it steady with one hand while taking one of the paper-wrapped cartridges from his ammunition pouch. Holding the ball end of the cartridge in his hand, he bit off the other end with his teeth, exposing the powder. He poured a little of this into the priming pan, and then poured the rest down the barrel. He would then shove the ball into the barrel and follow it with the paper wrapping. Removing his ramrod from its receptacle under the barrel, he would vigorously tamp powder, ball, and wadding down. Replacing the ramrod, he would lift the piece to his shoulder, cock the flintlock mechanism, aim after a fashion, and fire.

For maximum effectiveness, men using the Baker rifle "patched" their bullets with a bit of greased cloth, which made for greater accuracy, but this reduced the rate of fire from two rounds per minute to one.

There was much that could go wrong. It was extremely difficult to load these weapons in any but a standing position. In addition, in the heat of battle a man might spill some of the powder or drop the ball or the priming powder. One's powder could be damp or flint worn. Misfires were common and could be fatal, since the man might not realize that his piece had misfired, leading him to load it once again, with potentially disastrous results. Sometimes, men forgot to remove the ramrod from the barrel, thereby firing it off and rendering their weapon useless until they could secure a replacement, not necessarily a difficult task on a bloody battlefield.

These weapons were not very accurate, not even the rifles. In various tests, usually conducted against targets painted to resemble the front of an infantry battalion, it was determined that perhaps as few as 15 percent of the rounds fired seemed to have hit anyone. And range was important to lethality; beyond 100 yards serious casualties were relatively few, at 50 yards the slaughter could be terrific. It was these basic facts which molded tactics. Firepower could be lethal only if delivered in great volume on a relatively narrow front. As a result, armies were trained to fight with the troops lined up shoulder-to-shoulder, firing coordinated volleys at very short ranges against enemy troops similarly arrayed, which could be devastatingly effective. Of course, this didn't happen during the Texas Revolution, there being only one open field battle, San Jacinto. At San Jacinto, Houston did array his men more or less shoulder to shoulder, in two lines, right out of the textbook, but the Mexicans were caught wholly unprepared and never managed to form a line. Had they been deployed in line at the time the Texians attacked, the slaughter might have been less one-sided.

Artillery. The Texas War for Independence was essentially an infantryman's war. Artillery, although present, played a relatively minor role, even at the Alamo, where a proper artillery preparation would certainly have greatly reduced Mexican losses.

Altogether there were certainly fewer than 50 pieces of artillery in use during the entire war, and these were of an extremely hetero-geneous character. There was little standardization, and numerous types were in use. The Mexicans, for example, appear to have had Spanish and French guns, while the

Piece	Wt	Ln	Cal	Chg	Rng	RPM	Crew
12-Pdr	4.3	7.3	4.8"	4.2	2.3	1	15
8-Pdr	3.1	5.9	3.9	2.6	1.4	2	13
6-Pdr	2.6	5.9	3.5	2.0	1.4	2-3	11

Key: *Piece* is the weapon, normally identified by its "poundage," which was in fact not a very useful guide to projectile weight, due to differences in the definition of the pound from country to country. The old French pound was some 8.3% heavier than the English one, while the Spanish pound was .003% lighter. The 7-inch howitzer fired a shell of about 12 pounds. *Wt* is the weight of the gun, with carriage, in thousands of pounds. *Ln* is the length of piece in feet. *Cal*, the caliber in inches. *Chg* is the normal powder charge, in pounds. *Rng*, maximum range in yards with solid shot; effective range was usually about half of this while for canister effective range was usually only about a third of this; effective range for explosive shell from the howitzer was about 1200 to 600 yards, depending upon fuse setting. *RPM* is sustainable rounds per minute. *Crew* is the number of men officially prescribed as required to serve the piece. In practice during the Texas campaign, the guns on both sides were generally served by only about half the indicated number of men. This did not seriously impede the service of the piece in action, unless casualties piled up, but it did greatly hamper the tactical mobility of the guns. With a full crew it required only about a minute for a piece to go into action from what might be termed "road mode," and only a bit more time to limber up and get away. With a partial crew the time required was greatly increased.

Texians had a few American-made pieces as well. As a result, the accompanying table is only intended to give some idea as to the general characteristics of artillery at the time, and is based on contemporary Spanish practice. It gives a general notion of the characteristics of artillery in the period, although omitting a number of pieces known to have been in use, such as the Alamo's famous 18-pounder and the equally famous "Come and Take It" piece from Gonzales. The latter, variously described as a 3-pounder or a 6-pounder, appears in fact to have been a very light infantry gun, perhaps a 1-pounder, designed as an anti-personnel weapon, firing a small number of grape shot or musket balls, rather than solid shot.

The process of serving a gun was complicated. Assuming the piece was already in action, as it recoiled from its last round, the spongemen damp swabbed the tube to quench any live embers, while the ammunition Handlers brought up a felt or serge-wrapped powder bag and the type of round indicated by the gunner. The loader inserted the bagged powder charge into the tube and the spongeman shoved it home with the ram end of his swab, while the ventman placed his leathercased thumb over the vent as further insurance against premature explosion due to unextinguished embers. The loader then placed the projectile with its loosely attached wooden wad into the tube. As the spongeman shoved this down, the ventman

jabbed a "pricker" through the vent into the powder bag to tear it, and then shoved a light metal or goose quill primer filled with high quality powder into the tear. The gunner then relaid the piece, adjusting elevation and deflection by the use of wedges, screws, or main force. When he was satisfied, a slow match was then applied to the primer, discharging the piece, and started the whole process over again.

Of course, prepared powder charges were not always available to either side during this campaign. As a result, the gunners often had to ladle loose powder into the tube. This meant that the proper measure of powder, generally from a fourth to a third of the weight of the projectile, was not always used. As a result, artillery accuracy suffered.

Although mechanical fiction primers, basically flintlocks, had been in use for some time by the British and French, it appears that they were not used in Texas. Indeed, the Texian artillerymen appear to have often primed a piece by the simple expedient of pouring loose powder down the touch hole, a very obsolete and potentially dangerous method.

The normal projectile for guns, which had relatively long barrels and could attain considerable range with a flat trajectory, was shot, or ball. This was a solid sphere of metal designed to smash into things, like walls or masses of men. Direct fire was what worked against walls, but all of the cannon used at the Alamo were too light to make much of an impression. Had Santa Anna waited for his 12-pounders he would have battered his way into the Alamo with minimal loss. Against troops, indirect fire was best, aiming the ball so that it struck relatively hard ground in front of the massed enemy, since the impact would throw rocks and gravel at the troops and the ball would then ricochet, or bounce, through the ranks, each leap covering slightly less than half the distance made by the former. Howitzers had a short barrel and were designed for high-angle fire. Their normal projectile was the shell, a hollow metal sphere filled with powder and provided with a fuse. Before inserting the shell in the tube the loader had to cut the fuse to a length suited to the range required and, usually, apply a match to it too, making his job considerably more hazardous than under normal circumstances. Howitzers were particularly useful for getting at places behind obstacles, such as villages, forests, and hills. This ought to have made them particularly valuable at the Alamo, but Santa Anna does not appear to have employed them properly. Both guns and howitzers were also provided with canister or grapeshot, for situations where the enemy was literally at point-blank range. The two types of ammunition are often confused, but are quite different. Canister was aptly named, for it was essentially a package which released numerous—50-75—musket balls upon leaving the barrel; grapeshot was similar, but consisted of fewer—

9-12—but larger balls. A "taste" or two of canister or a "whiff" of grapeshot discharged into the face of an attacking force could cause horrendous damage and quite possibly result in the failure of the attack. Had the Mexican cannon at San Jacinto managed to get off a few rounds of either the outcome of the battle might well have been different. Lacking canister or grapeshot, the Texians improvised by firing scrap metal, including chopped up horse shoes and bits of chain. This did little to enhance barrel life, but long term bureaucratic and financial concerns were not at the time uppermost in the minds of the men at the Alamo and San Jacinto.

Gunpowder. All of these weapons, muskets and artillery alike, used black powder. This generated lots of thick white smoke. As a result, after a few rounds everyone was literally shrouded in great clouds, making it difficult to observe one's targets. Particularly for the artillery, continuing to fire in such circumstances was merely a waste of ammunition.

The Mexicans apparently used a relatively cheap grade of powder. Certainly, the Texians generally refused to use it despite having captured considerable stocks at the Alamo and Goliad in December of 1835, preferring instead the standard powder in common use in the U.S., which consisted of 76% nitre, 14% willow or poplar charcoal, and 10% sulphur. This was slightly less effective than the optimal formula, 74.64% nitre, 13.51% charcoal, and

11.85% sulphur, but was cheaper and easier to make.

The standard U.S. powder burned somewhat more rapidly, and with somewhat more smoke and slightly less propellant power than powder produced according to the optimal formula. As the Mexican powder apparently produced even more smoke with even less propellant power, the formula in use was probably more generous with regard to charcoal than the American formula. Graft undoubtedly played a role here, as some lots of Mexican powder were described as "little more than charcoal" by knowledgeable observers.

Spiking. If a cannon was in danger of being captured it was standard policy to "spike" it. This was actually a fairly simple procedure, involving the hammering of an iron spike into the touch hole, rendering the piece temporarily unserviceable. A spiked gun could be repaired, usually by extracting the spike, but, if it was too firmly implanted, by drilling a new touch hole. This latter course was a tricky business, since using the piece could cause the spike to fly out of the original touch hole with fatal results, and in any case the spiked touch hole might not be fully sealed, thereby causing the loss of some of the piece's projecting power. Since spiked guns were repairable, when the Mexican Army dismantled the Alamo, guns were not merely spiked, but were worked over with a sledge hammer, so that trunnions, the axle-like projections which serve to mount the gun to the carriage, and cascabels, the ball-like projection at the rear of the piece which served to balance it, were smashed off. As a further precaution, the guns were then dumped into the San Antonio River.

CHAPTER VI

"¡Deguello!" — the Fall of the Alamo

5-6 March 1836

By the time Bonham rode into the Alamo, it was clear that the situation of the garrison had become desperate.

Travis had perhaps 190 men to hold a ramshackle fort in the face of an overwhelmingly superior foe. Everything that could be done had been done. Weak points in the walls had been strengthened, mostly by piling earth against their inner sides; rough parapets had been raised to provide some protection for the men on the walls, and some earthworks erected to cover the main gate. A breach in the northern wall, made at the time the Texians had taken the Alamo back in December, had been rudely patched with earth and timbers. But such repairs were at best crude; the walls of the Alamo had never been intended to withstand artillery fire, and, light as it was, the Mexican artillery was slowly chipping away at the adobe and stone walls. Some trenches had been dug in the interior to provide fall-back defenses should the enemy pierce the outer perimeter. Ammunition was running low, and the men were reminded to conserve it as much as possible. Supplies of food were dwindling too and would not last much longer. Even if the Mexican Army did not attack, the garrison's days were numbered.

Each day Santa Anna's noose grew tighter, his artillery moved closer. On the morning of 4 March Santa Anna received his long awaited reinforcements. Three battalions of the *First Infantry Brigade*, nearly 1,000 men, came up under Col. Francisco Duque, having been delayed largely because Brig. Gen. Gaona had given the men five day's rest in the face of Santa Anna's orders to make haste. This brought the Mexican strength before the Alamo to some 2,500 men and nine pieces of artillery. Santa Anna called a staff conference. His officers argued that the time was not yet ripe for a general assault. The balance of Gaona's command, some 700 men, with five guns, the badly needed pair of 12-pounders among them, would be along in two or three days, by the 7th at the latest. Surprisingly, no one suggested starving the garrison out, a matter that would take but a few days. Several of the senior officers did bring up the subject of prisoners, urging that a show of mercy be made. Santa Anna, the "President and Major General," listened attentively. Then he overruled them all, disposing of their objections with various arguments, but ultimately by the force of his authority. As he later put it, "Against the daring foreigners opposing us, the honor of our Nation and our Army is at stake." The troops would be rested for the 4th and 5th, and then the Alamo would be stormed on the morning of 6 March.

Santa Anna spent 4-5 March planning his attack. His orders, issued at 2:00 p.m. on the 5th, displayed his talent for careful and meticulous preparations. There would be four attacking columns plus a reserve and a pursuit and security force. The *First Column* would comprise 400 men under the command of Martin Cos, who was now back in the general's favor but was also serving in clear violation of the parole he had given the Texians in December; the column was to strike the northwest corner of the walls. The *Second Column*, 380 men under Col. Duque of the *Toluca Battalion*, would attack against the northern wall where it had been breached and

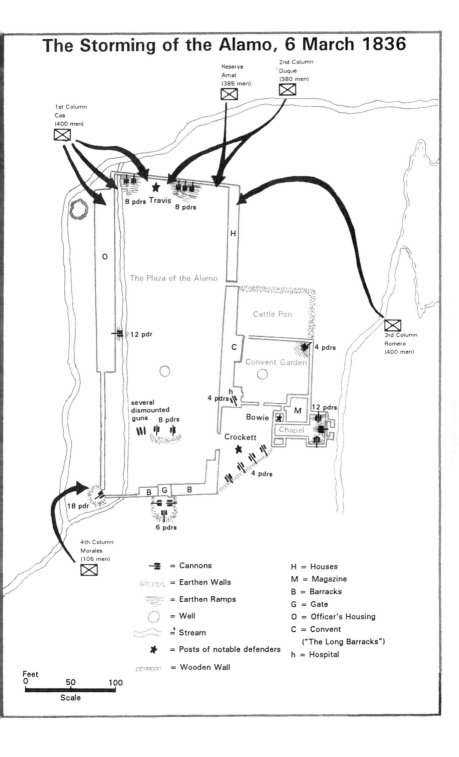

The Storming of the Alamo, 6 March 1836

Reserve
Amat
(385 men)

2nd Column
Duque
(380 men)

1st Column
Cos
(400 men)

8 pdrs   Travis   8 pdrs

H

O

The Plaza of the Alamo

Cattle Pen

12 pdr

C

Convent Garden

3rd Column
Romero
(400 men)

4 pdrs

h

4 pdrs

M   12 pdrs

Bowie

Chapel

several
dismounted
guns   8 pdrs

Crockett

4 pdrs

B   G   B

18 pdr

6 pdrs

4th Column
Morales
(105 men)

Feet
0   50   100

Scale

= Cannons

= Earthen Walls

= Earthen Ramps

= Well

= Stream

= Posts of notable defenders

= Wooden Wall

H = Houses

M = Magazine

B = Barracks

G = Gate

O = Officer's Housing

C = Convent
    ("The Long Barracks")

h = Hospital

Composition of Mexican Assault Columns
The Storming of the Alamo, 6 March 1836

First Column (Cos) 400 men, 10 ladders, 2 crowbars, and 2 axes
Aldama Battalion (300) less *Granaderos*
San Luis Potosi Battalion (100) *1st - 3rd Companies*

Second Column (Duque) 380 men, 10 ladders, 2 crowbars, 2 axes
1st Toluca Battalion (280) less *Granaderos*
San Luis Potosi Battalion (100) *4th - 6th Companies*

Third Column (Romero) 400 men
Jimenez Battalion (200) less *Cazadores* and *Granaderos*
Matamoros Battalion (200) less *Cazadores* and *Granaderos*

Fourth Column (Morales) 105 men, 2 ladders
Cazadores of the *Matamoros, Jimenez,* and *San Luis Potosi Battalions*

Reserve (Amat) 385 men
Zapadores Battalion (185)
Granaderos of the *Matamoros, Jimenez, Aldama, 1st Toluca,*
        and *San Luis Potosi Battalions*

Cavalry Pickets (Ramirez y Sesma) 380 men
Dolores Cavalry Regiment (285)
Presidiales del Rio Grande (55)
Coahuila Cavalry Regiment (30)
Vera Cruz Cavalry Regiment (10)

Unengaged (Santa Anna) 375-425 men
Escolta (26)
Artillery (Ampudia) 85 men, 10 guns
        (2) 8-pounders, (2) 6-pounders, (2) 4-pounders, (2) 7" howitzers
Recruits (265-315)

hastily repaired. The *Third Column*, 400 seasoned men under
Col. Jose Maria Romero of the *Matamoros Battalion*, would
attack the eastern wall in the vicinity of the animal enclosure;
and the *Fourth Column*, about 100 select *cazadores*—light infantrymen—under Col. Juan Morales of the *San Luis Potosi Battalion*, would attempt to take the rough palisade linking the
south wall to the chapel, which was Crockett's post. This
attack, the weakest of the four, was probably intended as a
diversion. Making provision even for the worst, Santa Anna
detailed which officers were to take command of each column

in the event that its commanding officer was slain, giving himself the task of leading Cos' men should the latter fall. The *Reserve* would total 385 of the finest men in the army, five companies of *granaderos* plus the elite *Zapadores Battalion* under Col. Augustin Amat. The cavalry, 350 men under Brig. Gen. Ramirez y Sesma, was to patrol the surrounding countryside, to ensure that no one escaped and that no surprise reinforcements arrived at an inopportune moment. Recognizing that the army had many green men in its ranks, Santa Anna ordered that only seasoned men were to participate in the assault, to guarantee that the attacking troops were physically and morally prepared. All recruits and untrained volunteers, perhaps 400 men, were to remain in camp. In addition, lest they fire upon friendly troops during the assault, he ordered that the artillery was to keep silent.

The broad generalities taken care of, Santa Anna then got down to the details. Ladders, axes, and crowbars were allocated in varying numbers to each column. *Granaderos* and *cazadores* were issued six extra rounds apiece, line troops four, with each to get two extra flints. Men were ordered to discard their overcoats, packs, and other impedimenta before mustering for the attack. Officers were instructed to see that muskets were clean, bayonets sharp, uniforms neat, chin straps properly in place. Santa Anna also ordered that harassing fire against the Alamo cease at 10:00 p.m., so that the troops could get as much rest as possible, to steel them for the coming ordeal. The troops were to be roused at midnight so that they would have plenty of time to arrive at their jumping off places by dawn. With his preparations made, Santa Anna himself retired. There was a fine repast waiting, prepared by his personal chef, a black American named Ben, and a bottle of fine wine as well.

Despite Santa Anna's intentions, many of the troops did not get much rest that night. By ordering a new trench dug, about halfway between the existing Mexican lines north of the Alamo and the fort itself, to provide a line of departure for the assault, he contradicted his own instructions. As a result, the men of the *Toluca* and *San Luis Potosi Battalions* spent much of the night entrenching under the direction of the chief of engineers, Capt. Ignacio La Bastica, and his two assistants. This was difficult work, which ought to have been performed by trained sappers, but there were none with the army, and so the task fell to the infantry. Noticing the activity, the Texians brought the Mexican troops under a harassing fire for a time. The men of the *Second Column* got little rest that night.

The arrival of the Mexican reinforcements was an ominous sign for Travis. Although Santa Anna had been in San Antonio since 23 February, Travis had discounted rumors to that effect. This was somewhat reassuring, since it was unlikely that the Mexican Army would undertake some decisive action in the general's absence. But when Duque's column arrived it was greeted with cheers of "¡*Viva Santa Anna!*" and later that day there were more cheers for the general, the news of Urrea's victories over the Texians having arrived. This convinced Travis that Santa Anna had finally arrived at San Antonio. During the 4th the Mexicans had managed to displace several cannon forward to within about 250 yards of the north face of the Alamo, and these guns spent the 5th pounding away at the northeastern corner of the walls. All of this suggested that something significant was afoot. There was only one thing this could mean: Santa Anna was making final preparations to storm the Alamo.

Travis ordered final preparations. By an enormous effort, the men managed to pile a mound of earth against the back of the northern wall, strengthening it against cannon fire. The available ammunition was issued, and the men on watch were given two or three additional muskets, to be kept loaded at their posts. Shortly after dusk on the 5th Travis dispatched one final courier, James L. Allen, at 16 apparently the youngest man in the Alamo, with a last appeal to Fannin to send aid. Although his appeal still rang with defiance, and concluded with "God and Texas! Victory or Death!" it appears that Travis at this point attempted to negotiate with Santa Anna. Militarily, there was no longer any point to holding the

Alamo. It had delayed the advance of the Mexican Army for nearly a fortnight, and its fall was now inevitable. Although men had slipped through the Mexican lines several times, and once even an entire company, when the Gonzales Mounted Volunteers rode in, escape seemed unlikely; the men of the garrison were tired, hungry, and would have to break out on foot in the face of an enemy who had hundreds of cavalry. The alternative was to attempt to surrender on honorable terms. Santa Anna's orders to offer "no quarter" was taken as rhetoric, for such a course was wholly out of keeping with the custom of war at the time. Surrender on terms was one of the many little traditions which had evolved over the centuries to mitigate the horrors of war: by doing so a beleaguered garrision preserved honor all around, while sparing lives on both sides. Some of Travis' men appear to have pressed him on the issue, and he seems to have concurred. Two witnesses, Maj. Gen. Vicente Filisola and Col. Jose de la Peña, recorded that Travis made an attempt to negotiate through intermediaries in San Antonio, it still being possible for men to pass over the walls and into the town. But Santa Anna spurned the offer, saying there could be "no guarantees for traitors" he demanded nothing less than surrender at discretion. This Travis was unwilling to do. So there was nothing now that could avert a final clash at the Alamo.

The night of 5-6 March was quite warm, a welcome relief from the freezing temperatures which had prevailed for a week. Although the moon was almost full, the sky was cloudy and it lent but a feeble light. Travis spent much of the night up and about. Accompanied by his man Joe, a 23-year-old black slave who toted a shotgun, he inspected the guard posts, conferred with the officer of the watch, talked to the sentries, and even played with some of the children, huddled in the church. He gave little Angelina Dickinson his gold ring with a cat's eye stone, threading a string through it so that he could hang it around the child's neck. Like many of the other men, he wrote one or two letters and made a simple will.

Then, around about 4:00 a.m. he went to his quarters, in a building on the west wall, near the northern corner of the Alamo, and bedded down. By then the vicinity of the Alamo was serenely quiet. But even before Travis turned in, the Mexican Army had begun to stir.

The cavalrymen were the first up, around midnight. They had much to do, feeding and watering their mounts, saddling up, and dispersing into the fields, to mop up any of the defenders who might escape from the Alamo, and along the roads, to give warning should anyone attempt a relief. The infantrymen began to stir as well. They too had much to do. As the men fell into ranks, their officers checked their equipment. Within an hour or so the infantry were marching to their assigned positions. By 4:00 a.m., even as Travis was turning in for the night, the assault columns were ready, each some 200-300 yards from the walls of the Alamo. The entire

Travis' Line in the Sand

Perhaps the greatest of Alamo myths is that regarding the famous "Line in the Sand."

The tale is simple. On the night of 3-4 March, with the Mexican Army making preparations for a final assault, Travis mustered his men, including the sick and wounded, in the Plaza of the Alamo. Making a short speech about the hopelessness of the situation, he announced that he was resolved to stay and die, but would not force any man to do so. Then, using his sword, he drew a line in the sand and invited all who wished to die with him to cross that line. The men hesitated for a moment. Then one, a 26-year-old named Tapley Holland, boldly stepped forward, to be followed by the rest of the men, in ones and twos and then in groups. As they walked across the line, the desperately ill Jim Bowie raised his head from his sick-bed, saying something like, "Boys, I can't make it across that line, will some of you give men a hand?" At once, four men sprang forward and, each taking a corner of his cot, carried him across the line. Within minutes it was over, as every man strode across. Every man, that is, save one, by name Louis Moses Rose, an older man and a veteran of Napoleon's retreat from Moscow.

Quietly, without harassment, Rose was allowed to gather his few belongings. Soon afterwards, with kind words from both Travis and Bowie, he slipped over the

114

movement had been made with extraordinary skill; although Travis had posted three men in the area between the walls of the Alamo and the Mexican lines, none raised the alarm.

Once in position, the troops of the assault columns were ordered to rest. With his staff, Santa Anna took up a position by his north battery, only some 250 yards from the Alamo. As the first streaks of dawn broke the eastern skies, shortly after 5:00 on Sunday the 6th, Santa Anna signaled to Bugler Jose Maria Gonzalez of the *Zapadores*. The *"¡Adelante! Forward!"* rang out, to be caught and echoed in an instant by all the buglers in the army. Swords in hand, officers screamed *"¡Arriba! Attack!"* And almost as one, the four columns sprang forward, racing to cross the 200 to 300 yards which separated their points of concentration from the Alamo walls.

In the Alamo, Capt. John Baugh, a Virginian, had just come on duty as officer of the day. He heard the trumpetings and

---

wall and away into the darkness.

Great theater, certainly, and done well in several celluloid versions of the Alamo, perhaps best of all in *The Last Command*. Unfortunately, not very good history.

Although the story of Travis' line in the sand has been accepted by many writers, even some who are hostile to the Texan cause, the tale is seriously flawed.

The incident is not mentioned by any of the known survivors of the Alamo. Neither Mrs. Dickinson, whose husband Almaron would have been among those who crossed the line, nor the teen-aged James Allen, whom Travis dispatched as a courier on the very last night of the siege, mentioned the incident, nor did Brigido Guerrero, who would also have had to cross the line, nor Travis' body servant Joe. There is other evidence to suggest that the tale is a fabrication. The touch about Bowie, for example, ignores the fact that during the siege, he was so ill as to be unable to recognize his friend Juan Seguin, when the latter asked to borrow his horse on the night of 25-26 February. Nor does it seem likely that the arrogant, self-important Travis, a fanatic on the matter of Texas independence and something of a martinet, would have had the nobility of character to have given his men a choice.

The story of the line in the sand did not come into circulation until a number of years after the fall of the Alamo, when a man identifying himself as Louis Rose gained some notoriety from it. It was perhaps inspired by Ben Milam's line at San Antonio the previous December.

the cries, and raised the alarm, "The Mexicans are coming!" As the Mexicans stormed across the open ground, the Texians on guard began to fire, while their sleeping comrades began to pour our of their barracks and race for their posts. Men began to fall.

The attacking troops came on in fair order, holding their fire for a time. But then the enthusiasm of the moment caused someone to shout "*¡Viva Santa Anna!*" and someone else shouted "*¡Viva La Republica!*" and immediately nearly 1,600 of Mexico's finest infantry took up the cry. The men began firing, emptying their muskets with no chance to reload.

Baugh's cry and the rattle of musketry woke Travis. Grabbing his weapons, he headed out the door of his room belting on his sword, with Joe following close behind. Exhorting his men, he reached his post by the 8-pounder battery near the breach in the northern wall just as the first Mexicans began putting up scaling ladders. The artillery was already cutting swathes in the Mexican ranks. Travis emptied his shotgun into the mass below. Joe too fired into the enemy ranks, and then turned to see his master tumbling over backwards with a musket ball in his forehead. As the stunned young man looked on, Travis, his sword still clutched in his hand, slipped down the earthen slope, then sat up, looked about for an instant and died, perhaps the first of the defenders to be killed. Joe fled to the safety of one of the buildings.

Firing became general. As their artillery belched repeated doses of scrap iron at the attacking Mexican troops, the Texians, many of whom had three or four loaded muskets at hand, poured on a deadly hail of bullets. Col. Duque fell, struck by some scrap metal, his men charging right over his body in their ardor for the attack. But the deadly fire from the wall was too much, and the *Second Column*, first to reach the wall, was the first to falter. The troops found that their hastily constructed ladders were too flimsy to bear the weight of several men at once, and they began bunching up in the relative safety of the dead ground beneath the walls, where the Texians could not fire without exposing themselves. The other columns, having a bit further to go, had an even more difficult time. The great 12-pounders atop the chapel poured a deadly fire on the *Third Column* and it veered away to its right. Cos' *First Column* received two charges of scrap iron full in the front, and the men veered away to their left, taking fire in their flank as they did so. The *Fourth Column*, composed of light infantry, raced for the jerry-built wall in front of the cemetery, but Crockett, with his Tennesseans and a few others, poured out a deadly fire from their muskets and 4-pounders. The *cazadores* went to ground. Within minutes it seemed as if the attack had failed. But it was merely a momentary lull and, with officers swearing and cursing, the troops began moving again.

With "*¡Vivas!*" for their country and general the attackers pressed on. The storm of Texian fire and lead from the Alamo was severely testing the mettle of the finest troops Mexico had, and the troops were up to the test. As the troops advanced, they assumed the instinctive "head to the wind" posture of men against fire. The columns began veering towards each other, the likewise instinctive tendency of men under fire to bunch up.

Romero's *Third Column* slipped rightwards toward the *Second*, now under the courageous old grafter Brig. Gen. Manuel Fernandez Castrillon. Cos' column veered leftwards, lapping around the northwestern corner of the Alamo. And the *cazadores* of the *Fourth Column* began to move obliquely across the south face, trying to get away from the murderous fire of Crockett's men. The troops pressed against the foot of the northern wall; Fernandez Castrillon's and now Romero's men found themselves safe from the artillery and somewhat sheltered from enemy fire, for it would take a brave Texian indeed to expose himself there, where so many Mexican muskets could bear that accuracy was no problem. Once again a lull set in. The battle had reached a critical phase.

Santa Anna intervened. He ordered Col. Amat's *Reserve* into action, to support Castrillon and Romero against the northwestern corner of the defenses. To inspire the men by example, Santa Anna also sent in the dandified members of his staff as well. And he ordered Bugler Gonzalez to play an ancient call, the "¡*Deguello!*", a bloodcurdling tune signifying "No mercy!"

As the other buglers in the army echoed the "¡*Deguello!*", the attackers took heart; Col. de la Peña, with the *Zapadores*, would later write that the call "inspired us to scorn life and to embrace death." Having changed the front to their right, Cos' men slammed against the northwestern corner of the Alamo, as the *cazadores* of Morales' *Fourth Column* continued their oblique movement across the front of the Alamo, taking advantage of the cover offered by the numerous half-burned *jacales* in the area. The last of the scaling ladders were brought up. The intermingled men of the *Third* and *Second Columns*, pressed against the northern wall, in what Col. de la

Louis Moses Rose

Traditionally regarded as "The only coward in the Alamo," Louis Rose is one of the more interesting of the Alamo legends. As tradition has it, Rose was, of course, the only man who refused to cross Travis' line in the sand.

The story of Louis—or Lewis—Rose was told by himself, some years after the Alamo fell, and, since Rose was illiterate, was written down by various people. According to Rose, who by some accounts was Jewish, as he prepared to escape, he spoke briefly with Bowie and Crockett, who had some gentle words for him. Then he slipped over the wall, clutching a small bundle of personal belongings. He landed, in some versions of his tale, in a pool of blood, got up, and began to make his way

carefully through the Mexican lines, several times having close calls with cavalry patrols.

Once Rose was away from the vicinity of San Antonio, he headed northwards across the prairie. It was tough going, especially since he had to move at night. Several times he ran into thickets of prickly pear and yucca, which tore his legs severely, the thorns working their way into his flesh. It took him several weeks to make his way to an American settlement. Near death from exhaustion and exposure, he was recognized by an acquaintance, who took him in and treated his wounds.

After the war, Rose went into business in northeastern Texas, but did not prosper, since his reputation as "The only coward in the

Peña, who was among them, called a "confused mass." Then, the men of the *Toluca Battalion* found that it was possible to scale the rough wood and stone patch which had been hastily thrown up to seal the old breach there. Men began to climb the wall. Heroically exposing themselves, the defenders poured down a deadly fire, but Mexican muskets kept up a counter fusillade, sweeping the walls of Texians. And, it must be said, the fire from the Mexican troops still to the rear was galling to their comrades in front for some of them fell, shot in the back by "friendly fire."

Led by Brig. Gen. Juan Amador, of Santa Anna's aides-de-camp, a handful of men from the *Toluca Battalion* attained the top of the northern wall. At almost the same moment Cos hurled the *Aldama Battalion* against the west corner of the Alamo, the men rapidly scaling the wall against almost no

---

Alamo" did not make him the most popular man in Texas. On one occasion a drunken assailant almost killed him, but Rose could find no legal recourse. Eventually, Texas being too inhospitable for him, Rose moved to Louisiana, where he died in 1850, aged about 70.

The story of Louis Rose is a curious blend of reality and fabrication. Certainly there really was a man named Louis Rose, who claimed to have been at the Alamo. It is possible that he was the man Mrs. Dickinson remembered as "Ross," who deserted one night. But if so, he certainly had not refused to cross Travis' line in the sand, since Travis had not drawn one. This would certainly suggest that much of the tale told by the historical Rose was a fabrication. To be sure, some aspects of Rose's account sound reasonable, such as his comment that it took several weeks to reach an American settlement. After all, he was traveling during the "Runaway Scrape," with the bulk of the American population in Texas fleeing for safety before the advancing Mexicans. On the other hand, some portions sound false. The touch about landing in a "pool of blood," for example, being rather melodramatic, and very unlikely given the nature of the soil in the area and the relative lightness of casualties hitherto. Aside from the "line in the sand" story, which is refuted by the lack of corroboration on the part of far more reliable witnesses, everything that Rose said about the Alamo was readily available in the public record. The best verdict that can be rendered as to the question of whether Rose was an Alamo survivor is "Not proven."

resistance. From the top of the wall, the troops began to jump down into the plaza of the Alamo below. One of them found a small postern gate, and opened it. Cos' men began to pour in even as Amador's cleared the 8-pounder battery on their left. Within minutes, the entire northern wall was in Mexican hands.

Atop the church, Capt. Dickinson and his men began swinging the 12-pounders so that they could play on the enemy troops pouring into the fortress from the north. Dickinson left the work for a moment, ran down the earthen ramp to the room where his wife was sheltering for a last embrace, then raced back to duty. The great guns belched grapeshot and scrap iron at the enemy. The 8-pounder battery at the center of the courtyard did likewise. Enemy casualties mounted, the attackers wavered, but only for a moment, for the *Fourth Column*, the *cazadores*, made themselves heard.

Having been repulsed from Crockett's position, the *cazadores* had moved obliquely across the south face of the Alamo, maintaining excellent discipline as they did. Reaching the southwestern corner of the mission, they stormed the earthen redoubt there, climbing up the rough sides to take the great 18-pounder cannon at the point of the bayonet. Now, the piece secured, they turned it upon the interior of the defenses. As some manned the powerful gun, the balance of the light infantrymen, Col. Morales at their head, stormed into the courtyard. Mexican troops were now pouring into the plaza of the Alamo from three points, across the north wall, through the postern near the northwestern corner, and across the 18-pounder position in the southwestern corner. The Texians, who had held bravely and well for nearly 45 minutes, fell back, as planned by the wily Travis.

The men fled first for the entrenchments that they had constructed so laboriously. Then they made for the security of the many buildings fringing the interior court. Crockett, whom Susanna Dickinson had moments before seen briefly entering the chapel to mutter a short prayer, denied his right flank, pulling men from the palisade on the south side of the

The Death of Crockett

Until early in the twentieth century, the generally accepted story of the death of Davy Crockett held that he was among the handful of prisoners saved by Brig. Gen. Manuel Fernandez Castrillion, only to be slaughtered at Santa Anna's order. By the 1950s, however, and particularly with the advent of various cinematic versions of the defense of the Alamo, there gradually arose the notion that Crockett had gone down fighting, clubbing Mexicans after he ran out of ammunition until Old Betsy was smashed, and then falling atop the bodies of a dozen foes, pierced by the enemy's bayonets. The story of the half dozen prisoners is confirmed in various Mexican sources, such as that by Francisco Becerra, the Mexican sergeant who subsequently settled down in Texas, as is the fact that the eldest of the prisoners was Crockett. The clearest and most detailed of the Mexican accounts of the death of Crockett is that of Col. Jose Enrique de la Peña, *La Rebelion de Texas*. This was first published in Mexico City in 1836, not long after the conclusion of the Texas Campaign, but attracted no attention. Upon its reissue in the 1950s, it caused a sensation among Texanophiles and -phobes in the U.S. and again when it was published in English in the 1970s. De la Peña's account is in most other respects quite accurate, which argues in favor of his version of the fate of Crockett. According to de la Peña, the man admitted to being Crockett, and spun a complex tale apparently intended to get himself off the hook which, of course, didn't work. This sounds pretty convincing. Moreover, it does not contradict the evidence of Susanna Dickinson, who said that she had seen Crockett's body near the front of the church, where the executions are said to have taken place, though it does run contrary to Joe's account, in which he saw Crockett's body atop a pile of dead Mexicans, in the northwestern corner of the cemetery, near the hospital. Despite this, it is probable that the story told by de la Peña is accurate.

Arguing in favor of de la Peña's account is the fact that the earlier, pre-cinematic tradition had Crockett and the others being taken prisoner and dying defiantly and bravely, precisely as de la Peña says they did.

cemetery to cover the low wall that divided it from the main plaza. Heavily beset, his men began falling back towards the hospital, only to be trapped against the wall and, in a furious hand-to-hand fight, cut down. But other Texians still held out. Many men had made it to the relative safety of the buildings fringing the plaza. Here they made their stands, two or three to a room, or all alone, in the barracks and the hospital, and the other buildings. Some men retreated from room to room, for during the siege much effort had been spent in preparing the buildings for just such a last-ditch defense. It was fighting of the most difficult sort, house-to-house and room-to-room. One structure was so soundly fortified that the Mexican infantrymen dragged up a cannon, apparently the Alamo's own 18-pounder, blew in the door, and went in with cold steel. And so, one by one, the defenders were ferreted out and killed. Some of the defenders tried to surrender, but as always in such fighting, others in the same party wanted to fight on, and all were slain.

Shortly after 6:00, about an hour into the assault, with the sun beginning to lighten the scene, a struggle developed on the roof of the Long Barracks. From a flag staff atop the roof the garrison's colors were displayed. As some men of the *Jimenez Battalion* charged towards the Texian banner, a detachment of the *Zapadores* gained the roof of the barracks. Three men of the *Zapadores* were cut down as they tried to reach the Texian colors. Then a young subaltern of their battalion, Jose Maria Torres, not yet 19 years of age, leaped forward. Grabbing the lanyards, Torres hauled down the flag of rebellion. Then, aided by the mortally wounded and equally young Lt. Damaso Martinez, he raised his battalion's colors, the angry eagle and tricolor of Mexico. Scant moments later, still clutching the Texian colors, young Torres fell.

The battle was now drawing to a close. The last Texians were being rousted from their hiding places and killed. Some of the defenders apparently attempted to flee. Col. de la Peña noted that at least five men were seen to flee over the walls. Finally, only Almeron Dickinson's post in the chapel remained, from whence the 12-pounders still poured death into the courtyard. Taking the slab-sided building would require extraordinary courage. And it was to be found in full measure.

Col. Juan Morales, leading the *cazadores* of the *Fourth Column*, had his men drag up the captured 18-pounder. They opened fire, pouring round after round right into the front entrance and down the nave of the old church, while other troops poured on a withering fire. Gradually the countering fire from the chapel grew less. Then the light companies of the *Matamoros* and *Jimenez Battalions*, together numbering less than 50 men now, stormed in with the bayonet. The surviving defenders were shot down or bayoneted, one, Robert Evans, in the act of throwing a torch into the powder magazine. Bowie, desperately ill and unable to leave his sick bed, was shot and bayoneted where he lay. Others fell where they were found, whether resisting or surrendering or too wounded to know the difference. Some troops got out of hand, and two older boys huddled among the women and children were butchered, and Susanna Dickinson was slightly wounded. But then the officers asserted their authority. As the women and children were offered protection, the *cazadores* went in search of more legitimate enemies.

Soon the firing fell off, from a steady roar to an occasional bang, and then to silence. Santa Anna entered the mission, surrounded by toadies and officers. Near the front of the church General Fernandez Castrillon came up to report that several of the defenders had been mistakenly taken alive, a pathetic half dozen men, one a mere boy, another a bent and aged man. Fernandez Castrillon suggested that perhaps a show of mercy might be in order. Angrily Santa Anna demurred, his instructions had been that no prisoners be taken and he ordered the men slain immediately. Col. Jose de la Peña, who was present, recounted what took place: "Several officers who were with the President, who perhaps had not been present at the point of the danger...pushed forward, in order to impress their general, and, with swords in hand, fell upon these miserable, defenseless men...[who]...died without complaining and without humiliating themselves...." As the survivors were so brutally cut down, silence fell upon the Alamo. It was a bit past 7:00 a.m., little more than two hours from Jose Maria Gonzalez' first bugle call, and the Alamo was securely and completely Mexican once again.

The Death of Bowie

One of the hoariest myths of the Alamo concerns the death of Bowie. To begin with, Bowie's location at the time the Mexican Army overran the Alamo is often erroneously given. Although he spent most of the siege in his quarters in the barracks just east of the main gate, it appears that in the last day or so he was moved to one of the rooms on the ground floor of the chapel, perhaps to provide some security from artillery fire. It was here that he met his end.

By tradition, when the Mexican soldiers burst into Bowie's room, they found the sick man sitting up in his bed, with a brace of pistols in his hands and his famed "Arkansas toothpick" on his lap. As the soldiers raced across the room to attack him, Bowie felled two with pistol shots, and then, as his assailants plunged their bayonets into him, cut a few more to pieces with his knife before giving up the ghost, whereupon his body was tossed in the air on the points of Mexican bayonets.

There are several problems with this account. While a man of undoubted courage and remarkable skill as a brawler, Bowie was terminally ill at the time. His physical condition during the last days of the siege was extremely poor, and it seems highly unlikely that he was in any condition to defend himself. Moreover, a bayonet has

a considerably longer reach than a bowie knife. And even the strongest troops are likely to have found "tossing" a six-foot, 200-pound man about with bayonets quite impossible.

A slightly different version of the death of Bowie was told by Andrea Castañon Ramirez Villanueva, better known as *Sra.* Candelaria. *Sra.* Candelaria claimed to have nursed Bowie in his final hours. "I had hard work keeping Colonel Bowie on his couch. He got hold of his two pistols and began firing them off, shouting all the while to his men not to give up. He was raving....Finally a bullet whizzed through the door, grazing my chin—see, it left a scar which is still there today—and killed Bowie. I had the Colonel in my arms. I was just giving him a drink." Unfortunately, although *Sra.* Candelaria mentions Mrs. Dickinson in her account, the latter did not mention *Sra.* Candelaria in her version of the battle, and specifically branded her a fraud. This need not necessarily be considered conclusive proof, but there are other problems with *Sra.* Candelaria's account. For example, she said, "Davy Crockett died fighting like a wild beast, within a few feet of me, and brave Colonel Travis within a few feet the other way," adding, "Poor Davy Crockett was killed near the entrance to the Church, his rifle in his hands. He was the last to die." If indeed, *Sra.* Candelaria was present at Bowie's deathbed, she would not have had knowledge of how or where any of these men died. Moreover, Crockett probably survived the actual assault, only to perish in the massacre of prisoners ordered by Santa Anna soon afterwards. And Travis certainly did not die a "few feet" from the church. But there is more evidence to suggest that her story was a fabrication.

By her account, *Sra.* Candelaria was living in San Antonio when the Mexican Army marched up. On the fifth day of the siege, that is on 28 February, she claimed to have received a letter from Houston himself, which read, "Candelarita, go and take care of Bowie, my brother, in the Alamo," a request which she "took as an order and obeyed immediately." It seems highly unlikely that she would have been able to make her way into the Alamo at a time when the Mexican Army was increasing its hold on the place.

Although *Sra.* Candelaria was treated with great respect in her old age, even receiving a modest pension from the State of Texas, her tale is to be rejected. The fact that most of her story is quite accurate cannot stand in the way of the obvious flaws. The tale of the Alamo's last days was quite well known and she could easily have picked up a good deal of accurate information. Indeed, since she

also claimed to have been born in 1785 during an Indian raid, and since she died in 1899, it is surprising that anyone believed her at all.

Another legend has it that Bowie was taken alive and interrogated by a Mexican officer. On the strength of Bowie's Mexican citizenship, the officer accused him of treason. Bowie is said to have replied that it was not he who was the traitor, but those who fought to uphold Santa Anna's usurpation of power. This infuriated the officer, who had Bowie subjected to various tortures, including the cutting out of his tongue, before he was finally killed. This tale too can be dismissed, as it flies in the face of the testimony of the only two reliable witnesses, Mrs. Dickinson and Travis' slave Joe.

Other versions of the death of Bowie have him succumbing to his illness just hours before the Alamo was stormed or committing suicide in the last moments, a tale also told about Travis. None of these can stand up to scrutiny.

According to both Mrs. Dickinson—who admittedly gave more heroic versions of the events as time went on—and Joe, Bowie was apparently comatose at the time he died. When the Mexican troops entered his room, they found him in his bed, and blew out his brains. Dr. Sutherland, who subsequently visited the Alamo, later recorded that bloodstains could still be seen on the wall where Bowie's bed had been.

Surprisingly, a few men of the garrison survived. Brigido Guerrero had been with Cos' army back in December, but deserted to enter Texian service, enlisting as a private in Juan Seguin's company. When all was lost, he had fled to a cell, locked himself in, and, when Santa Anna's troops arrived had managed to convince them that he was a prisoner. Although wounded, Joe, Travis' black man-servant, was spared despite his participation in the defense on the grounds that he was a slave, as also was Sam, Bowie's freedman, who never told his story. At least one man, Henry Warnell, seems to have gotten clear away. He was one of the five men whom de la Peña recorded as having gone over the wall during the assault; of the other four, three were cut down by the cavalry and one survived for a time by hiding under a culvert, only to be discovered and slain the next day. But others apparently made at least a temporary escape from the disaster, for a number of bodies were later found in the fields to the north of the Alamo, men who had made good their escape from the slaughter within the walls, only to be slain by the cavalry as they attempted to flee.

The survivors, Mrs. Dickinson, and Bowie's sisters-in-law, *Sra.* Gertrudis Navarro and Mrs. Juana Navarro Alsbury, and the rest were well treated. Santa Anna even offered to adopt the charming infant Angelina Dickinson. When her proud and defiant mother refused, he gave her some money and told her she was free to go. But before he released her, Santa Anna paraded the army in Mrs. Dickinson's honor, and also because she would certainly spread word of its strength to all whom she encountered. Then he sent her and Angelina and Travis' man Joe off towards the Texian lines, guided by his cook, the black American Ben.

Altogether about 189 men died in the defense of the Alamo. They died for something about which they knew nothing, word of the Texian Declaration of Independence on 2 March never having reached the garrison. Among the Mexican troops, about 70 men seem to have died in taking the Alamo. But there were also some 300 or so men who were seriously

Susanna Dickinson

Susanna Dickinson (1814-1883) was born Susanna Wilkerson in Tennessee. In May of 1829, at the age of 15, the illiterate black-haired, blue-eyed beauty eloped with Almeron Dickinson (c. 1800-1836), a promising young black-smith originally from Pennsylvania who had served in the U.S. artillery. In 1831 the couple settled in Gonzales, Texas, where their daughter Angelina was born about three years later. By the fortunes of war, Susannah was the only American woman in the Alamo. Until age and the growing Alamo myth began to cloud her recollection she was one of the most reliable witnesses to the events. After the fall of the Alamo she was briefly famous throughout Texas, but then faded from view. Despite her status as a widow of one of the heroes of the Alamo, she received nothing from the Republic of Texas beyond her husband's land allotment. Her later life was an almost continuing disaster, characterized by poverty, repeated marriages, brutality, and prostitution. Her fifth marriage wrought a significant change in her life, and she settled down with her new husband, with whom she went into the cabinet-making business. After a scandalous life, in her old age Susanna Dickinson became quite "respectable." As a young woman strikingly beautiful, with black hair and blue eyes, she became quite stout as she grew older.

If anything, the life of "The Babe of the Alamo," Angelina Dickinson (1834-1869), was even worse than her mother's, under whose unfortunate influence she was raised. In 1843 several members of the Texas Senate attempted to secure a pension for the child, so that she could be raised and educated as befit the offspring of one of the heroes of the Alamo, rather than continue to be "educated in vice" under her mother's care, but those who could genuinely "Remember the Alamo" were greatly outnumbered by newcomers to Texas, and the attempt led nowhere. A marriage at age sixteen ended in divorce when Angelina's husband discovered that she bestowed her "favor" with great generosity. She eventually became a prostitute, had several children, and finally died of a uterine hemorrhage.

The two most important heroines of the Alamo both suffered neglect and abuse from the Texas for which the one gave her husband and the other her father.

wounded during the assault. And the army's lack of medical personnel began to tell. Without proper medical attention, even by the relatively unsophisticated standards of the day, most of the seriously wounded would die over the next few weeks from infection and shock, exposure, and loss of blood, as also would some of the slightly injured. They died not for Mexico, but for the greater glory of Jose Antonio Lopez de Santa Anna, who could have taken the Alamo with little or no bloodshed by merely waiting a few days more. So in their deaths, Travis and each of his comrades had managed to at least take two of their foes with them, no mean feat in any war. Of course, the disparity in the losses, indeed, the losses themselves, had not bothered Santa Anna in the least. He had won, after all, and he still had more men at hand, men of whom he had said: "What are the lives of soldiers more than so many chickens?" With these men, Santa Anna intended to extirpate the Texian Revolution. A decision on the fate of an independent Texas could not long be deferred.

Stephen F. Austin, in a formal portrait. Although sometimes depicted in "frontier dress," buckskins and such, by the time of the Texas Revolution Austin seems to have most often worn the mid-nine-teenth century equivalent of a business suit, as was the case with many of the other leaders of the Texas Revolution. *Courtesy of the Institute of Texan Cultures.*

Antonio Lopez de Santa Anna uncharacteristically out of uniform, in an engraving made for a Mexican history book about twenty years after the Texas Revolution, when he was a bit stouter. Definitively out of power, his countenance shows little of the arrogance found in many more commonly seen likenesses. *Courtesy of the Nettie Lee Benson Latin American Collection.*

William Barret Travis, in the only known likeness from life, a drawing made by Wiley Martin in December of 1835, when he had already achieved a measure of fame. The sketch is believed to be rather accurate, as it was said to bear a great resemblance to Travis' nephew, who was supposed to look a great deal like his uncle. *Courtesy of the Daughters of The Republic of Texas Library.*

Although this portrait of Martin Perfecto de Cos suggests a dashing, capable military commander, the reality was something entirely different. *Courtesy of the Institute of Texan Cultures.*

Ben Milam, more formally Benjamin Rush Milam, in a portrait painted after his death, showing him in the uniform of a Texas colonel, which he probably never wore. *Courtesy of the Texas State Library.*

James Bowie about the time of the Texas Revolution, in a portrait painted when he was thirty-six years old. The steady gaze, the folded arms, and the barely concealed hilt of the knife invented by his brother Rezin, all suggest a certain authority and determination. Note also that, like Austin and most other Texas heroes, Bowie is wearing what passed for a business suit at the time, rather than the frontier garb with which he is usually portrayed in films. *Courtesy of the Daughters of the Republic of Texas Library.*

David Crockett, in a full length painting by William H. Huddle. Depicted in his prime, perhaps a dozen years younger and rather thinner than he was at the Alamo, Crockett's buckskin outfit and coonskin cap, as well as his favorite musket "Betsy" and the forested backgound, suggest nothing less than the self-reliant, tough and independent frontiersman which, despite nineteenth century equivalent of "media hype," he really was. *Courtesy of the Institute of Texan Cultures.*

Juan Seguin, tragic *Tejano* hero of the Texas Revolution, depicted in his uniform as a colonel of the Texas Army, painted in 1838. *Courtesy of the Nettie Lee Benson Latin American Collection.*

Sussana Dickinson in middle age, after she regained some measure of respectability. A raven-haired, blue-eyed beauty of about twenty-two at the time of the fall of the Alamo, the cumulative effects of poverty, drink, and dissolution had taken their toll. *Courtesy of the Daughters of the Republic of Texas Library.*

Major General Vincente Filisola, shown in an engraving which appeared in his memoirs, published in 1852. One of the best Mexican officers, and one of the few apolitical ones, Filisola's decisions to obey Santa Anna's orders to evacuate Texas, issued while the latter was a prisoner of the Texians, was in error, but probably unavoidable, given that he lacked a genuine following among other Mexican commanders. *Courtesy of the Nettie Lee Benson Latin American Collection.*

Col. Juan Almonte in his old age, by which time the illegitimate son of the revolutionary Father Jose Morales had become a supporter of the ephemeral empire of Maximilian von Habsburg. Although not a great soldier, Almonte's diary of the campaign in Texas, in which he served as an aide-de-camp to Jose Antonio de Santa Anna, is a valuable primary source. *Courtesy of the Nettie Lee Benson Latin American Collection.*

Brigadier General Juan Jose Urrea, perhaps the ablest officer in the Mexican Army in Texas, from a photograph. A tough, no-nonsense professional soldier, Urrea was appalled at Santa Anna's orders to execute the hundreds of prisoners whom he had captured between the Rio Grande and Goliad, and managed to save many of them. *Courtesy of the Nettie Lee Benson Latin American Collection.*

"The March to the Massacre," an heroic painting by Col. Andrew J. Houston, showing Col. James W. Fannin's men being marched off to their execution on Palm Sunday, 1836. *Courtesy of the Texas State Library.*

"The Surrender of Santa Anna," a large painting by William Henry Huddle, 1886. Santa Anna, the man in the dark tunic and light trousers, is being addressed by Houston, who is lying on a blanket in deference to his wounded foot. Virtually all of the men in this painting are readily identifiable, most notably Erastus "Deaf" Smith, who is just to the right of Houston. Note the general absence of uniforms among the Texians, and that Houston is wearing a dark suit. *Courtesy of the Daughters of the Republic of Texas Library.*

Samuel P. Houston, in a photograph taken in 1837, at the age of forty-four, by which time he was president of Texas. *Courtesy of the Daughters of the Republic of Texas Library.*

Sam Houston in his old age. Although his successful conduct of the San Jacinto campaign resulted in a Texian victory and brought him numerous honors—twice president of Texas, senator and later governor—his life ended in tragedy when he opposed the Texas secession from the Union. Deposed from the statehouse by an illegal proceeding when he refused to take the oath of allegiance to the Confederacy in 1861, he died a broken man two years later. His last words were "Texas." *Courtesy of the Institute of Texan Cultures.*

The Alamo Flag

The Texians used several flags during the Revolution. A Mexican flag emblazoned with the year "1824," a reference to the federalist constitution of that year, had some use early in the Revolution. Other designs in use included one with a broad blue band charged with a single white star, with 13 alternating red and white stripes. Yet another is that which became the flag of the Republic and the State of Texas, a starred blue band and two broad stripes, white over red.

Altogether there may have been at least four flags in use at the Alamo. Tradition has it that the men of the Alamo died fighting under a Mexican flag emblazoned with "1824," which is by no means certain, but is a possibility. In addition, Travis had purchased a flag of uncertain design for his Cavalry Corps, which presumably was in the Alamo at the time of its fall. And at least two of the volunteer companies which comprised the garrison, the 1st and the 2nd New Orleans Grays, each possessed a flag of their own.

The only flag definitely known to have been used by the defenders was a blue-gray silk banner borne by the 1st Company of New Orleans Grays. After the fall of the Alamo, Santa Anna sent this flag to the Mexican Congress in token of his victory. Although several of the deputies trampled upon the banner in triumph, it was subsequently preserved in a museum.

When Santa Anna dispatched the flag of the New Orleans Grays to Mexico City, he wrote that it was "one of the flags of the enemy" taken in the storming of the Alamo. This indicates that there were other flags captured at the time. However, the design and the ultimate fate of these flags is, and will probably forever remain, unknown. It is perfectly possible that one of the others was the "1824" flag. Santa Anna would not have sent that to Congress, since its federalist message would have been too obvious. Certainly the flag of the New Orleans Grays was *not* the one around which considerable fighting occurred, and for which the young Lt. Jose Maria Torres of the *Zapadores* and several other men died during the assault.

Although neglected for many years, the flag of the New Orleans Grays was eventually put on display in an historical museum in Mexico City. It was very carefully examined and several times photographed. Although it deteriorated very badly after 1920 and had to be restored, descriptions and photographs of the original flag show that it was reasonably clean and stain free. If it had been flying over the Alamo on 6 March 1836 it almost certainly would have been soiled by smoke and stained by the blood of Lt. Torres, who was shot as he ripped it from the staff.

So the matter of the flag that flew over the Alamo remains unresolved.

The Men of the Alamo

By tradition 189 men died in the Alamo. They were a mixed lot. Some were illiterate frontiersmen, others educated professionals. There were at least six physicians and at least a dozen lawyers in the group. Most were unknowns, part of the faceless crowd that passes unheralded through history, while others had already made an indelible mark upon history, such as Crockett. Some were quite young; the youngest was probably Galba Fuqua, just 16; and some were rather old for such heroics: Gordon C. Jennings was 57. Among the Alamo dead were three brothers, James, George, and Edward Taylor, from Tennessee, who had gone to Texas to seek their fortune.

Although there is some uncertainty as to the geographic origins of many of them, the defenders appear to have come from at least 28 different states and countries.

Alabama	3
Arkansas	3
Connecticut	1
Denmark	1
England	12
Germany	2
Georgia	4
Illinois	1
Ireland	12
Kentucky	12
Louisiana	4
Maryland	1
Massachusetts	5
Mississippi	4
Missouri	5
New Jersey	1
New York	7
North Carolina	7
Ohio	3
Pennsylvania	9
Rhode Island	1
Scotland	4
South Carolina	7
Tennessee	34
Texas	9
Vermont	1
Virginia	13
Wales	1
Unknown	23

Although generally regarded as a bunch of agents of the slavocracy of the South, of the 166 men whose geographic origins are more or less known, only 97 (58.4%) hailed from states in which slavery was legal. What is more interesting is the significant number of men from Tennessee, 34 (17.9%), a contingent larger than that of the next three largest combined. Also interesting is the fact that save for Tennessee and Virginia, no state sent more men to the Alamo than England or Ireland. The little Texas town of Gonzales, where the Revolution had begun, contributed 38 of its residents, including many of its fathers, husbands, and sons to the defense, 32 of whom rode into the Alamo on the night of 1 March, long after all hope of relief had evaporated.

This list is actually highly inaccurate. Americans were already the most mobile people in the world at that time. Gordon C. Jennings, for example, is variously listed as having been born in Connecticut or, as his family claims, Pennsylvania, and in any case had long been resident in Missouri before going on to Texas. Similarly, James L. Ewing is usually listed as being from Tennessee, but was born in New York: Almeron Dickinson, usually given as hailing from Tennessee, was actually born in Pennsylvania; and Micajah Autry was born in North Carolina, but had been living in Tennessee for over a decade before moving on to Texas. At least one of those listed as having been born in Texas was actually born south of the Rio Grande. The rest of the men of Seguin's company were all local men from San Antonio.

At least one of the Alamo dead was Jewish, Antony—or Avram—Wolfe, originally from England. Considering the proportion of Jewish persons in the population of the United States at the time, this was a significant presence, the more so if the shadowy Louis Rose was also Jewish, as is sometimes asserted.

One of the men killed in the Alamo was black, by name John. John was the slave of Francis de Sauque, whom Travis sent off with dispatches on 22 February, the day before the Mexican Army arrived at the Alamo. It seems reasonable to assume that he was an active participant in the defense. There were several other black people in the Alamo at the time it was stormed, including Travis' man Joe and Bowie's freedman Sam, both of whom certainly were active in the defense, as well as a black woman whom Joe recalled seeing dead from a gunshot wound when some Mexican officers led him around to identify the corpses. This unfortunate woman is the only non-combatant known to have died in the assault. There may well have been other black people present, women as well as men, since Joe's account, which was not recorded verbatim, rather ambiguously refers to "several Negroes and women," which may be taken to mean "several black men and women" or "several black men and several women." Sam, who was literate and Bowie's trusted confidant, unfortunately left no account of the battle.

The number of people who survived the storming of the Alamo has never been properly tallied. A handful of the men defending the place are either known or rumored to have survived. At least three of these are certain, the two black men, Joe and Sam, as well as Brigido Guerrero, the Mexican Army deserter who had joined the garrison and managed to convince his erstwhile comrades that he had been kept in the Alamo against his will. In addition, Henry Wornell or Warnell, a 24-year-old from Arkansas, a jockey and rumored dealer in "horses of questionable ownership," also seems to have escaped, though precisely how is unclear. The evidence for his escape is found in land claims filed by his son, John Warnell, beginning in 1858. In one version of the claim the younger Warnell stated that his father was sent out of the Alamo with a message for Houston, a mission which he accomplished, although wounded in the process. If true, this would mean that Travis had dispatched a second messenger after he sent out James Allen on the last night of the siege. However, in another version of the claim, John Warnell indicated that his father was one of the three men whom Travis assigned to observation posts outside the walls, which permitted him to escape, although wounded. Although the latter story is probably the more likely, in either case, it does seem that Warnell managed to escape, albeit that he died of his wounds about three months later. Despite this he is generally listed among the 189 who fell at the Alamo. In addition, in mid-March two men, one of them badly wounded, showed up at Nacogdoches claiming to be survivors, and reporting that the Alamo had fallen and that they alone had survived the "general massacre." The accuracy of this report cannot be ascertained. It rests on but one source, a story published in the *Arkansas Gazette* of 29 March 1836, and such slender evidence is not usually reliable, but the general details of the events were more or less accurate. On the other hand, word of the Alamo disaster had spread with considerable speed, sparking the "Runaway Scrape,"

so it is not beyond the realm of possibility that the story is a fabrication, particularly since it is 350 miles from San Antonio to Nacogdoches, a tough trip for a wounded man, who would have had to spend part of the time dodging Mexican cavalry patrols, and still reach the latter place in time for the journalist to get his story, write it up, and send it off to distant Arkansas so that it could be published on 29 March. It has been suggested that the wounded man in question was Henry Warnell. Given the serious nature of Warnell's wounds—he died from them in May—this seems unlikely. In his condition he would have had to have been a tough man indeed to have made the long trek from San Antonio to Nacogdoches.

The survivors also included a number of women in addition to Susanna Dickinson: Bowie's sisters-in-law, Juana Alsbury and Gertrudis Navarro; an attractive young woman named Trinidad Saucedo; an older one known only as Doña Petra, and a few others who remain nameless. And there were several children: at least two infants, Angelina Dickinson, then about 15 months old, and Juana Alsbury's recently born baby, plus Enrique, the son of Gregorio Esparza, one of the gunners, and one of Anthony Wolfe's two sons, the other, big for his age, having been cut down during the storming of the chapel, and probably some others as well. Taken together, the number of survivors seems to have been around 20 or so.

Casualties at the Alamo

One of the continuing questions concerning the storming of the Alamo on 6 March 1836 is that of the number of casualties. How many men were defending the mission-fortress? And how many of those who took part in the attack became casualties?

The question is of some historical importance, but even more significant in terms of the Alamo legend. The tendency has been for pro-Texan writers to greatly inflate the number of Mexican dead at the hands of the garrison, while pro-Mexican authors tend to inflate the size of the garrison, and downplay Mexican losses.

Some notion of the magnitude of the problem may be gained by comparing the testimony of various persons who were more or less eyewitnesses.

Casualties

	Texans	Mexican
Mexican Eyewitnessess	Killed	Total (K/MW)
Col. Juan Almonte	250	288 (65)
BGen. Juan Andrade	*	311 (260)
Sgt. Francisco Becerra	*	2300 (2000)
Ramon Maritnez Caro	182	400+ (400)
MGen. Vicente Filisola	182-202	311 (60)
Col. Jose de la Peña	253	313 (60)
Col. Jose Sanchez Navarro	257	387 (121)
MGen. Antonio Lopez de Santa Anna, 1836	606	370 (70)
MGen. Antonio Lopez de Santa Anna, 1874	*	1000 (*)
Other Eyewitnesses		
Dr. John Bernard	*	500-700 (300-400)
Anselmo Borgara	*	521 (*)
Pablo Diaz	*	6000 (*)
Susanna Dickinson	160+	1600 (*)
Francisco Ruiz	182	1600 (*)

An asterisk (*) indicates that no figure was given. K/MW means "killed or mortally wounded."

The men listed as *Mexican Eyewitnesses* were present at the Alamo in various capacities with the Mexican Army. Almonte and Sanchez Navarro were on Santa Anna's staff; de la Peña was with the *Zapadores*, and Becerra was a sergeant in the *Matamoros Battalion*. Although not present at the time of the assault, Filisola was second-in-command of the army and Andrade commanded the cavalry, which meant that both had access to official documents, as did Ramon Martinez Caro, Santa Anna's private secretary. Both de la Peña and Sanchez Navarro attempted to count the Texian bodies, which were being cremated. The people listed under *Other Eyewitnesses* were present in various capacities. Dr. Bernard was one of the American surgeons captured at Goliad and pressed into service by Urrea, who shortly dispatched him to the Mexican military hospital at San Antonio. Anselmo Borgara, Pablo Diaz, and Francisco Ruiz were local residents, the last being the *alcalde* of San Antonio. And, of course, Mrs. Dickinson was inside the Alamo itself.

At first glance most of the figures given by these various witnesses appear irreconcilable. However, from various sources it is possible to determine the actual figures more closely.

It appears that Travis had about 170-180 men at the time Santa Anna's army marched up on 23 February, perhaps a few more. This number fell over the next few days, as Travis dispatched a number of couriers, apparently about 16; among them Dr. John Sutherland, John W. Smith, Juan Seguin and his aide Antonio Cruz, James Allen, and James Bonham. In addition, it seems certain that several men deserted during the siege. These were probably mostly Mexican-Texans, local men, with kinfolk in the vicinity, who would not have found it difficult to slip away safely. However, some Americo-Texans were probably among them: Mrs. Dickinson recalled a man named "Ross" who disappeared one night. But men also managed to slip into the Alamo during the siege. On 1 March, some 30 men rode up with Capt. George Kimbell and John W. Smith. Two nights later James Bonham returned, but Smith was sent out again. These comings and goings make difficult any determination as to how many men were present. Nevertheless, it would seem that the garrison had between 180-190 men, somewhat more than the number with which Travis began the siege. This is fairly close to the traditional figure, derived from various lists of those who fell in the assault, which puts the number of defenders who died at 189. Despite the fact that these figures seem to omit several men, such as Brigido Guerrero, Bowie's man Sam, and Travis' slave Joe, all of whom survived the fall of the Alamo, they seem to be reasonably accurate. However, it seems likely that there were also a number of non-combatants killed during the assault: Joe, for example, reported a black woman among the dead, and there were probably other non-combatants killed as well. Filisola gives the dead as including "150 volunteers, 32 people of the town of Gonzales, who under cover of darkness joined the group two days before the attack on the fortress, and about 20 citizens and tradesmen of the town of Bexar," which would appear to include some people who had the misfortune to have been caught in the Alamo. It is interesting to note that the traditional figure for the number of defenders killed, 189, more or less conforms with those of the more reliable references, Mrs. Dickinson and Filisola.

The question of Mexican losses is a much thornier one. Figures as high as 2,500 dead have been reported in the storming of the Alamo, a number which considerably exceeded the total of the troops engaged, about 1950 or so, including the *Dolores Cavalry Regiment*, which incurred some losses picking off fugitives fleeing the cattle pen and the gunners. The actual figure appears to have been over 300 but probably not more than about 400, including men killed outright or mortally wounded, and those who died from less severe wounds which went untreated since Santa Anna had neglected to bring any medical personnel along on the expedition, but excluding those men who died from disease or exposure, both among the troops present at the time of the assault and among those who arrived over the next few days.

The critical witness in the matter of Mexican combat casualties at the Alamo is certainly Filisola, who gives a detailed breakdown of the casualties by unit:

Regiment	Engaged	K/MW	Wounded	Surviving
Aldama	340	11	46	283
Dolores Cavalry	285	1	3	281
Jimenez	275	9	25	241
Matamoros	275	7	37	231
San Luis Potosi	275	9	37	239
Toluca	320	20	79	221
Zapadores	185	3	24	158
Total	1955	60	251	1644

While in another place, Filisola gives somewhat higher casualty figures, 70 dead and about 300 wounded, the difference between the two sets of figures is not great, and may be based on information available at different times. What is particularly interesting about his account of the battle is that Filisola adds the comment, "A large number of the wounded died due to poor care and lack of medical supplies." Since men who were lightly wounded were rarely counted among the casualties, such things being considered of little account in those days by most armies, the possibility that most of the seriously wounded died—and, given the dangers of gangrene, some of the lightly wounded as well—is reasonable, which means that the total of Mexican dead was certainly 300. It is interesting to note that, keeping in mind his proviso concerning men who subsequently died of wounds, Filisola's figures are roughly confirmed by those of Andrade and de la Peña, and even by those Santa Anna gave in 1836.

Some idea of the accuracy of this estimate may be obtained by noting the strengths of the regiments which were at both the Alamo and San Jacinto. At the latter battle, the *Aldama* appears to have had only about 210 men, some 75% of its strength after the Alamo, while *Matamoros* had about 240, slightly more than its total after the Alamo, and *Toluca*, 210, only slightly less. Although the figure for the *Aldama* is somewhat out of line, those for the other two regiments are not unreasonable.

So it seems reasonable to conclude that the Mexican Army's battle deaths at the Alamo numbered at least 300 and possibly somewhat in excess of 400.

CHAPTER VII

"The Runaway Scrape"

7 March-20 April 1836

The fall of the Alamo found the defenses of Texas in disarray. Had Santa Anna moved immediately he would have found the Texians largely incapable of defending themselves. But Santa Anna could not move for some days. Even with the arrival of the balance of Gaona's *First Brigade* on 7 March, he had with him at San Antonio only about half the army. The men needed rest, particularly those who had taken part in the storming of the Alamo. The wounded had to be tended, however hopeless their prospects, and the dead had to be disposed of, an unpleasant and difficult task which was accomplished mostly by mass cremation. In addition, supplies were running low, and he needed time to revictual from local resources. So the best that he could do immediately was to send out his cavalry, with the dual missions of scouring the countryside for the enemy and foraging for supplies, while encouraging Urrea to continue his successful advance near the coast.

When the Alamo fell, Texas had under arms perhaps 1,100 to 1,300 men. The largest concentration was at Goliad, nearly 500 men under James W. Fannin. There were also about 275 at Gonzales, another 200 at Matagorda on the coast, and a further 300 to 400 scattered all over the countryside in tiny

packets. Technically the men concentrating at Gonzales constituted the main army of the Republic. They were lacking in
almost everything, clothing, ammunition, rations, training,
discipline. Although no word had been received from the
Alamo in many days, there was a growing uneasiness as to its
fate: Travis had promised to fire the great 18-pounder three
times a day to signal that the Alamo still held out, and it had
been many days since the big gun's deep throated roar had
been heard. On 11 March Houston rode into town, his work
at the Convention finished, bringing with him about 100 men.
That same day came word of the fall of the Alamo. At about
4:00 in the afternoon two *Tejanos* arrived in town, Andres
Barcenas, a rancher, and Anselmo Bergaras, one of Seguin's
men, fleeing Santa Anna's cavalry patrols. A day or two
previously they had spoken with a man who had just come
from San Antonio, and he had told them a chilling tale: the
Alamo was fallen and all within it slain, plus 521 Mexicans as
well. Panic reared its head among the troops. Acting quickly,
Houston charged the pair with being agents of Santa Anna
and had them arrested. But he clearly believed that their
story was true. Indeed, the details which they provided
would be confirmed later, even down to the execution of the
handful of prisoners and the mass cremation of the dead,
though the identity of their informant, also a *Tejano*, would
never be established. That very night Houston wrote to Fannin, "I have little doubt but that the Alamo has fallen," and
ordered him to fall back from Goliad, after blowing up the
defenses. The very next day, Houston took the first steps
towards turning the mass of men at his disposal into a military organization. He created the "1st Texas Volunteer Regiment," with Col. Edward Burleson in command and Lt. Col.
Sidney Sherman, a Kentuckian who had come to Texas with
50 fully equipped volunteers, as second-in-command. On the
13th Houston dispatched "Deaf" Smith, Henry Karnes, and
R.E. Handy to scout westward to confirm the tale told by
Barcenas and Bergaras. Within hours they had returned, having encountered Susanna Dickinson and several of the other

women and children who had survived the Alamo, escorted by the black chef Ben and Travis' man Joe. The story told by Mrs. Dickinson and the others sparked contradictory reactions among the men; some despaired, others panicked, and still others demanded to be led immediately against the enemy. Houston ordered a general retreat. Some cries of anger were raised, but he stuck to his decision. The army would fall back to more heavily settled areas, in order to gain time in which to build up its numbers, procure equipment, obtain supplies, and engage in some training. At midnight on 13 March the 1st Texas, now numbering about 400 men as additional volunteers came in from the surrounding farms and ranches, pulled out of Gonzales. With it went a large number of refugees, mostly the women and children of the town, whose menfolk had perished at the Alamo. Meanwhile, Houston sent couriers with orders that all Texian personnel were to concentrate on the main army as soon as practical.

Fannin, meanwhile, had been sitting idle since his abortive attempt to march to the relief of the Alamo on 27 February. The disasters which had overtaken Johnson and Grant appear to have paralyzed his will. The hapless West Point drop-out was proved wholly inept in a crisis. When Houston's orders to evacuate Goliad came through on 12 March, he wasted time trying to get the local settlers moving, rather than just announcing he was pulling out, which probably would have worked wonders toward sparking a panicked flight from the area. Worse, he had divided his command. Some days earlier he had sent Capt. Amon B. King with a score of men to the Refugio area to organize the evacuation of the settlers there. On the 12th, the same day on which he received Houston's message, Fannin learned that King was having some difficulties. Rather than abandon the hapless captain to his fate, Fannin sent Col. William Ward with nearly 150 men of his Georgia Battalion to lend King a hand. As these troops approached the Refugio, they ran into Brig. Gen. Jose Urrea's column. Urrea, a fast moving no-nonsense professional soldier, had already gobbled up King's little band, and was looking for bigger prey. His troops skirmished with Ward's men on 14 March, chasing them into Refugio, and then invested the place. Unwilling to attempt a stand in the ruined mission at Refugio, later that same night Ward ordered his men to escape as best they could, taking advantage of a driving rainstorm. Urrea pursued, and managed to sweep up most of the fugitives. By this time Urrea found himself burdened with prisoners. Although reluctant to do so, his officers pressed him to execute the lot in obedience of Santa Anna's "no quarter" orders. He compromised, ordering that all prisoners who were Mexican citizens be sent to the rear for trial, he had the rest shot. As the prisoners were being readied for the appropriate disposition, Urrea took the bulk of his troops and headed for Goliad, where Fannin was still idling away the days.

Ward and the other fugitives from the disaster at Refugio reached Goliad on 16 March. Fannin immediately convened a council-of-war. After some debate, the council opted for immediate retreat. In other circumstances this would have been sage advice. Indeed, had Fannin put his army on the road when he received Houston's orders to withdraw from Goliad, he might have gotten clean away. Unfortunately, the time for an orderly withdrawal had passed. On the 17th, even as the troops were getting ready to move, Urrea came up, his cavalry skirmishing with Fannin's outposts. The Texian position at Goliad was strong. Unlike the Alamo, the post at Goliad, Presidio La Bahia, had been constructed as a military installation. The presidio stood atop a prominent hill. Built of stone, the roughly square fort had full bastions on two corners and small guard posts on the other two. The walls, which had proper parapets and embrasures, were between eight and ten feet high, and enclosed an area of about 3.5 acres; a good deal larger than the area of the Alamo, but as the plan of the post was square, the trace of the walls was actually not much greater than that of the Alamo. Enhancing Fannin's prospects, should he choose to hole up in the presidio, was the fact that his 350 or so men were not significantly inferior in numbers to Urrea's army, now reduced to only about 500 due to casualties and the necessity of providing escorts for prisoners. And Fannin had far more artillery than did Urrea, about a dozen pieces to one. Although food stocks at Goliad were relatively slender, with Urrea upon him, Fannin's best course was to hole up in the presidio and accept a siege. An attempt to hold Goliad would have kept Urrea pinned down for weeks, and probably forced Santa Anna to bring the main body of the army down from San Antonio. On the other hand, in the circumstances escape was highly risky, particularly since half of Urrea's troops were seasoned cavalrymen. In the same situation Travis would not have hesitated. But Fannin was not Travis. He chose to escape, abiding by the decision of the council-of-war. And even then he dithered.

In preparation for the retreat, Fannin ordered the heaviest pieces of artillery dismounted and buried. Then he changed his mind and decided not to retreat, and so ordered the pieces dug up again. Then he once more changed his mind. Eventually the army was ready. On the rainy morning of 18 March the troops were formed up to begin their retreat, with oxen hitched to the supply wagons and artillery, and his small contingent of cavalry ready to cover the movement. Then a Mexican cavalry patrol came in sight. Fannin dispatched Col. Albert C. Horton with his cavalry troop to drive off the enemy patrol. The Mexican cavalrymen fell back as Horton came up, drawing him towards a larger body of troopers, who then chased the Texian cavalry back towards the presidio. The Mexicans then drew off, and Horton chased after them once again. This provoked the inevitable response, and Horton was soon being pursued back to the presidio. All of this transpired in full view of Fannin's troops, who lined the walls of the presidio to watch. Unfortunately, they so enjoyed the spectacle, which lasted for a couple of hours, that they neglected to outspan the oxen, nor had anyone bothered to feed or water them. As a result, when Horton's tired troopers finally returned to the presidio, Fannin had to order the movement postponed until the next day. That night proved cold and rainy. Urrea's troops, who included many recruits from tropical Yucatan, were bivouacked in the fields and suffered terribly. This was a bit of luck for Fannin. During the night his men demolished major portions of the fortress, and burned all supplies and foodstuffs which could not be brought away. Under cover of the rain, which gradually melted into a fog, Fannin's little army slipped out of Goliad at about 9:00 on the morning of 19 March and set out on the road to Victoria.

Urrea did not learn of Fannin's departure for several hours. Delayed by weather, his patrols went out late, and did not reach the vicinity of the presidio until late morning. Not until about noon did his troopers discover that Fannin had flown. Urrea immediately put his men on Fannin's trail, intending to follow at a convenient distance until an opportunity offered itself to strike a crushing blow.

Fannin's retreat was badly conducted. He took far too much artillery with him, and failed to order the men to abandon their personal possessions. Worse, they had taken very little food with them, and apparently no fodder for the oxen. Within hours, Fannin's men and animals were exhausted. The sun had come up strong, burning away the fog, and by afternoon it became hot. With men and animals threatening to fall, Fannin called a halt only about seven miles from Goliad. As the oxen were outspanned, Horton's cavalrymen, who had been covering the rear, came in with word that Mexican patrols were only about four or five miles behind the army. Fannin ordered the march to resume. But the army had scarce gone two miles when the oxen began to fall out. Fannin once more ordered the army to halt, about a mile from Coleto Creek. Although his officers immediately protested that by pressing on the extra mile they would gain the security of the creek's heavily wooded banks, Fannin overruled them. As a result, the army took up a position in a slight hollow on the open prairie with no natural cover and no water. Urrea's men were soon upon them. Scattering Horton's cavalry, many of whom fled across the prairie never to be heard from again, Urrea's troopers began to harass the Texian camp, aided by occasional balls from his lone 4-pounder. Texian response was feeble. Fannin managed to get his men moving towards the creek, but they barely made it half way before going to ground again, under the harassing fire of the Mexican troops. Although they had more artillery than did Urrea, the Texian fire was slow, there being no water to sponge the pieces between shots; worse, the only trained gunner with them fell wounded. Urrea also made several errors. Anxious to get the business over with, he attempted several frontal attacks, both with cavalry and infantry, which the Texians were able to beat off. Finally he decided to let time do his work for him, and called off the attacks.

The battle continued though the afternoon and into the night, as the Mexicans kept up their harassing fire. The Texians began running out of ammunition, and food. There was no water, and the cries of the thirsty wounded grew. By daylight on 20 March Fannin decided that his men were spent. He asked for terms. Urrea offered none. So Fannin agreed to surrender "at discretion"—without terms. Urrea, an honorable officer, certainly believed that the Texians would be well treated. Indeed, he arranged for care for the wounded. Texian medical personnel worked in the same makeshift ward as did the Mexicans, treating men indiscriminantly. A few of the prisoners were shipped southward under light escort. A few others were brought in: men from Refugio and other small actions, including a party of volunteers from Tennessee who had landed at Copano Bay a few days earlier, thinking it was still in Texian hands, only to be scooped by one of Urrea's patrols. Urrea almost certainly did not know what was coming. For on 27 March, orders arrived from Santa Anna that all 442 of the prisoners were to be executed as "pirates." Urrea saved those few he could, the medical personnel, with the excuse that he needed them to tend his wounded, and those already shipped out. Among those saved were Dr. Benjamin Harrison, the son and father of future Presidents of the United States, whom Urrea had known when he and William Henry Harrison had both been diplomats in Colombia. Other men were saved by the individual acts of brave officers and a brave woman, *Sra.* Francisca Alvarez, wife of a Mexican officer. But most were doomed; on that Palm Sunday 342 men were taken down a road a little ways and shot. Fannin was taken back to Goliad, and shot there.

As Fannin's army came to its dramatic end, Santa Anna was preparing to sweep away the last vestiges of rebellion in Texas. After resting the army at San Antonio, he began to send out columns in various directions. On 14 March the *First Brigade* under Brig. Gen. Antonio Gaona was sent off to the northwest, with orders to harry the Texians from the area between San Antonio and the Colorado River, before turning southeastwards to sweep down the right side of the Brazos. A few days later, even as Urrea was finishing with Fannin, he was reinforced with several battalion of infantry and ordered to continue his advance along the coast. And finally, Santa Anna and the main body of the army moved out from San Antonio on 29 March, heading eastwards towards Gonzales, with the intention of finding and crushing the main Texian forces. The overall strategic plan envisioned the three columns effecting a juncture along the lower reaches of the Brazos in late April, whereupon the newly reunited army would press eastwards to secure Texas right up to the Sabine River. But while Santa Anna was scattering his army across all of Texas, Houston was slowly building his.

The Texian retreat was well handled. Houston kept his men well in hand, while constantly sending out "Deaf" Smith and other fine scouts to keep him apprised of the whereabouts of the Mexican Army. As a result, at no time did the Mexican columns ever approach the main body of Texian forces. Flying before the retreating army, panicked crowds of settlers—and the new government of Texas—headed for the relative safety of East Texas. Fairfax Gray, a wealthy Virginian who was in Texas to help float a loan to the Republic, recorded "...thousands are moving off to the east. A constant stream of women and children, and some men, with wagons, carts and pack mules, are rushing across the Brazos night and day." During this panic—dubbed the "Runaway Scrape" by irreverent Texians—Houston's army grew by fits and starts. It lost strength as some men deserted to go to the aid of their families. Nevertheless, overall strength rose, as new volunteers arrived from the United States. By 26 March, when Houston reached the Colorado River, he had about 1,200 men. Over the next few days there were many desertions, and Houston was forced to assign some troops to help cover the flight of the settlers, among them Juan Seguin's mounted *Tejanos*, so that on 30 March, when he reached the Brazos River at Groce's Ferry, he had only about 800 men with him. At Groce's Crossing, Houston made camp. He spent 12 days at Groce's Crossing, organizing the 2nd Texas Volunteer Regiment, which included a troop of 60 cavalrymen, and gave it to Col. Sherman. Some 200 deserters from the American Army of Observation along the Sabine River came in, all armed and many still with their full kit, and they were formed into the Texas Regular Battalion. For nearly two weeks, the little army drilled and marched and learned to soldier. A pair of cannon came up, the "Twin Sisters," 6-pounders donated by the city of Cincinnati. Slowly the army took shape under Houston's demanding eye. The men were good and tough, but disliked discipline, and were openly contemptuous of Houston's unwillingness to lead them into action immediately. On 12 April, even as Santa Anna's columns spread all across Texas in a broad fanlike pattern heading northeastward, the army took to the roads again.

The Mexicans were confident of final victory. The Alamo, Goliad, and now the evidence of a vast, panic-stricken evacuation of Texas by the American settlers all boded victory. So confident was Santa Anna that he proposed returning home to take other matters in hand, but his officers convinced him to see the business through. They pressed on. The troops, though tired, were in good spirits. Food and drink and loot were plentiful, the fighting almost non-existent.

When the army reached the Brazos, there to be reunited with Gaona's *First Brigade*, Santa Anna decided to press on ahead. He was anxious to put an end to the business, and didn't want any more close calls. On 15 April he had failed to capture President Burnet and most of the Texian government by scant minutes, the Texians escaping by ferry as they traded shots with a patrol led by Col. Juan Almonte. He joined the vanguard, some 600-700 men, moving out before the army. On 18 April he arrived at New Washington, a small town on the San Jacinto River. The main body, under Maj. Gen. Filisola, was some 45 miles behind, at Fort Bend on the Brazos. Unbeknownst to him, Houston, with over 1200 men, was at Harrisburg, not 30 miles away. And Houston knew where Santa Anna was. On 18 April "Deaf" Smith—who could not hear very well but could out-track anyone—had intercepted Capt. Miguel Bachiller, who was serving as a courier. In saddle bags stamped "W. B. Travis," Smith found dispatches for Santa Anna from Filisola. These gave full details as to the deployment and strength of the army, including the probability that Santa Anna would be reinforced by some 600 additional troops under Martin Cos within a few days.

On 19 April, Houston crossed Buffalo Bayou, bringing his army on the next day to the plain of the San Jacinto, where that river runs into the bayou, not a dozen miles from Santa Anna at New Washington. Santa Anna spent two days at New Washington, gathering food, including 100 beeves that were rounded up by the lancers of his escort. On the morning of 20 April he ordered the town burned and marched northwards towards the San Jacinto plain. About 2:00 p.m. the outposts of the two armies began a desultory skirmish, with the lancers of Santa Anna's escort and the *granaderos* of the *Toluca Battalion*, supported by the single Mexican gun, tangling with some Texian cavalry supported by their own artillery. Although Santa Anna thought about luring Houston into an attack, nothing came of it. Towards evening the Mexican troops pulled back and the indecisive fight came to an end, a few men having been wounded on each side. Night fell and the armies bedded down; Santa Anna's confident of victory on the morrow, and Houston's angry and frustrated that he had not taken on the hated Mexicans then and there.

CHAPTER VIII

"Remember the Alamo!"
The Battle of San Jacinto

21 April 1836

The field of San Jacinto is small, barely three square miles. It is roughly triangular, bounded on the northeast and north-west by the San Jacinto River and Buffalo Bayou, and open on the southwest by the Texas coastal plain. As neither stream is fordable, the position is essentially a dead end save for Lynch's Ferry, crossing the San Jacinto from the northern apex of the triangle to the like named hamlet on the opposite bank. The ground itself is rather marshy along the margins of the waterways and is cut by two shallow ravines. There are occasional pools of open water in the marshes and, on the east, a considerable lake. Much of the plain is grassy, but there are substantial stands of live oak forest running along the bayou and ravines and scattered about in several other places.

On the night of 20-21 April, Santa Anna encamped his troops in the southeastern corner of the plain, up against an arm of the San Jacinto. There was a small copse of live oak in front of his position, and this was haphazardly fortified with a breastwork of pack saddles and other impedimenta to provide a battery position for his single 6-pounder, which had been slightly damaged during the skirmishing on the previous afternoon. The *Matamoros Battalion*, only 240 men, was assigned to cover the front, which extended from the edge of Lake Peggy, on the east, about 1200 yards in a shallow arc that ran northwestwards through the little copse of woods and then curved towards the southwest. The 6-pounder was sited approximately in the center of this line, amidst the trees. Just behind his right flank Santa Anna posted five companies of *cazadores*, while over behind his left he positioned five companies of *granaderos*, and, somewhat further back, the lancers of his escort. These dispositions effectively consumed his entire force, roughly 600-650 men. He thus had no reserve, save himself and his staff, who camped in the rear. This did not bother him greatly, as he was confident the forces he had, the best men in the army, could handle any Texian attack. Moreover, he expected some 600 reinforcements under the ubiquitous Cos to arrive within a few hours and did not anticipate any serious enemy action before then. The troops rested on the field as best they could, and Santa Anna retired to his tent.

Sam Houston and the Texian Army was camped little more than 1200 yards from Santa Anna's front, among the live oaks fringing Buffalo Bayou. Superficially, Houston's position at San Jacinto was hardly favorable. He had only about 800-850 men present, with little prospect of reinforcement, beyond two companies of infantry and some cavalry left at Harrisburg to guard the sick and stores, and some recruits still en route. He also had no line of retreat, for Lynch's Ferry was not suitable to the rapid movement of relatively large numbers of men, while Santa Anna's army effectively cut off the only other practical routes out of the position. However, all of this appears to be precisely what Houston wanted. His army was hot for a fight, nearly mutinous, in fact. But while he had managed to instill a modest degree of discipline and order on his men, they were hardly regulars. In a battle they would fight well, but lacking the sturdiness of regulars might easily panic and fly. If he gave them no option but to win or die, he knew they would acquit themselves well. He was taking no chances. And he was extending his own.

Houston went to his tent. He appears to have passed part of the night reading, from the two books which had given him much comfort and companionship during the campaign, Swift's *Gulliver's Travels* and Caesar's *Gallic Wars*.

Dawn on 21 April found the Texians stirring far more energetically than the Mexicans. Houston might have attacked right then, but he held off. From the captured dispatches he was aware that Cos was expected to reinforce Santa Anna shortly, and preferred to attack after these reinforcements had reached the Mexican Army, rather than have them arrive in the midst of a battle, which would probably be devastating to the morale of his own men. Of course the army was ready, and becoming hourly more restless. The men were anxious to be led into action: so hot for action were the men that Pvt. William P. Zuber, one of those ordered to remain at Harrisburg, actually wept over the matter and tried to bribe his friend, Alphonso Steele, to trade places with him. Houston went among the men sounding their opinion, hearing murmurings that he should be replaced. But he kept his own counsel, not once declaring his own intentions. Sometime during the morning, "Deaf" Smith came to Houston. He had been talking with some of the men, and they had suggested that perhaps destroying Vince's Bridge, some miles to the west, might be a good idea. Houston thought about it for a moment; doing so would cut off any possibility of retreat by his own army, and hamper the flight of the enemy should they be defeated. He looked up at Smith.

"Can you do it without being cut to pieces by the Mexican cavalry?"

"Give me six men and I will try."

Houston assented. Smith went off to seek volunteers among the cavalrymen. Getting more than he needed, he selected six men whom he knew, and rode westwards. Soon after the bridge began blazing merrily, Smith and his men returned, not having once seen a Mexican soldier.

Cos's column, four reduced infantry battalions, marched up around 9:00 a.m., bringing Santa Anna's army to some 1,200-1,300 men. Santa Anna welcomed his brother-in-law and ordered the new arrivals to make camp behind his loosely held front. Time passed. Noon found both armies resting in camp, but the Mexicans were largely asleep, taking their ease, while the Texians were complaining and griping about the inactivity. Houston called a council-of-war at noon. He announced that he intended to attack the next day! The staff agreed. The troops did not. Mutiny threatened, and the wily Houston responded, "Very well, get your dinners and I will lead you into the fight, and if you whip the enemy every one of you shall be a captain."

The army took its time getting ready. The men had their "dinners," Houston's prepared by Ben, Santa Anna's former cook. That done, they readied their equipment and formed their companies. Only at about 3:00 p.m.. did they begin to get into battle line, at the edge of the live oaks which fringed Buffalo Bayou. Their preparations took about half an hour. On the left was Col. Sidney Sherman's 2nd Texas with about 260 men; next to them came Col. Edward Burleson's 1st Regiment with about 220; then the "Twin Sisters" of the Cincinnati Battery and some 31 men; to their right came the 240 bayonet-equipped troops of the Texas Regular Battalion under Lt. Col. Henry Millard; and beyond them at some distance were approximately 50 cavalrymen under Col. Mirabeau Bonaparte Lamar, who scant hours before had been a private.

The whole army stood in two thin lines stretching perhaps 1,000 yards, each man ready for action, many armed not merely with a musket, but also with two or three pistols and a sword or a bowie knife. Astride Saracen, his big white stallion, Houston took up a position in the center of the line, a few yards out in front. At 3:30, sword in hand, he waved the army forward. As the men stepped forward, the color bearer of the 2nd Texas unfurled the regimental banner, a bare breasted Liberty wielding a saber from which dangled a ribbon inscribed "Liberty or Death," the only flag the Texians

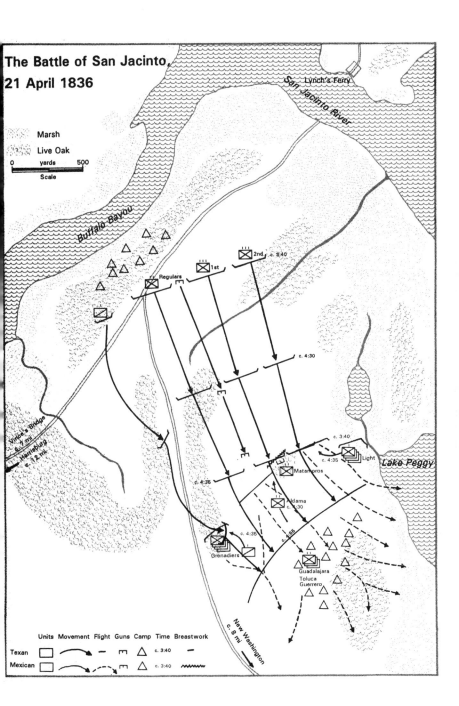

The Battle of San Jacinto,
21 April 1836

Marsh

Live Oak

0   yards   500
Scale

Lynch's Ferry

San Jacinto River

Buffalo Bayou

Regulars

1st

2nd c. 3:40

c. 4:30

Vince's Bridge
c. 7 mi.
Harrisburg
c. 12 mi.

c. 3:40

c. 4:35   Light

Lake Peggy

c. 4:35

Matamoros

Aldama
c. 4:30

c. 4:35   c. 4:55

Grenadiers

Guadalajara
Toluca
Guerrero

New Washington
c. 8 mi.

	Units	Movement	Flight	Guns	Camp	Time	Breastwork
Texan	□		—	⌐	△	c. 3:40	—
Mexican	□			⌐	△	c. 3:40	﹀﹀﹀

had that day. The army's band, a black drummer and a German fifer, played a naughty tune just then popular for lack of anything else common to them both

> *Will you come to the Bow'r I have shaded for you?*
> *Our bed shall be roses all spangled with dew.*
> *There under the bow'r on roses you'll lie*
> *With a blush on your cheek but a smile in your eye!*

Remarkably, all of this activity went unnoticed in the Mexican camp. To be sure, there was a modest patch of rising ground between the two armies and some thin stands of live oak, but even so, the failure of the Mexican Army to detect the Texian preparations was extraordinary. So overconfident were Santa Anna and his subordinates that they had neglected the most elementary measures for security in the face of the enemy. No scouts had been dispatched, no men posted as sentries. The lancers of the general's escort, about 60 men, were idling away the afternoon, their horses unsaddled and strung out cropping grass. Most of the troops were either asleep or resting under arms. None of the senior officers present appears to have been in charge, though in the circumstances command devolved upon Brig. Gen. Manuel Fernandez Castrillon, who was half dressed and shaving, as Santa Anna himself was taking siesta in his tent, some say with the aid of opium and a young woman named Emily Morgan. So as the Texians approached, moving at a very easy pace so as not to lose their cohesion, no one in the Mexican camp noticed them.

At about 4:30, the Texians emerged from the thin woods running through a ravine in the center of the plain, not 550 yards in front of the Mexican lines.

A bugler on the right of the *Matamoros* was the first to sound the alarm. As other buglers sounded the alert, the single Mexican cannon cut loose with grapeshot and the men of the *Matamoros Battalion*, a mere outpost line, began to fire. But in their haste both infantrymen and artillerymen alike fired high, and few of the Texians were hit.

Hearing the bugles and the firing, Fernandez Castrillon

stopped shaving, snatched up his sword, and ran to the front shouting orders. The *Aldama Battalion* was to move instantly to support the *Matamoros* on its right. The *granaderos* and *cazadores* were to form up for immediate employment. The cavalrymen were to saddle up. The *Guadalajara, Toluca,* and *Guerrero Battalions* were to form columns for counterattacks. But it was already too late. Even as the alarm was being raised, Houston attacked.

The Texian artillery open up first, the gunners hauling the "Twin Sisters" out ahead of the infantry, then quickly unlimbering and letting fly at a mere 200 yards from the Mexican lines. Lamar's cavalry began swinging around to the right, in a feint against the Mexican left. Then the infantry went forward. As the Texian line swept forward, the gunners manhandled the "Twin Sisters" forward to within 70 yards of the Mexicans, and then quickly brought them back into action. As they did, the Texian infantry came up, and after one or two rounds more, the "Twin Sisters" fell silent. Saracen took a round, falling heavily to earth. Houston quickly mounted another horse, and rode on. This steed too was soon hit, and Houston took a round of grapeshot in his right ankle. Ignoring the pain, he mounted a third horse and pressed on.

Within minutes the 2nd Regiment made contact, driving into the thin front offered by the *Matamoros Battalion*, its 240 men strung out across 1,200 yards. Seconds later, the 1st Regiment came up to its right. Together the two regiments overran the single Mexican gun, which had managed to get off only five rounds, taking the breastworks and the copse of woods quickly. The Mexicans tried to rally but failed. The *Aldama* came up in fair order, only to be overrun by fugitives from the shattered *Matamoros*, on whose heels the Texians followed. As the Regular Battalion came up, Lamar's cavalry overran the *granaderos* on Santa Anna's left as they struggled to form up, sending the men streaming back in panic.

Although wounded in the leg, Fernandez Castrillon leaped on an ammunition box shouting encouragement to the men in an effort to rally them. They ignored him, streaming to the

Manuel Fernandez Castrillon

Manuel Fernandez Castrillon (178?-1836) was born into a prosperous *criollo* family from Havana, Cuba. After an excellent education, he entered the Spanish colonial army and was eventually posted to Mexico, where he served with some distinction in various assignments, first in Royal service, helping to crush the Mexican Revolution, then with Iturbide's Imperial government and finally with the Republic, in the process rising to brigadier general. Although a well-trained, professional officer, and a veritable lion in battle, much of his career was spent in staff positions, as he was unsuccessful in independent command. Like many Mexican officers, he had his hand in the till, and was one of the most heroic grafters in the army, lending money on military con-tracts via third parties at 60 percent annual interest.

From about 1822 Castrillon was one of Santa Anna's closest advisors and confidants. By no means a "yes-man," he had the courage to challenge decisions that he disagreed with, as when he objected to Santa Anna's orders to execute prisoners as immoral or when he challenged Santa Anna's decision to storm the Alamo without waiting for the arrival of his 12-pounders. Castrillon was among those who believed that the Texas Revolution was a trifling affair. A tall, strong man, with a full head of thick, curly hair despite being in his late-50s, Castrillon refused to flee the field when the Mexican Army broke at San Jacinto, and fell bravely trying to rally the troops.

rear. Broken-hearted, he stood his ground, shouting "I have been in forty battles and never once showed my back! I'm too old to do it now!" Col. Tom Rusk, Texian Secretary of War, tried to save the old campaigner, but there would be no mercy this day. The Texians, their blood up, cut him down, crying "Remember the Alamo! Remember Goliad!"

The panicked fugitives fled through the Mexican camp, disrupting the *Guadalajara, Toluca,* and *Guerrero Battalions* as they struggled to form ranks. Col. Pedro Delgado would later observe that "Mexican soldiers, once demoralized, cannot be controlled." And so it was. With its cohesion gone, Santa Anna's army disintegrated as men fled in all directions. From battle, the fight turned to slaughter, the Texians killing indiscriminately, "Remember the Alamo! Remember Goliad!" on their lips. Untold scores fled into the marshes and the lake and the river. Others ran until exhausted, sank down, and were cut to pieces where they lay by Texian swords or bayonets or bowie knives. Within 18 minutes it was over but for the massacre. Hundreds were cut down crying "Me no Alamo!" Taking one look at the slaughter, Santa Anna grabbed the nearest horse and fled. Showing more honor and devotion, Juan Almonte managed to rally some men, bringing them away into some marshy woods along the bayou.

Some men tried to show mercy.

"This is my Mexican," cried John Wharton, a cavalryman, as he pulled one of the pathetic fugitives up behind him on his horse, but seconds later the man was shot anyway. Pedro Delgado and several other men were more fortunate, for a "Col. Allen of the cavalry" took them under his protection. Alas for history and honor, this man cannot be identified, there being no such officer with the Texian Army that day. Other officers also tried to intervene, but discretion overcame their scruples. Not even Houston could stem the blood lust, and, shouting, "Gentlemen, I applaud your bravery, but damn your manners!", rode off. The men would only be sated by blood. And finally, toward sundown their bloodlust was exhausted. As calm returned, Almonte managed to surrender some 600 men, a third of them wounded.

Altogether, some 600-650 Mexicans perished at San Jacinto and a further 730 were taken prisoner, no more than 70 or 80 having succeeded in escaping. The Texian loss was small, two killed outright, six mortally wounded, another 18 less seriously so, among them Houston himself. Although the figures on both sides are at best approximations, they certainly are close to the actual numbers. The booty was great, for the Texians captured virtually all of the Mexican equipment: four stand of colors, one 6-pounder, 600 functional muskets, 200 pistols, 300 swords, scores of horses and mules, and a considerable sum in gold, some of which promptly evaporated. Nevertheless, there was enough left so that, after allocating some gold to cover the army's immediate expenses and having set aside some funds for the navy, Houston was

The Texas War for Independence, 1835-1836
Battles, Engagements, and Skirmishes on Land

Date	Action	Forces Engaged (% Losses)	
		Texians	**Mexicans**
29 Jun 1835	Anahuac	26 (0%)*	45 (100% *p*)
30 Sep	Gonzales	18 (0%)*	80 (0%)
1 Oct	Guadalupe Ford	150 (0%)*	80 (1-2%)
9 Oct	Goliad	300 (0%)*	100 (100% *p*)
28 Oct	Mission Concepcion	92 (1%)*	200-300 (20-25%)
1 Nov-4 Dec	San Antonio (Siege)	600-800 (1-2%)*	1000-1200 (1-2%)
9 Nov	Lipantitlan	150 (0%)*	100 (1-2%)
26 Nov	"The Grass Fight"	60 (0%)*	100 (50%)
5-11 Dec	San Antonio (Fall)	600-800 (2-3%)*	1000-1200 (67% *p*)
23 Feb-5 Mar	The Alamo (Siege)	185 (1-2%)	2100 (1-2%)*
28 Feb	San Patricio	45 (90% *p*)	100 (0%)*
3 Mar	Agua Dulce	25 (90% *p*)	80 (0%)*
6 Mar	The Alamo (Fall)	185 (100%)	1800 (16-18%)*
13 Mar	King's Defeat	20 (100% *p*)	80 (1-2%)*
14 Mar	Refugio	150 (1-2%)	400 (40%)*
16 Mar	Refugio	145 (50% *p*)	400 (1-2%)*
18 Mar	Goliad	50 (O%)	100 (0%)
20 Mar	Coleto Creek	350 (100% *p*)	400 (1-2%)*
21 Mar	Copano	83 (100% *p*)	100 (5%)*
25 Mar	Rocky Creek	6 (0%)*	14 (16%)
7 Apr	San Felipe Ford	20-30 (10-15%)	70 (1-2%)*
15 Apr	New Washington	20-30 (0%)	60 (0%)
20 Apr	San Jacinto	100-200 (1-2%)	200-250 (1-2%)
21 Apr	San Jacinto	850 (2-3%)*	1200-1300 (90% *p*)

The table includes all identifiable engagements on land during the period of the revolutionary struggle in Texas, not all of which have been discussed in the text. Naval actions are listed separately. *Forces Engaged* includes only troops active in the action shown. *Losses* are shown as a percentage of those engaged, with the *p* indicating that most of the losses were prisoners. The Mexican troops taken at Goliad on 9 October 1835 and San Antonio on 11 December 1835 were largely released on parole over the next few days, while those taken at San Jacinto on 21 April 1836 were released after as much as a year in custody. Most of the Texians taken prisoner by the Mexicans were shot. An asterisk (*) indicates the victor, in those actions where one is discernible.

able to give each man $11.00 in gold, a goodly sum for the day. The best prize came the next day.

Sweeping through the surrounding countryside, cavalry patrols gathered up about 40 more prisoners. The arrival of one of them at the camp caused a stir. Although unshaven and dirty, the man wearing a Mexican private's tunic was quickly recognized by the other prisoners. Despite his efforts to keep them silent, word soon spread that Santa Anna was present. The Texian guards took notice, and dragged him off to where Houston sat, under an old tree, nursing his injured ankle. A mob gathered, clamoring that Santa Anna be hanged at once. But Houston had other ideas. There were still over 4,000 effective Mexican troops in Texas, some 2,500 within 50 miles. Lynching "The Napoleon of the West" would not free Texas. Negotiating with him would.

Houston and Santa Anna got along surprisingly well, apparently even sharing a pipe of opium. The terms were simple: in return for his life, Santa Anna was to order the Mexican Army out of Texas and conclude a treaty recognizing the Republic's independence. This Santa Anna was perfectly willing to do. By doing so, he ensured Texian independence.

The Santa Anna Legend

A legend in his own lifetime, Santa Anna was the subject of many tales as soldier, grafter, womanizer, and generally admirable bad guy. Some of these stories were actually true, most mere fabrications. Herewith is a sampler of Santa Anna stories.

The Washington's Birthday Ball. One tradition holds that Santa Anna appeared in mufti at the Washington's Birthday ball held in San Antonio on the evening before his army camped before the mission, engaging in conversation with many of the guests, taking a turn or two around the dance floor with some of the ladies, thoroughly enjoying himself, while gathering some valuable intelligence. This seems highly unlikely, since several of the people at the *fandango*, such as the Seguins, father and son, would have been personally acquainted with the President. Besides which, if Santa Anna had managed to arrive that evening, he would probably have been able to capture the Alamo single-handedly, since all but ten men of the garrison were at the party, and, according to one hostile tradition, most of them were beastly drunk by midnight. The story probably grew out of other, and truer tales of Santa Anna's adventures in earlier campaigns, when he had once disguised himself as a woman to reconnoiter enemy positions and on another occasion es-

caped from an enemy-held town by openly striding about proclaiming that he had just won a great victory.

The Affair of the General's Decorations. On one occasion Santa Anna is said to have stiffed a professional woman of her fee. In revenge, the woman stole his numerous decorations—including his *Gran Cruz del Orden de Isabel la Catolica*, his *Orden de Guadalupe*, and his *Orden de Carlos III*—and bestowed them on whomsoever she passed as she fled his palace in Mexico City. As a result, Santa Anna was forced to run about town and buy back his orders from the beggars and drunks and prostitutes of the capital. This tale may very well have been true.

Santa Anna's Mock Wedding. While encamped before the Alamo Santa Anna is said to have developed a passion for a local *señorita*. He decided to pay her court, only to find his advances rebuffed by her mother, who asserted that the road to her daughter's bed lay down the aisle. One of his officers, not wishing to see his general disconsolate, suggested a little ruse, on the theory that "all's fair in love and war." Observing that there was a man in his outfit who could perfectly imitate a priest going about his duties, the officer suggested that Santa Anna propose to the young lady, and marry her. This was done, and the trick worked perfectly, so that the good general spent a part of the siege enjoying his "honeymoon." All good things must come to and en, of course, and when the general had to resume his military duties, he dispatched his new "wife" to one of his estates where she was in time delivered of his child.

Although an amusing tale, much of this story is certainly false. Santa Anna was so prominent a public figure that neither the young lady nor her mother could have been unaware of his marital status. To be sure, there does seem to have been a young lady with whom Santa Anna passed his nights while at San Antonio, and who eventually did bear his child. Alas for romance, however, her objections to the liaison seem to have been overcome by a gift of 2,000 *pesos*.

The Court Martial of Santa Anna. Once, whilst still a relatively junior officer during the Revolution, Santa Anna, an inveterate wagerer, found himself faced with some enormous gambling debts. Unable to find the money to pay off his creditors, and fearful of the consequences, he forged the names of two very senior officers on some military payment vouchers. This enabled him to pay his debts. Normally such a deed might have gone unnoticed, given the inefficiency and graft rampant in the Spanish Army of the day. Unfortunately for Santa Anna, the forgery was discovered. Disgrace loomed, as the young lieutenant's superiors spoke of a court martial.

However, at the last moment Santa Anna was able to avoid disaster. He talked a kindly, and wealthy, regimental surgeon into staking him the necessary funds with which to reimburse the army and the matter was dropped. True to form, Santa Anna never did pay back the money he owed to the generous medical officer.

Santa Anna's Adopted American Son. The story of Santa Anna's offer to adopt Angelina Dickinson, the "Babe of the Alamo," shortly after his troops had made her fatherless, may sound like a legend but is certainly true, as it is attested in several sources. The General seems to have had a hankering to adopt someone, however, for he eventually did adopt an American child, a boy. In 1842 there were a series of incidents along the ill-defined Texas-Mexican border, with the result that twice Mexican troops actually occupied San Antonio. But they were both times withdrawn. Then, in December of that year, about six companies of Texan troops deserted to go on a freelance invasion of Mexico. This was smashed by Mexican troops under Brig. Gen. Pedro Ampudia, who had commanded Santa Anna's artillery during the Campaign of 1836. Among the prisoners was a 12-year old boy, John Christopher Columbus Hill, who had accompanied his father and older brother. Rather than surrender his musket, he smashed it against a rock. This bold gesture, and his brave answers when ques-

161

tioned about his presence among the filibusters so impressed Ampudia that he sent the boy on to Santa Anna, by then once more President of Mexico.

Young Hill also impressed Santa Anna, who made him an offer: Remain in Mexico as Santa Anna's ward, to train for a military career in Mexican service, and his father and brother would be released. Rather than flatly accept or refuse the offer, the lad brazenly decided to bargain with his captor, saying that he would accept upon condition that he be trained as an engineer, since he would never lead Mexican troops against Americans. This appears to have impressed Santa Anna still more, and he accepted. Both Santa Anna and young Hill were true to their word. The general released the boy's father and brother and saw to it that he had the finest education possible in Mexico at the time, while the young man had a long and honorable career as an engineer in Mexico. But in the end, young Hill abandoned Santa Anna for a greater man, Benito Juarez.

The General's Leg. Santa Anna lost a portion of his left leg to a French artillery shot during the "Pastry War." It was an event of considerable importance to his political life, since it proved his loyalty and dedication to the *patria*. To ensure that all and sundry were aware of his loss for the fatherland, Santa Anna had the leg encased in a richly decorated silver casket. For some time thereafter, he always kept the leg with him,

making a particular point to display it prominently when his political fortunes needed shoring up. Occasionally he would attempt to get a priest or bishop to say a mass over the limb, as though it were the relic of some great saint, but without success. Although one uncharitable tale says that he once attempted to stake the leg in a card game, this seems unlikely. In any case, in 1841 Santa Anna returned to power. The following year he had the leg entombed in an elaborate monument amidst spectacular ceremonies, civil, military, and religious. Unfortunately, when he was thrown out of power in 1844, the tomb was demolished and the leg disappeared. Many years later, after the aged Santa Anna had returned to Mexico to die, an old soldier approached him and presented him with his leg, which he had rescued from the mob and guarded for some thirty years. It is said that Santa Anna wept.

Santa Anna Courts Iturbide's Spinster Sister. Allegedly desiring to curry favor with the newly installed Emperor Agustin I Iturbide, Santa Anna is said to have courted the latter's 60-ish spinster sister Nicolasa. Whatever *Doña* Nicolasa thought of the romantic attentions of the young—28 year old—brigadier general, her imperial brother is supposed to have squelched the proposal with some remarks which so wounded Santa Anna that he henceforth turned against his recently acquired sovereign. Like many other tales about Santa Anna, this one may have a germ of truth to it. Santa Anna may well have paid some court to the emperor's sister, but the difference in their ages was by no means as great as suggested. At the time *Doña* Nicolasa was in her early 40s, not sixty.

Santa Anna Founds an American Institution. Shortly after the American Civil War, Santa Anna, who had been out of power and in exile since 1855, briefly took up residence in the United States, settling down on Staten Island, New York. He passed his time plotting a return to power, and, since this was the period of the French intervention in Mexico, angling for a commission from the Emperor Maximilian, to whom he gave unsolicited, but probably valuable advice. Nothing came of these machinations, but Santa Anna did make a major contribution to American industry and popular culture. While living on Staten Island, he was from time to time wont to take a bit of chicle and chew on it. This impressed the general's American secretary, one James Adams. Since the young man expressed an interest in the stuff, Santa Anna gave him his supply of chicle when he left to continue his wanderings. Adams conducted various experiments with the substance and by adding a little sugar and a sugar coating and calling it "Chiclets" founded the American chewing gum industry. The extent to which there is truth in this tale is open to some question, since chewing gum was already known in the U.S. at the time. But it may perhaps be true that Adams acquired an interest in the product through his contact with Santa Anna.

The General's Saintly Grandson. Santa Anna's grandson by his second marriage, Antonio Lopez de Santa Anna III (1881-1965) entered the Jesuit order in 1897. Ordained a priest in 1913, he embarked upon a distinguished academic career, teaching at various Jesuit institutions in Europe for many years. Retiring from academe in 1939, after 26 years, he took up the life of a missionary, serving on the wild and mountainous frontier of Santo Domingo and Haiti, where he acquired a well-deserved reputation for dedication and devoutness, while pondering the sins of his notorious grandfather, of whom he was quite appalled. The saintly Santa Anna retired from this work after more than 20 years, and died in a Jesuit residence in San Juan, Puerto Rico, shortly after authorizing an English edition of his grandsire's wonderfully self-serving memoirs.

Santa Anna, Houston, and the Masonic Conspiracy. When Houston refused to shoot Santa Anna out of hand after his capture, some people suggested that it was because Santa Anna had made a secret Masonic sign, which alerted Houston to his status. It is true, of course, that Santa Anna was a Mason, of the York rite, as befitted a liberal Mexican, the more conservative ones being mostly of the Scottish rite. And Houston was also a Freemason. But this was of little political importance. Freemasonry was extremely popular at the time, and considerable numbers of men on both sides in the war were members. Indeed, when Ben Milam died, he was given a Masonic funeral in full regalia. So the tale that Santa Anna flashed a secret Masonic sign so that Houston could save his life has no foundation.

Santa Anna Marries the Wrong Daughter. According to legend, while still a bachelor, Santa Anna became enamored of the beautiful younger daughter of the prosperous and well-connected Garcias of his native Vera Cruz. However, when he raised the question of marriage with her father, his proposal was so clumsy that *Sr.* Garcia thought the handsome young general was proposing marriage to his older daughter. As the tale is told, neither gentleman became aware of the confusion. It being a proper courtship in the old Iberian style, the engaged couple were not permitted to meet, so that the mistake remained undetected until the two arrived at the altar. When Santa Anna discovered that he was about to wed the older daughter, Inez, he is said to have remarked "It's all the same to me," and gone on with the ceremony. If the tale is true, the mistake appears to have been a fortunate one, for the marriage seems to have been fairly happy. The marriage was a fruitful one, the pair having five children who survived infancy. By all accounts, the general's wife was a patient, if long suffering companion, who overlooked her husband's numerous affairs. Immensely popular in Mexico, for her good works and her devotion to her husband, she died in 1844. The extent to which Santa Anna was devoted to his wife is difficult to determine. Although upon her untimely death the 50-year old general was for a time quite disconsolate, after about a month he cut short his mourning in order to marry a woman of 15, with whom he had several more children.

Santa Anna and the Cannibals. Upon his ouster from power in 1844, Santa Anna found himself once more a fugitive. While fleeing alone through the mountains above Vera Cruz he was captured by a band of Indians. Recognizing the former *Benemerito de la Patria* ("Well-Deserving of the Fatherland"), the Indians decided to play a delicious joke on him. Setting a large cauldron aboiling, they gathered herbs and spices and chilis and set about preparing an elaborate meal, with Santa Anna scheduled to be cooked up and served as a gigantic tamale. It looked bad for the general. But then the good fortune which ever seemed to smile on him in such tight spots did so yet again. The local priest got wind of the goings-on and hastened to the place. Scolding the Indians, and elevating the Sacred Host, he rescued Santa Anna from certain death.

While this tale seems true, it is generally told with the assumption that the Indians in question were going to present the Santa Anna tamale to the government.

In fact, there is no reason to assume this. There were a number of anthroprophaginous tribes resident along the west coast of the Gulf of Mexico, from Vera Cruz up into Texas, and it is equally reasonable to assume that Santa Anna was going to be principal *entre* in a festive cannibal feast.

Santa Anna and the "Yellow Rose of Texas." Several reasons have been given for Santa Anna's indolence on the day of San Jacinto. His passion for opium is often referred to, as is the effects of a heavy lunch and a hot day. But there is also one Emily Morgan, a young, of course, and beautiful mulatto-girl, with whom Santa Anna is said in some accounts to have whiled away the mid-day hours in sexual bliss. There are even versions of the tale which suggest that Ms. Morgan was dispatched to Santa Anna's camp by none other than Sam Houston, who, knowing of the general's predeliction for younger women, supposedly calculated that he might tarry with her at a critical moment.

It is an old tale, but it is not mentioned in the earliest treatments of the campaign, nor in the diary of Juan Nepomuceno Almonte, who was present as Santa Anna's aide. But it is credited by a number of Mexican historians. So perhaps the tale is true. That Houston had a hand in setting up the liaison may be doubted, however. The Mexican Army had been passing through some relatively thickly settled regions, and Santa Anna could easily have acquired a female companion without much ado, particularly one seeking an escape from slavery. Unfortunately, Emily Morgan flits in and out of history with this single episode, and the story of her historic dalliance with Santa Anna can neither be confirmed nor refuted.

Interestingly, the tale is the basis of the equally old song "The Yellow Rose of Texas," a reference to Ms. Morgan's "yellow" coloring, a matter about which some of those among whom the song has been most popular might perhaps find distasteful.

CHAPTER IX

Afterwards

Actually, Santa Anna's orders to evacuate Texas, and his recognition of the independence of the Republic were wholly invalid, since he was acting while in enemy hands. Brig. Gen. Jose Urrea and several other senior officers urged Maj. Gen. Vicente Filisola, now in command of Mexican forces in Texas, to disobey. But Filisola was reluctant to do so. He was unsure of his authority. Although one of the seniormost officers in the Mexican Army, he was still essentially a foreigner. Rather than disobey, he issued the appropriate orders. Soon the balance of the Mexican Army, more than 4,000 undefeated men, was marching south.

Santa Anna remained a guest of the Texans for some time. He alternately charmed and disgusted Houston and his other hosts. When questioned as to the most suitable method of disposing of the numerous Mexican corpses that littered the San Jacinto, one witness noted that Santa Anna was "wholly indifferent and cared not what disposition was made of the bodies." Asked to explain his defeat, he noted that it "was not the result of the plans, movements, or actions of the commander-in-chief," but rather because "Fortune had turned her back to me." An attempt to send him to the U.S. came to naught when some newly arrived volunteers carried him off the ship and tried to lynch him. It was not until November that the government of Texas was able to send him to New Orleans. Before leaving, Santa Anna penned a little

Numbers and Losses during the Texas War for Independence

Neither side in the War for Texas can be accused of being overly meticulous in the matter of record keeping. Indeed, record keeping was poor in the Mexican Army and virtually nonexistent in the Texian Army. However, by drawing upon various more or less official sources and the diaries and memoirs of various of the participants, it is possible to get some notion of the numbers of men involved in the war and of the number who fell.

Prior to the outbreak of the Texas Revolution, there were some 1,000-1,200 Mexican troops in Texas. Aside from perhaps 50-100 dead, these men mostly returned south of the Rio Grande in December of 1835, either as fugitives or on parole. Back in Mexico some 600-900 of these forces were incorporated into the army which Santa Anna was concentrating at Saltillo. As he intended to bring with him to Monclova about 5,050-5,100 men, the total force which he anticipated having under command when he arrived there would have been about 5,650-6,000. And in fact, when Santa Anna reorganized the army on 15 January 1836, the total "effective" manpower was about 6,050 officers and men, to whom should be added perhaps 50-100 more for staffs and technical personnel. So, allowing for some loss due to desertion, straggling, and illness, the total force which Santa Anna brought with him into Texas was certainly somewhat in excess of 6,000 men. There were, in addition, several thousand camp followers, mostly women and children.

Figures for the Texians are more difficult to come by. Since Texian staff work was non-existent, the best source for the strength of the Texas forces comes from the records relating to veterans' land grants, claims for which continued to be filed until 1874. On the basis of these, some 3,500 to 3,600 men served in the Revolutionary forces, including the Navy, at some time during the war, not all of them at the same time. Many of these men did not serve more than a few days. Roughly speaking, about 1,200 men served during the various operations in 1835, a substantial proportion of whom were Texas residents. At peak strength, at about the time of San Jacinto, there were probably no more than 2,000 men under arms, many of

note to his hosts, "My friends, I consider you brave on the field of battle, and generous after it. You can always count on my friendship, and you may never regret the consideration which you have shown to me." From New Orleans, Santa whom were newly arrived American volunteers. These totaled roughly 1100 with Houston at San Jacinto and Harrisburg, 200 more at Fort Bend, another 150 at San Felipe, and small numbers at Velasco, Galveston, and east of the Trinity River. About 5% of the manpower of the Texas forces was composed of *Tejanos*. This appears to have been more or less in keeping with the *Tejano* proportion of the military-eligible male population. Although *Tejanos* constituted about 10 percent-15 percent of the total population, the Americo-Texans were disproportionately male.

As with the numbers engaged, the number of casualties is also rather difficult to ascertain, particularly for the Texas forces.

Based on very uncertain figures, it appears that the Texians lost some 850-950 men, killed and wounded. The heaviest losses were the 350 men killed with Fannin and the 189 or so who perished at the Alamo. Probably no more than 50-100 other men were killed or died of wounds in all the other actions of the war. So about 600 of the Texian casualties were dead.

Mexican losses can be calculated with somewhat greater precision. Shortly after San Jacinto, Maj.-Gen Vicente Filisola, upon whom command of the Mexican forces in Texas devolved when Santa Anna became a prisoner of war, reported that his effectives totaled 4,078. Since Santa Anna entered Texas with somewhat more than 6,000 men, the Mexican Army had lost about 1,950 men killed, wounded, or prisoner. Add in the 50-100 who died during the operations in 1835, and the total certainly rises to about 2,000-2,100. At least half of these were dead, some 350, probably more, at the Alamo, plus about 600 at San Jacinto, and perhaps 100-150 more in the other actions of the war. In addition, there were about 700 or so prisoners taken at San Jacinto. So Mexican losses were some 1,000-1,200 dead, 700 or so prisoners, and perhaps 400 otherwise ineffective due to wounds. Nor do these figures take into account men who succumbed to disease. By the time of San Jacinto the *Yucatan* battalion, which had seen very little action, was down to 239 men, a loss of about 21% since January.

Casualties on both sides were heavy, and more or less of the same magnitude. In both armies the ratio of men killed to those wounded was about 2:1, a testament to the ferocity with which prisoners were treated, particularly after the Alamo. The Texians suffered about 25% casualties, with about 17% dead. Mexican losses were about 33% casualties, and about 18% dead. By any accounting it was a bloody war.

Anna made a surprisingly triumphal progress across the United States, eventually charming Washington society, before finally being released.

Almost as soon as he was free, Santa Anna disavowed

every agreement concerning Texian independence which he had entered into while a prisoner. The fate of Texas was still in question, but the Texians jubilantly ignored the possibility of a renewed Mexican invasion as they set about establishing a proper government and getting into some traditional American style cut-throat politics. Meanwhile, Mexico ran into some serious difficulties of its own. Those difficulties endured for the entire life of the "Lone Star Republic," which was fortunate, for the Republic led a very unstable life. Even during the Revolution, the native *Tejanos* and the original American settlers were being shoved aside by the newer waves of immigrants from the United States. These soon

The Pastry War

In 1828 the newly elected, but not yet inaugurated, President of Mexico, Manuel Gomez Pedraza, a *moderado* liberal, used the army to eject the governor of the State of Mexico, none other than Lorenzo de Zavala. Not a man to take such high-handed and illegal treatment lying down, in December, supported by Santa Anna, Zavala rallied most of the garrison of Mexico City to his side. There followed four days of bloody fighting. Zavala's men won the fight, and installed a liberal, Vicente Guerrero, as President. Now, during the fighting there was considerable looting on the part of the city's underclass, aided and abetted by soldiers and even officers. When the property owners sought redress, they were ignored. For those among the victimized who were Mexicans there was no further recourse. However, many of those who had lost property were

foreigners, and took their cases to their consuls. The French government claimed that its citizens had lost some 600,000 *pesos*, a goodly sum at a time when a common workman's daily pay was only about one *peso*. One of the claims was filed by a pastrycook who had lost a thousand *pesos* when his shop was sacked by some drunken army officers. Despite repeated demands for action, the French government did not seem inclined to press the case beyond occasional protests to the Mexican government. So it appeared that the matter was dead. But a decade later, someone in Paris decided to do something.

One morning in April of 1838, a French fleet appeared off Vera Cruz, belligerently demanding immediate settlement of the claims for damages inflicted in 1828. The President of the moment, Anastasio Bustamante, refused. So the came to dominate Texan political life, which more often resembled a public brawl than an orderly process. For the first couple of years Texan independence was preserved more by the fact that revolts and separatist movements in Northern Mexico and the Yucatan kept the central government too busy to think about recovering Texas. The French intervention of 1837-1838, the so-called "Pastry War," brought Santa Anna back into power, but it also conveniently eliminated the Mexican Navy for the next few years and brought formal French recognition of Texan independence, an action which was soon also taken by Britain, Belgium, and the Netherlands.

Santa Anna was the prime threat to Texas, but by assisting

French promptly bombarded and then seized the fortress of San Juan de Ulua, which guarded the harbor of Vera Cruz, 16 April. This marked the beginning of "The Pastry War." Some desultory fighting followed, as the French made raids into the interior to "sting" the Mexicans into cooperating. The biggest French victory was the capture, by *coup de main*, of virtually the entire Mexican Navy on 5 December 1838 as it lay at anchor at Vera Cruz, a matter of considerable importance to the fate of Texas. Eventually, the Bustamante government promised payment in full, and the French politely sailed home on 9 March 1839.

The historic importance of the Pastry War has nothing to do with the moneys involved or with the violation of Mexican territoriality by the French. Rather, it marked the return of Santa Anna as a force in Mexican politics, after his disgrace following the disaster in Texas. When the French occu-pied San Juan de Ulua, Santa Anna emerged from retirement at his hacienda at Jalapa, above the city and illegally took command of the Mexican forces. Although Santa Anna was almost captured when the French took Vera Cruz in December of 1838—legend has it that he fled naked from his tent—he managed to turn even this disaster to his profit. When the French, having completed the capture of the Mexican ships, pulled out of Vera Cruz, Santa Anna led some troops in pursuit through the streets of the city. His men tangled with a French rear guard, and the general had the good fortune to have his left leg mangled by some French grapeshot, necessitating an amputation which left him in considerable pain for the rest of his life. The circumstances of the injury lost nothing in the telling, and immediately restored his status as hero of the nation, a loss which he was ever after never loathe to mention.

---

separatists in the Yucatan and other areas, the Texans managed to keep him off balance for a few years more. Nevertheless, the early 1840s were a dangerous time for the Republic. After considerable border skirmishing, in 1842 Mexican armies twice briefly occupied San Antonio, which caused the Republic to reestablish a regular army. Several efforts to take the offensive against Mexico, with the object of annexing Santa Fe and Coahuila, were as abortive as the Mexican attempts at reconquest. Meanwhile, Texas grew rapidly in population as new settlers arrived from United States, to which the Republic several times sought annexation. This was finally achieved in 1845, thereby firmly securing Texan independence from Mexico.

It also led to the Mexican-American War of 1846-1848.

Veterans of The Texas War in the American Civil War

A quarter century after the Texas War for Independence a number of men who had soldiered for the fledgling Republic, either during the war or immediately after it, attained some distinction during the Civil War, all in the ranks of the Confederacy.

Thomas Green (1814-1864) was born in Virginia, but raised in Tennessee, where he studied law. In 1835 he joined the flood of volunteers for Texas, fighting alongside Ben McCulloch in the artillery at San Jacinto. In 1841 he was appointed Clerk of the Texas Supreme Court, a post which he held until 1861, save for the period of the Mexican-American War, when he served with some distinction as a captain of the 1st Texas Rifles. In 1861 Green helped raise the 5th Texas Cavalry, and fought at Valverde, in New Mexico, at Galveston, and later in Louisiana, under Richard Taylor, by which time he had been promoted to brigadier general. Green was killed in action during the Red River Campaign, on 12 April 1864.

Ben McCulloch (1811-1862) was born in Tennessee. Haphazardly educated, and with no particular profession, in 1836 he volunteered for the Texas Army, and fought at San Jacinto in the artillery. He took up surveying, a valuable

trade in the booming Texas land market, and became a notable Indian fighter, two not incompatible skills. Joining the Texas Rangers during the Mexican-American War, McCulloch rendered excellent service as a scout for Zachary Taylor. In 1849 he caught "gold fever" and went to California, but soon afterwards returned to his adopted state, where he served as a U.S. Marshal and in other government posts until the outbreak of the Civil War, when he was appointed colonel of the state militia, in which capacity he forced the surrender of U.S. troops at San Antonio in February of 1861. Shortly appointed a brigadier general, he fought in Arkansas, where he won the Battle of Wilson's Creek (10 August 1861). He was killed leading a brigade at the Battle of Pea Ridge (7 March 1862). Ben McCulloch's brother, Henry Eustace (1816-1895), followed him to Texas in 1837. In addition to farming, he dabbled in local politics, serving as a legislator and county sheriff. During the Mexican-American War he served as a captain of the Texas Rangers. After the war he served in the state legislature for several years. At the outbreak of the Civil War the younger McCulloch, by then a U.S. Marshal, was appointed colonel of the 1st Texas Mounted Rifles. Promoted to brigadier general early in 1862, his principal activities during the war were associated with the Vicksburg Campaign, during which he commanded the brigade which was soundly thrashed by some newly recruited black troops at Milliken's Bend (6-8 June 1863). After the war the younger McCulloch returned to farming.

Jerome Bonaparte Robertson (1815-1891) was a native of Kentucky. In his youth apprenticed to a hatter, Robertson nevertheless managed to study medicine at Transylvania College, from which he graduated in 1835. The following year he went to Texas, where he saw some service as a volunteer. He afterwards practiced medicine in Washington County, while gaining some distinction as an Indian fighter and politician. A delegate to the secession convention in 1861, Robertson voted for secession. He was shortly appointed a captain of the 5th Texas Infantry, part of the Texas Brigade of the Army of Northern Virginia. Robertson rose rapidly thereafter, so that by November of 1862 he was a brigadier general. A tough, tenacious fighter, Robertson was several times wounded in action. In late 1863, there being some charges of dereliction of duty while serving under James Longstreet in the Knoxville Campaign, Robertson was transferred to Texas, where he assumed command of the state reserves. After the war he resumed the practice of medicine, became active in railroading, and served in a variety of state posts. His son, Felix Huston

Robertson (1839-1928), was the only native-born Texan to attain a generalcy in the Confederate Army, when he was promoted to brigadier general in 1864, at the age of 25.

George B. Crittenden (1812-1880), a native of Kentucky, graduated from West Point in 1832, and immediately afterwards saw service in the Black Hawk War. After several years of garrison duty, Crittenden resigned his commission and went to Texas, where he joined the small regular army. During the Mier Expedition of 1842, he was captured, but shortly afterwards released. He later fought in the Mexican-American War, winning a brevet to major. Continuing in the U.S. Army after the war, Crittenden, by then a lieutenant colonel, resigned to "Go South" in 1861. In Confederate service he rose to the rank of major general. However, after troops under his command suffered a disastrous reverse at Fishing Creek, Kentucky (19 January 1862), Crittenden resigned amid charges that he had been "in a beastly state of intoxication" during the battle. He served out the war in various minor posts and was later State Librarian of Kentucky.

Joseph L. Hogg (1806-1862) was born in Georgia into a prosperous planter family which relocated to Alabama when he was 12. Hogg studied law, dabbled in politics, and joined the militia. In 1839 he went to Texas, where he was shortly elected to Congress. During the Mexican-American War, Hogg served as a private. He afterwards became active in state politics and railroading. A member of the Texas secession convention, Hogg voted to dissolve the Union. Appointed a colonel, he was at first engaged in organizing and training new regiments. In early 1862 he was made a brigadier general. Early in May of 1862, shortly after reaching Corinth, Mississippi, with a brigade destined to reinforce Pierre G.T. Beauregard's army which was reorganizing after its defeat at Shiloh, Hogg took sick with dysentery and died. According to one tradition, he had never worn his brigadier general's uniform. He certainly had never served the Confederacy in combat.

Albert Sidney Johnston (1803-1862) was undoubtedly the most distinguished veteran of the Texas Revolution to see service in the Civil War. Johnston, a native of Kentucky, graduated from West Point in 1826. After several years of garrison duty and service in the Black Hawk War (1832), he resigned from the Army in 1834 to care for his ailing wife, who shortly died. In 1836, he went to Texas, enlisting as a private. Within a year he was named commander-in-chief of the Republic's Army, with the rank of brigadier general. This was a difficult assignment, due partially to the poverty of the Texas Republic and partially to the "rampant individualism" of Texans; in February of 1838 Johnston was seriously wounded in a duel with Brigadier General Felix Huston, a jealous subordinate, an injury which left him slightly lame, and subject to occasional numbness or pain in his right hip and leg. Later that same year Johnston was named Secretary of War, a post which he held until 1840, when he resigned to take up farming. Although appointed colonel of the 1st Texas Volunteer Foot Rifles on the outbreak of the Mexican-American War, Johnston's principal duties were as a staff officer. At the end of the war he was commissioned a colonel in the U.S. cavalry, and was eventually given the newly raised 2nd Cavalry [now the 5th] in 1855. In 1857 he was appointed a brevet brigadier general and placed in command of the so-called "Mormon Expedition." The outbreak of the Civil War found him commanding all U.S. forces on the West Coast. He promptly resigned, was shortly commissioned a full general in the Confederate Regular Army, and given command of all Confederate forces west of the Allegheny mountains. Johnston brought considerable energy to the task of raising and organizing his forces, and establishing control of Kentucky. However, in February of 1862, his "front" was ruptured by U.S. Grant's capture of Forts Henry and Donelson. His effort to rectify this reverse led to the Battle of Shiloh (6-7 April). At about 2:30 p.m. on the first day of the battle, as he was personally commanding the troops on his left flank, Johnston was struck in the leg by a musket ball which severed the femoral artery. None of his staff officers having the presence of mind to apply a tourniquet, the general bled to death in minutes.

Francisco Becerra (1810-1876) Although other veterans of the Texas War may have attained greater distinction in the service of the Confederacy, none may be said to have had a more interesting or more unusual career than Francisco Becerra. Becerra came to Texas with Santa Anna, being at the time a sergeant in the *Matamoros Battalion* of the Mexican Army. He was present at the storming of the Alamo, and at San Jacinto, where he had the good fortune to be captured, rather than cut down in the slaughter which followed the Mexican defeat. Rather than return to Mexico, Becerra settled down in Texas, being employed for a time by Reuben Marmaduke Potter, the first serious historian of the Alamo. Becerra several times returned to a military career, fighting Indians in the Texas Army, Mexicans in the Mexican War, and, when the Civil War broke out, Yankees as a second lieutenant in the Confederate Army. In 1875, Col. John S. Ford, who had mustered Becerra into Confederate service in 1861, recorded his reminiscences of the Alamo and San Jacinto, which have since been published several times. Becerra, who in latter life was a policeman in Brownsville, died shortly afterwards from the lingering effects of a bayonet wound which he had incurred while attempting to arrest an unruly soldier.

The Texas Revolution, American Imperialism, and the Slavocratic Conspiracy

Most Mexican historians, and not a few American ones, are of the belief that the independence movement in Texas was all part of a carefully orchestrated conspiracy to expand the slaveholding interests in the United States, a conspiracy aided and abetted by President Andrew Jackson. Indeed, most Mexican historians charge that the entire history of American settlement in Texas, going right back to the original land grants to Moses Austin by the Spanish Crown, was part of an elaborate plot to separate Texas from Mexico.

This is a convenient theory. It satisfies Mexican nationalist feeling, and makes anti-slavery and anti-imperialist Americans smugly happy as well. Unfortunately, it doesn't really stand up in court very well.

Liberal Mexicans consistently sought assistance from Americans and other foreigners during the revolutionary period 1810-1821. Indeed, American interest in Texas was sparked as much by Mexican nationalists as by American greed. Seeking assistance in their struggle against Spain, Mexican revolutionaries actively recruited on U.S. soil. One result of this desire for American aid by the Mexican revolutionaries was that there were a number of American filibustering expeditions into Texas. In August of 1813, for example, a column of American adventurers and Mexi-

can *emigres* raised by one of the leading Mexican rebels, Bernardo Gutierrez de Lara, invaded Texas from Louisiana. Although "The Republican Army of the North" managed to capture San Antonio, the following August it was defeated by Royalist troops, who slaughtered their prisoners, and the *Tejanos* who supported them with great brutality. Although the object of this expedition was to support the Republican revolutionary forces in Mexico, many Mexicans contended that this was merely a "cover plan" to mask the annexation of Texas by the United States.

In 1818, there was yet another such expedition, about 300 men under a Dr. James Long, who held a commission as a general from one of the republican factions in Mexico. This force, in which Jim Bowie briefly served, had mixed success. After occupying Nacogdoches, Dr. Long put his men on ships and landed them down the coast. He then marched inland for Goliad and San Antonio. Royalist reaction was swift, however. After a brief skirmish, Long and his men were all captured and sent to Mexico City, where they were incarcerated. Although Dr. Long himself was eventually shot, most of the men with him were released when the Mexican Republic came into existence.

And indeed, even independent

177

Mexico continued to make foreigners welcome in the Army, where, for example, the Belgian Adrian Woll, the Italian Vicente Filisola, and the American John D. Bradburn all attained generalcies, and even in the Navy, in which the American David Porter, a naval hero of the War of 1812, served as commander-in-chief during the late 1820s.

The prominence of Americans in the Texas secessionist movement obscures the fact that centralist governments in Mexico were consistently plagued by separatist movements. At the very same time that Texas was in secession from Mexico, both Yucatan and New Mexico were in rebellion as well. It took several years for the central government to suppress these two unruly provinces. That Texas succeeded where Yucatan and New Mexico failed may be attributed to the fact that they were able to tap into a major source of foreign support, in the United States. As it was, prominent Mexican liberals supported the revolutionaries, such as Lorenzo de Zavala, who, of course, was a signer of the Texas Declaration of Independence and the first vice-president of Texas, and Valentin Gomez Farias, who had briefly been President of Mexico after Santa Anna's resignation in 1833, who helped raise money for Texas in the United States. Torn between his loyalty to Mexico and his disgust at Santa Anna's usurpation of power, Jose Manuel Rafael Simeon de Mier y Teran, one of the most liberal generals, committed suicide.

Of course, Americans who contributed funds and equipment to Texas and who volunteered for service did so in violation of the nation's Neutrality Acts. Legally, the U.S. government was obligated to prevent any such American participation in the war. This it failed to do. However, the U.S. government also failed to impede the purchase of military supplies in the U.S. by the Mexican government and the transport of such supplies by American merchantmen, both of which were also illegal under the Neutrality Acts, nor did the U.S. strip Americans in Mexican service of their citizenship, as would have been proper under the terms of the Neutrality Acts. Despite the U.S. failure to enforce the Neutrality Acts, men such as Felix Huston and John A. Quitman, who recruited volunteers for Texas in the U.S., warned their men to take some care to avoid drawing attention to themselves or their destination.

It is true, of course, that most of the Americans in Texas favored the institution of slavery. Slavery was illegal under all versions of the Mexican constitution, a matter which, as apologists for the Mexican view consistently point out, was a source of contention between Mexico and the settlers. However, despite legal prohibition, various forms of "involuntary servitude" flourished in Mexico. Contract labor was specifially permitted under Mexican law, but there was no legal limit on the duration of an indenture. So 99-year contracts were not unknown, and, indeed, were the ruse by which the American settlers in Texas were able to keep their slaves. In addition, there was penal servitude for debt, with the debtor and members of his family over the age of 10 being contracted out to work off the indebtedness. This amounted to a life sentence, since the debtor had to provide his own upkeep, or reimburse his master through additional labor. In addition, the bulk of Mexico's *Indios* were peons, held in more or less feudal subjugation by the landowning classes. And despite the law, outright chattel slavery existed as well. There was a thriving trade in the children of "wild" Indians, such as Apaches, to provide exotic and expensive house servants for the wealthy.

Nor was the political atmosphere in the U.S. favorable to the annexation of Texas, and the probable war with Mexico which would follow. The debate over slavery was heating up, and even President Jackson, who certainly qualified as an expansionist, was reluctant to exacerbate sectional tensions more than was necessary, having just brought an unruly South Carolina to heel in the "Nullification Crisis."

If there had been a coherent U.S.-based conspiracy to separate Texas from Mexico, the matter would probably have proceeded much more smoothly.

The Texan Revolution at Sea

1835-1836

Texas has a rich and varied maritime history. Yet the importance of the sea in the Texas War for Independence is often overlooked. Although it is the glorious defeat at the Alamo (6 March 1836) and the spectacular victory of San Jacinto (21 April 1836) that have grabbed the attention of history, it was through command of the sea that Texas' independence was assured.

In practical terms, at the time of the Texas Revolution, the most efficient way of going to Texas, whether from Mexico or the United States, was by sea. The journey by sea, through the Gulf of Mexico to Anahuac or Brazoria or any of the numerous other inlets and bays common along the territory's 400-mile long coastline, was not only easier, faster, and cheaper than the various possible overland routes, but it was also healthier; the overland route from Mexico ran across seemingly endless semi-desert terrain, while that from the United States was partially across somewhat less extensive malarial marshlands and partially across wonderfully flat prairies. Spanish rule in Texas had been maintained from the sea and Mexico adopted the practice as a matter of course upon attaining independence. If troops had to be brought into the territory, even to San Antonio, some 100 miles inland, they went by sea. And, indeed, most of the American settlers in Texas arrived by sea.

The sea was also intimately bound up in the causes of the Texas Revolution. Almost as soon as they had settled in Texas, the Americo-Texans, like most Anglo-Saxons heartily committed to free-trade, clashed repeatedly with the customs authorities of protectionist Mexico. Given that they were also heirs of the great Anglo-Saxon maritime tradition, it was not surprising that when they took up arms against Mexico, they immediately turned their attention to the sea. But even before the break with Mexico had become an open one there had already been action at sea.

The first maritime engagement of the Texas Revolution took place off Velasco on 1 September 1835. The Mexican armed transport *Correo de Mejico* seized an American-owned merchantman outward bound from Velasco, the ship having improper papers. Seeing this, a band of heavily armed Texians boarded the small, unarmed steamer *Laura* and put to sea intending to retake the merchant ship. A relatively bloodless exchange of fire ensued, which ended when the Texians "liberated" the merchant vessel after *Correo de Mejico* became becalmed.

The next morning the Americo-Texan owned armed schooner *San Felipe*, Capt. W.A. Hurd commanding, turned up off Velasco, bearing as its precious cargo Stephen Austin, founding father of American settlement in Texas, and a load of arms. The local winds being deficient, *Laura* sortied again, in order to take *San Felipe* in tow and bring her into port. As this was taking place, the skipper of *Correo de Mejico*, Thomas M. Thompson, a Mexican naval officer of English birth formerly resident in the United States, took advantage of some light airs to maneuver his ship so as to bring *San Felipe* under fire. *San Felipe*, still under tow, responded in kind. Meanwhile, *Laura* brought *San Felipe* into port, so that Austin could disembark, a critical event in the course of the Texas Revolution, since his intention was to deliver the call to arms against

Mexican centralism. Then, having landed their precious cargo, *Laura* towed *San Felipe* back to sea so that she could engage the Mexican vessel more seriously. There ensued a desultory action which lasted for much of the afternoon of 2 September, during which Thompson was lightly wounded. Nightfall found both ships on a southerly course, with *San Felipe* more or less in pursuit of *Correo de Mejico*. During the night both ships were becalmed not far apart. The action resumed the next morning, and *Correo de Mejico* had the worst of it and struck her colors. In a bit of pettiness, the Americo-Texans accused Thompson of being a pirate and hauled him off to New Orleans, where sympathetic American authorities kept him and his crew in jail for some time before pressure from Washington effected their release. In any case, the first round at sea had gone to the rebellious settlers.

As the political situation deteriorated into open rebellion over the next few weeks, the Mexican Minister of War and Marine, Jose Maria Tornal, developed a plan to crush the rebellion. He proposed concentrating a sizable squadron— two brigs and six schooners, plus some smaller vessels—in the Gulf and using it to cover the landing of upwards of 20,000 men on the Texas coast. It was an excellent plan, for it combined protection of the lines of supply of any Mexican forces in Texas with an offensive movement, and its merits were recognized not only by several prominent civilian politicians but also by virtually everyone in the high command of the army. But neither Tornal nor anyone else was able to convince Santa Anna of its merits. Tornal's plan required time. Ships and troops would have to be concentrated at Vera Cruz, and the operation would have to be timed for the optimal season, which would require several months. Santa Anna, who can hardly be said to have understood naval operations any better than he understood military operations, was in a hurry to crush the rebels. Since in the autumn of 1835 he had a substantial army in Zacatecas, having just crushed a rebellion there, he ignored Tornal's advice and committed his army to an overland invasion of Texas.

Meanwhile, the Mexican Navy increased its activity off Texas. Within a few weeks the armed schooners *Moctezuma* and *Veracruzana* were in Texas waters, covering the maritime lines of communication of Mexican forces already in Texas by escorting supply and troop ships. These ships more or less controlled the seas for Mexico for nearly two months.

During this period, of course, the Texians made their final break with Mexico. In early November their provisional General Council adopted resolutions calling for the purchase of warships—"two schooners of twelve guns each and two schooners of six"—and the issuance of letters of marque and reprisal, piracy licenses frequently issued by inferior naval powers into the early nineteenth century. Within weeks Texas privateers were wrecking havoc with Mexican merchant shipping. Although there were never more than six of these licensed pirates, they seriously interfered with Mexican communications. Of course, since their primary purpose was to make a profit, the skippers of privateering vessels were not inclined to undertake actions such as coast defense or pursuit of Mexican warships. So command of the seas remained in Mexican hands, and both *Moctezuma*, which was eventually renamed *Bravo*, and *Veracruzana* several times harassed coastal settlements and interfered with Texian shipping. As a result, in late November the armed schooner *William S. Robbins* was purchased by the Committee of Safety at Matagorda. Intending to use her for local defense, the Committee of Safety applied for and on 5 December was granted a letter of marque. She was the first publicly owned vessel, and thus effectively the first ship of the infant Texas Navy.

The first and only action in which *Robbins* took part under her letter of marque occurred in mid-December 1835. An American schooner, *Hannah Alexander*, inbound with arms for the Texas forces, was intercepted and run aground off Paso Caballo by the Mexican *Bravo*. The Mexican skipper put a prize crew aboard the schooner and made preparations to take her off. But the winds rising, he stood away, lest *Bravo* herself run aground. Meanwhile, *Robbins'* skipper, the same

Capt. Hurd who had commanded *San Felipe* off Velasco, got word of the incident and immediately set sail for Paso Caballo. On 19 December he retook *Hannah Alexander* virtually without a shot, *Bravo* standing too far out to sea to interfere.

While these events were unfolding, agents of the provisional government were in New Orleans, negotiating the purchase of various vessels under the provisions of the legislation calling for the acquisition of four schooners. They were quite successful. By mid-January they had picked up a former U.S. Revenue cutter, which was commissioned as *Independence* under Capt. Charles E. Hawkins, a veteran of both the U.S. and Mexican naval service, and the armed schooner *Brutus*, which went to sea with the ubiquitous Hurd in command early the following month, after various pro-Mexican interests had exhausted attempts to block her departure by legal means. To balance out the "fleet," two privateers, *William S. Robbins*—renamed *Liberty*—and *Invincible*, were also purchased, putting to sea under a pair of brothers, Captains W.S. Brown and Jeremiah Brown, both veteran merchant skippers.

The new Texas Navy soon took the offensive. On her first voyage, 10 January-1 March, *Independence* operated clear down to Tampico, taking numerous small Mexican vessels, and earning her skipper a promotion to commodore. Meanwhile, *Liberty* found the large unarmed merchantman *Pelicano* lying off Sisal. On the night of 3-4 March Capt. Brown sent two long boats full of men, intending to capture *Pelicano*. However, the local Mexican garrison commander realized what was about and reinforced the merchant vessel with about 20 men. As a result the cutting out party had a brisk fight on its hands before it secured control of the ship.

During the "Runaway Scrape," Commodore Hawkins kept most of his squadron in the vicinity of Matagorda Bay, to keep Texian maritime supply lines to the U.S. open, and to help guard what was fast becoming the principal munitions dump of the nascent republic. Off course, Hawkins had no intention of remaining inactive, but regularly dispatched some of his ships on patrols.

On one of these, on about 25 March, *Liberty* was patrolling in the Gulf. There she encountered an American-owned brig, *Durango*, under charter to the Mexican Army and ladened with military supplies. The vessel made a fine prize. Hawkins also dispatched *Invincible* to patrol off the mouth of the Rio Grande, with the intention of interfering in the movement of ships upriver to Matamoros, the principal Mexican supply base for the Texas campaign.

There, on 3 April, *Invincible* encountered *Bravo* sailing into the Gulf, escorting the lightly armed merchant ship *Correo Segundo*. By a bit of bad luck, *Bravo* damaged her rudder in crossing the bar at the mouth of the river, and was soon wallowing in the swells, unable to steer. Rather than attack, *Invincible's* skipper, Jeremiah Brown, decided on a ruse that would enable him to take the Mexican ship without fighting, while permitting him to gather whatever intelligence might be available. He hoisted the American flag, and sent a junior officer over in a small boat. Welcomed aboard *Bravo* by Capt. Jose Maria Espino, the young man announced that his vessel was a U.S. Revenue cutter, sent to investigate charges that the American consul and American shipping at Matamoros had been subject to some harassment. Capt. Espino proved a friendly sort, and agreed that *Invincible* should proceed upriver to Matamoros. The ruse might well have worked. However, one of the officers aboard *Bravo* was Lt. Thomas M. Thompson, former skipper of *Correo de Mejico*, recently released from custody in New Orleans. And it was he whom Capt. Espino sent aboard *Invincible* to facilitate the latter's movement up the river. Of course, as soon as Thompson boarded the Texian vessel he was recognized. Capt. Brown promptly clapped him in irons and gave *Bravo* a broadside. Capt. Espino responded in kind, tossing Brown's emissary into the brig and returning the cannonade. The battle lasted about an hour, with neither vessel incurring much damage. Then a large brig appeared on the horizon. Figuring the vessel was Mexican, Brown decided to deal with it first, and then return to finish off the still-rudderless *Bravo* at his leisure. The ship turned out to be an American merchantman, *Pocket*, under charter to the Mexican government. Not only was she loaded with military supplies, but she had aboard a number of Mexican naval officers returning home from the U.S., and a valuable map of the Texas coast, the product of a recent survey conducted by none other than Thomas M. Thompson. All in all, a highly profitable engagement.

As it turned out, Matagorda Bay did not prove the most secure anchorage. Towards the end of March, two Mexican men-of-war had turned up off the port, *Bravo* and *General Urrea*. They had a brief encounter with *Independence*, which soon withdrew. The Mexican vessels stood to sea and did not return, but their presence was disturbing. Then just a few days later, Hawkins learned that a Mexican column under Brig. Gen. Jose Urrea was advancing up the coast towards Matagorda Bay. It was this column which accounted for the earlier visit of *Bravo* and *Urrea*, which had been escorting a supply ship for Urrea's benefit. Hawkins decided to withdraw the fleet to Galveston, which he accomplished about the time *Invincible* was taking *Pocket*.

The capture of Santa Anna at San Jacinto on 21 April wrote *finis* to the war at sea, at least for a time. The Texians had done well. Although they did not win complete command of the seas off their shores, they were able to secure their lines of communication to the United States and to interfere somewhat with those of the Mexican Army.

Although Mexico technically had the larger fleet, Santa Anna's demands for immediate action meant that the Mexican Navy, which also had to concern itself with separatists in Yucatan, was unable to concentrate sufficient strength in Texas waters to secure command of the seas. Nevertheless, Tornal's efforts paid off to the extent that during the February-April 1836 campaign in Mexico, Brig. Gen. Jose Urrea's column was able to advance up the coast, from the vicinity of

Corpus Christi Bay to Brazoria without having to endure the suffering which plagued the main body under Santa Anna.

So ultimately, the war at sea had been indecisive. But that was enough to help the Texians win the war on land.

Afterwards. San Jacinto did not really mark the end of the Texas-Mexican conflict. Desultory operations continued on both land and sea for some years. In these, Texas used its little navy, its only permanent military force, to best advantage. Nevertheless, despite several victories over the Mexicans, the odds were against the Texians. By heroic efforts, Tornal managed to put together a reasonably impressive squadron by 1837, over a dozen moderately well-armed schooners and brigs, including *Independence*, taken in a hot little action in April of that very year, and with these vessels he imposed a fairly effective blockade on the Texas coast, from Galveston southwards. However, in 1838 the "Pastry War" broke out with the French, who raided Vera Cruz and managed to capture or destroy virtually the entire Mexican fleet, a matter which helped preserve Texan independence for several years more.

Over the next few years the Texas Navy was more than able to hold its own. For a time in 1842-1844 the "fleet" was under lease—at $8,000 a month—to separatist rebels in Yucatan, during which service it engaged in one of the first actions involving steam powered ships, when a Texan squadron of sailing vessels met and defeated a Mexican one composed mostly of steam powered ships. The Texas Navy also found time to become the first military service to adopt a repeating firearm, the famous "Navy" Colt, .44-caliber revolver.

In 1845 the Texas Navy was incorporated into that of the United States.

Naval Actions of the Texas War for Independence

Date	Location	Texan	Mexican
1 Sep '35	Velasco	*Laura*	*Correo de Mejico*
1-2 Sep	Velasco	*S. Felipe*	*Correo de Mejico*
1 Nov	Matagorda	*S. Felipe*	*Bravo*
19 Dec	Paso Caballo	*Robbins*	*Bravo*
3 Mar '36	Sisal	*Liberty*	*Pelicano*
25 Mar	Matagorda	*Independence*	*Bravo, Urrea*
25 Mar	Gulf	*Liberty*	*Durango*
3 Apr	Rio Grande	*Invincible*	*Bravo, Pocket*

The dates of the actions listed for 1 November and 25 March are uncertain.

Warships of the Texas War for Independence

Name	Type	Guns	
TEXAS			
Brutus	schooner	10	
Independence	schooner	10	ex-USRC Ingham
Invincible	schooner	7	"fast"
Laura	steamer	0	
Liberty	schooner	6	ex-William S.Robbins
San Felipe	brig	1	
MEXICO			
Bravo	schooner	5	ex-*Moctezuma*
Correo de Mejico	schooner	2	
Correo Segundo	schooner	?	
General Urrea	brig	10	
Veracruzana	schooner	5	

Note that this listing omits Mexican vessels which were not involved in operations off Texas. There were a number of these, mostly engaged in operations off Yucatan, which was also restive at this time.

The Mexican Army

American perceptions notwithstanding, the Mexican Army was a relatively experienced and more or less professional force. During the period of the Texas Revolution the Mexican Army actually consisted of several contingents. There were the regular forces, or *permanentes*, the garrison troops, or *presidiales* and *auxiliares*, and the semi-regular state troops, or *activos*. All three contingents were quite good. The *permanentes*, of course, were the regular force, supported by the central government. The *presidiales* and *auxiliares* were usually stationed at frontier outposts, such as the Presidio del Rio Grande or San Antonio, and were often quite busy dealing with the Indians, in consequence of which they were probably the best troops in the Mexican Army. The *activos* were frequently embodied for service during rebellions and as a result some of them were fairly professional. The total regular force of the Mexican Army comprised eight regiments of infantry, the elite *Zapadores*, eight regiments of cavalry, and a substantial corps of field artillery. The numbers of *activos*, *presidiales*, and *auxiliares* varied depending upon the political situation: Only states loyal to Santa Anna were permitted to have *activos*, as Zacatecas found to its sorrow in 1834, when it attempted to create *activo* regiments.

Organization. The internal economy of all three components was essentially the same.

Infantry regiments normally consisted of one battalion,

which comprised eight companies. Each company was supposed to have 120 men, which with a staff of 25 made for a
total battalion strength of 985 officers and men. However, it
was rare for a regiment to be at full strength, as casualties,
disease, and desertion were common. Indeed, unless active
operations were imminent it was not uncommon for most
infantry regiments to exist in cadre form, with as little as 10%
of their official manpower. Normally, companies had from 35
to 65 men, with battalions running about 275 to 500 men. Two
of the companies in each battalion were "elite" companies, in
Spanish *compañias de preferencia*, one of *granaderos*—"grenadiers" or heavy infantry, and one of *cazadores*—"hunters" or
light infantry. The former were traditionally recruited from
the biggest and bravest men in the regiment, while the latter
were drawn from the smaller of the bravest men. In battle the
elite companies were normally deployed on the extreme right
and left of their regiments, for which they were sometimes
known as "flank" companies. Since the men were usually
more skillful and more experienced, it was often the case that
the elite companies from several regiments would be combined into provisional battalions for special missions. Usually the elite companies were more showily uniformed and
better trained than the line companies, but essentially all
three types of infantrymen were equipped in the same fashion, and most were armed with the British "Brown Bess"
musket. This was old, but reliable, and not particularly inferior to the muskets used by most of the Texians. In addition
to the Brown Bess, some of the elite companies during the
Texas Campaign were issued the British Baker Rifle, a very
good weapon which had a low rate of fire. The *Zapadores*,
although technically sappers, or engineering troops, were the
elite regiment of the Mexican Army, and were organized and
most often served as an infantry battalion.

On paper cavalry regiments consisted of four squadrons.
Each squadron had a staff of three, plus two troops of 71
mounted and 8 dismounted men each, for a total of 151 officers and men. A regiment, with four full squadrons, plus its

staff of 20 and service detachment of 14 technicians, ran to 678 officers and men. In practice however, regiments normally ran to between 200-300 men due to the exigencies of the service, with squadrons often of no more than 50-75 men, and troops of only about 25-35 or so. In each regiment, the first troop was equipped with lances and carbines, while the balance had sabers and carbines.

The artillery of the Mexican Army was rather rudimentary. Batteries were essentially *ad hoc* organizations, comprising a varying number of guns, each of which had a crew of eight or ten men. Most of the guns were light pieces. During the Texas Campaign, Santa Anna had with him 21 guns, comprising four 7-inch howitzers, seven 4-pounders, four 6-pounders, four 8-pounders, and two 12-pounders. This was not normally a tactical handicap, as the most probable opponents of a Mexican Army were not likely to be provided with superior artillery. However, save for the 12-pounders, these guns were too light to effectively batter down even the simple defenses of the Alamo.

Although there were several well trained engineer officers with the Mexican Army in Texas, it lacked any properly trained engineering troops, since the *Zapadores* were actually infantrymen. This hampered operations on several occasions, since the engineers had to undertake their work using unskilled infantrymen. The construction of a bridge to replace one burned by the Texians on the Nueces River required two days. And the emplacement of the artillery batteries at the Alamo took far longer than was necessary.

Another serious problem in Texas was the lack of any medical personnel. Although the Mexican Army had a medical corps, in his haste to get the expedition into Texas going, Santa Anna wholly neglected to make provisions for it to be accompanied by any medical personnel. As a result, virtually all of those who were seriously wounded during the campaign appear to have died.

Manpower and Training. Most Mexican troops were of Indian stock, with a sprinkling of *mestizos*. Volunteers were rare, and forced recruiting was the norm. On one occasion a recruiting officer wrote to a senior officer, "Here are 300 volunteers. I will send you 300 more if you return the chains." Many of the men so conscripted were too old or too young to make proper soldiers, and not a few of them were the sweepings of the local jails. Once in the army, however, these men generally were pretty good. Accustomed to obedience, they were docile and were relatively amenable to military training. Though smaller than the average American, 5'1" as against 5'8", they were inured to hardship and physically tough men. There were some problems, however. Since they were given no musketry training, the men did not know how to aim their weapons. They lacked motivation, a logical consequence of recruiting from the peasant classes, were uniformly illiterate, and had to be supervised constantly. In battle, their morale tended to be brittle, so that they were much more effective in the attack than in the defense.

Since recruit training was performed in the regiment, it was often the case that there were many untrained men present in a battalion about to go into action. During the Texas Campaign two whole battalions were composed almost entirely of green men, as was most of a third, and about 25% of two others, with significant numbers of recruits in the remaining battalions. As a result, a third of the infantry battalions were heavily composed of recruits, and many of the infantrymen were so green that Santa Anna ordered that they be kept out of the assault columns at the Alamo. One curious problem manifested itself in Texas with regard to the *Yucatan* battalion. It was almost entirely composed of men recently recruited in tropical Yucatan, and as a result the troops suffered very seriously from the unusually cold weather which plagued the army during its approach march. In his diary Brig. Gen. Jose Urrea recorded the deaths from exposure of six men of the *Yucatan* within hours of the onset of the Blue Norther of 25 February.

With something like 130 generals and other ranks in proportion, the Mexican Army was overly supplied with officers.

The Mexican Army was about four times larger than the U.S. Army, but had 33 times more generals. The officers came mostly from the *criollo* classes, with a few *mestizos*. Recruiting was a very political affair, since it was wise for the government to satisfy the need for gentlemanly employment of the offspring of the better-connected families in what was still essentially a feudal society. As a result, a lot of men became officers who were intellectually or temperamentally unsuited for such responsibilities. Most of the officers were brave enough, which was a major requisite when leading troops lacking initiative, and, given their family backgrounds, had the habit of command, another useful asset. But many of the officers were themselves lacking in initiative, as demonstrated by Cos' inactivity at San Antonio in December of 1835. In addition, many were indolent and negligent of their duties; not a few were abusive of the troops, and many were grafters on a sometimes heroic scale. During the Texas Campaign Brig. Gen. Antonio Gaona, by origin a Cuban, had managed to corner the supply contracts for the army, and was raking in about 100% over cost. Worse still, officer training was generally poor, and even many senior personnel had only a rudimentary professional education. This was one reason why Santa Anna paid meticulous attention to the details of organizing the assault columns at the Alamo. As a result, few possessed the skills necessary to deal with all contingencies likely to confront the army. The disaster at San Jacinto, for example, was clearly the result of an extraordinary neglect of the most elementary principles of castramentation.

Tactics. On paper, the Mexican Army was essentially a Napoleonic-style force. It was theoretically trained to use relatively flexible tactics combining infantry, cavalry, and artillery. In practice, however, the training of both officers and men was so rudimentary that the only tactic most knew was the frontal attack, with the men firing their muskets from the hip as they advanced, and then closing with the bayonet. This generally worked well against rebel peasants. It worked much less well against the Texas rebels, who, although no more professional, were more experienced and more determined. A decade later the inadequacies of the Mexican Army would be fully revealed when it confronted the much smaller, but much better trained and professionally led U.S. Army.

APPENDIX

The Texas Army

One of the first acts of the rebellious Texians when they established their provisional government in November of 1835 was to authorize the creation of an army, which was to be commanded by Sam Houston as major general and commander-in-chief, under the authority of "Governor" Henry Smith. As finally worked out, the new army was to consist of 1,120 men plus some headquarters personnel and regimental staffs. Half of the army was composed of regulars enlisted for two years and half of volunteers enlisted for the duration of the war or two years, whichever was less. This army was to include a small general staff, one regular and two volunteer regiments of infantry, and a regular regiment of artillery. Provision was also made for the raising of a paramilitary force of 150 Rangers. Soon afterwards, at the urging of William B. Travis, who desired and secured its command, the delegates authorized the creation of a "Cavalry Corps" of 384 men. This brought the authorized strength of the army, with the Rangers, to about 1,700 men, including staffs. In addition, all able-bodied men in Texas between the ages of 16 and 50 were liable for militia service, to be organized on a local basis, with provision for the election of officers. Further legislation provided for the enlistment of additional troops into an "Auxiliary Corps of Volunteers," and the creation of a "Reserve Army," which was to be raised in the United States. So, in effect, the Texas Army had six principal contingents, a regular force, a regularly enlisted volunteer force, an auxiliary volunteer force, a reserve army, and a militia, plus the Rangers. In practice, during the war, only the regular army, the regular volunteers, and the auxiliary army amounted to anything, the reserve army not enrolling a single man before the end of the war.

Organization. Since most of the delegates to the convention at San Felipe de Austin, and to the later provisional congress of the new Republic, were Americans, many of whom had done some militia service in their home states, they very reasonably adopted the regulations of the United States Army for use by their new creation, in so far as these suited the needs of Texas.

The staff of the army was to comprise the commander-in-chief plus an adjutant general, an inspector general, a quartermaster general, a surgeon general, and four aides-de-camp. Regiments of infantry, whether regular, volunteer, auxiliary, or militia, were to consist of five companies of 56 men, with a staff of five. The artillery regiment was to consist of five batteries of 56 men, with a staff of four. Travis' cavalry corps was to consist of six companies of 64 troopers each, plus a staff of three or four. In practice, due to problems of materiel, recruiting, and training, neither the artillery nor the regular cavalry played much of a role in the war. Travis was only able to recruit about 30 men into his "Cavalry Corps."

Manpower, Training, and Tactics. Every man who fought for Texas was a volunteer. Most of the men who fought in the campaign of 1835 had been settled in Texas for some time. But most of these men returned to care for their families through the winter. As a result, the bulk of those who fought in the Campaign of 1836, which ended before the harvest would have released the old-time Texians for service, were newcomers. These new men were primarily from the southern United States, but with many from other parts of the country and a sprinkling of men from other lands as well. Only 41 of the men who fell at the Alamo, including nine *Tejanos*, four of Fannin's men, three of those who perished with Grant, and 57 of those who were at San Jacinto, including 20-21 *Tejanos*, had been permanent residents of Texas prior to 1835. As a general rule, the longer a man had been in Texas the more likely he was to hold the native *Tejanos* in high regard. As a result, although the influx of volunteers from the United States was essential to the success of Texian arms, it marked the beginning of a steady decline in the fortunes of the native *Tejanos*, many of whom appear to have been enthusiastic supporters of the Revolution.

These were mostly tough, healthy men, possessed of enormous self-confidence, crude and bigoted though they certainly were, in an age considerably less genteel than it is usually pictured. Tradition to the contrary notwithstanding, most of them were not seasoned frontiersmen or crack shots in the mold of Davy Crockett or even Houston himself. Indeed, many were farmers or country boys, some were tradesmen and artisans. Their social origins ran the gamut from the wealthiest to the most impoverished. Most were no more than semi-literate, but many were quite well educated, sophisticated men. They had many faults, being almost uniformly ethnocentric, undoubted racists, brutal, casual with other people's property, and partial to drink. Although their devotion to rugged individualism made them difficult to handle, they made good fighting men, if not fine soldiers. Whatever their faults, and they were many, the men who fought for Texas were tough.

There was little formal training given to these men. In that regard it was fortunate that many of them possessed some militia, with a good many having seen action in Indian fights, since it meant that they had at least undergone what passed for "basic training" in the mid-nineteenth century. Since they lacked formal training in tactics, Houston was correct to use them offensively at San Jacinto. To have tried to accept a Mexican attack might well have been disastrous.

Numbers. At the time of the siege of the Alamo the principal contingents of the Texas Army totalled about 1900-1950 men:

With Travis and Bowie at the Alamo: about 180-190 men, organized into about five companies of volunteers, one of Travis' cavalrymen (the only one actually raised), and one of artillerymen.

With Fannin at Goliad: about 465 men, organized into one company of regulars, two "battalions" of five companies of volunteers each, constituting the "First Volunteer Regiment," plus an odd half-company and 15 miscellaneous volunteers not attached to any particular company. Average company size was about 38 men.

With Grant and Johnson at Refugio: about 150 men, constituting the Matamoros expedition.

Assigned to Houston: the main army, with about 275 men at Gonzales, plus about 100 more en route with Houston, who arrived on the 11th, the two forces comprising about eight miscellaneous companies.

Other forces: Perhaps 650 more, principally near Velasco (c. 200) and Matagorda (c. 100-150), and scattered all the way back to the U.S. frontier.

The multiple disasters of the Alamo, the Matamoros expedition, and Goliad reduced the army to about 1,100 men. On 12 March Houston organized his army, by then grown to about 400 men, into the 1st Volunteer Regiment. The next day he commenced his retreat. Despite desertions, his army had reached about 1,200 men by the time he arrived at the Colorado River, on 26 March. Desertions again mounted when he retired behind the Colorado to the Brazos, as Texians decided to tend to their families. This loss of manpower was offset by the arrival of new volunteers and of contingents from Velasco and other areas. On 2 April Houston brought his army to Groce's Ferry. There he halted his retreat for 12 days to reorganize and rest his army. He created the Regular Battalion, the core of which consisted of many of the 200 men who had deserted from the U.S. Army of Observation along the Sabine and the 2nd Volunteer Regiment, and put the army through some training, the only formal drilling it would receive. By this time the main army numbered about 1,300-1,400 men, and there were perhaps another 400-600 men scattered across the rest of Texas. Although he reported that he had just 783 men at San Jacinto, based on the land grant records Houston seems to have had about 800-850 men, having left about some 250 mostly ill or inept troops at Harrisburg, to guard supplies.

Mexican Order of Battle in Texas

The *Army of Operations*

Command and Staff
Commander-in-Chief: Maj. Gen. Antonio Lopez de Santa Anna

Second-in-Command: Maj. Gen. Vicente Filisola
Chief-of-Staff: Brig. Gen. Juan Arago
Aides-de-Camp: Brig. Gen. Manuel Fernandez Castrillon, Brig. Gen. Martin Perfecto de Cos, Brig. Gen. Juan Valentin Amador, Col. Juan Nepomuceno Almonte: Col. Juan Bringas, Col. Jose Bates.

Quartermaster: Col. (brevet Brig. Gen.) Adrian Woll
Chief of Artillery: Lt. Col. Tomas Requena
Chief of Engineers: Capt. (Brevet Lt. Col.) Ignacio Labastica
Staff: 16 officers

Vanguard Brigade: Brig. Gen. Joaquin Ramierez y Sesma
Matamoros Permanente Infantry Battalion (272 men)
Jimenez Permanente Infantry Battalion (274 men)
San Luis Potosi Activo Infantry Battalion (452 men)
Dolores Permanente Cavalry Regiment (290 men)
Artillery (8 pieces, with 62 men)
Total: 1400 men and 8 guns

First Brigade: Col. (brevet Brig. Gen.) Antonio Gaona

Aldama Permanente Infantry Battalion (390 men)
1st Toluca Activo Infantry Battalion (320 men)
Queretaro Activo Infantry Battalion (370 men)
Guajanuato Activo Infantry Battalion (390 men)
Rio Grande Presidial Company (60 men)
Zapadores Battalion (185)
Artillery (6 pieces, with 63 men)
Total: 1750 men and 6 guns

Second Brigade: Col. (brevet Brig. Gen.) Eugenio Tolosa
Morelos Permanente Infantry Battalion (300 men)
Guerrero Permanente Infantry Battalion (400 men)
1st Mexico Activo Infantry Battalion (350 men)
Guadalajara Activo Infantry Battalion (420 men)
Tres Villas Activo Infantry Battalion (189 men)
Artillery (6 pieces and 60 men)
Total: 1700 men and 6 guns

Cavalry Brigade: Brig. Gen. Juan Jose Andrade
Tampico Permanente Cavalry Regiment (250 men)
Guanajuato Activo Cavalry Regiment (180 men)
Total: 430 men
Independent Division: Brig. Gen. Jose Urrea
Yucatan Activo Infantry Battalion (300 men)
Cuautla Permanente Cavalry Regiment (180 men)
San Luis Potosi Auxiliary Cavalry Troop (40 men)
Bajio Auxiliary Cavalry Troop (30 men)
Artillery (1 piece and 8 men)
Total: 550 men and 1 gun

Summary
      c. 4,500 Infantry
         185 *Zapadores*
      c. 1,120 Cavalry
      c.   190 Artillery
      c.   50 Command and Staff
Total: c. 6,050

The strength of an army can never be ascertained with absolute precision. At the time of the Texas Campaign, for example, there was no standard method of calculating the number of troops in an army. As a result, every army used a different system. Some, for example, did not count the officers, while others failed to count not only the officers but also the field musicians, who were an integral part of the combat effectives, since they relayed the commands to the troops. Similarly, some armies carried ill men on the rolls, while others did not. The figures given here are at best approximate, being based on the strength of the army on 15 January 1836, as reported in Filisola's memoirs. However, Filisola's figures are certainly in error, since he did not record the presence of several small detachments of troops from an odd assortment of commands, such as a contingent of 39 cavalrymen, nine from the *Vera Cruz Permanente Cavalry Regiment*, and another 30 from the *Coahuila Permanente Cavalry Regiment*, who appear to have been attached to the *Dolores Cavalry Regiment*, and the 26 lancers who formed Santa Anna's personal bodyguard. So the army probably ran to something in excess of 6,100 officers and men when it set out from Saltillo for San Antonio. The march was accomplished by brigades, each setting out independently at intervals of two or three days. On the march, some troops fell out, being unable to endure the hardships of the unusually cold weather, so that the army probably lost 1-2% of its manpower, if not more. Losses among the camp followers were certainly greater.

To avoid possible confusion, Spanish military terminology has largely been rendered into English. Thus, the Spanish *general de division* is given as "major general," *general de brigada* as "brigadier general," and *general mayor* as "chief-of-staff." Note that a "brevet" was an honorary rank, which conferred certain privileges on the holder, such as the right to command formations of all arms in which there was no officer of higher brevet.

A substantial proportion of the infantry were recruits, as can be seen from the accompanying table.

Battalion	Strength	Recruits (%)
Aldama Permanente	390	113 (29.0)
Guadalajara Permanente	420	
Guajanuato Activo	390	
Guerrero Permanente	400	
Jimenez Permanente	274	26 (9.4)
Matamoros Permanente	272	78 (28.9)
1st Mexico Activo	350	
Morelos Permanente	300	
Queretaro Activo	370	
San Luis Potosi Activo	452	200 (44.2)
1st Toluca Activo	320	40 (12.5)
Tres Villas Activo	189	185 (100.0)
Yucatan Activo	300	250 (83.0)

There were, in addition, a good many recruits scattered through the balance of the infantry battalions. As a result, it is probable that of the approximately 4425-4430 men in the 13 infantry battalions which comprised the bulk of the army, perhaps 1000-1100 were green recruits, 18%-25% of the total.

The cadres of the *permanente* battalions were all seasoned men. Among the *activos*, the *Toluca* battalion had been involved in the fighting at Zacatecas in May of 1835, and was the equal of any of the *permanente* battalions, as was the cadre of the *San Luis Potosi* battalion, leaving aside its recruits.

The artillery of the army comprised four 7-inch howitzers, seven 4-pounders, four 6-pounders, four 8-pounders, and two 12-pounders. The distribution of these among the various brigades is somewhat unclear, and so the allotment indicated on the accompanying table should be taken as only approximately correct.

Vanguard	two 7" hwtzr, two 8-pdr, two 6-pdr, two 4-pdr
1st Brigade	two 7" hwtzr, two 12-pdr, two 4-pdr
2nd Brigade	two 8-pdr, two 6-pdr, two 4-pdr
Independent Div.	one 4-pdr

Order of Battle at San Jacinto

21 April 1836

The Army of Texas (Houston), 800-850 [1,150] men, 2 guns
Headquarters Staff, 11 [12] men
Medical Staff, 5 [6] men
Artillery, 31 [37] men, two 6-pounders
Cavalry, 50 [57] men
Regular Battalion (4 companies), c. 240 [389] men
1st Volunteer Regiment (6 companies), c. 220 [317] men
2nd Volunteer Regiment (9 companies), c. 260 [331] men

The Mexican Army of Operations (Santa Anna); 1,250 men, 1 gun

Headquarters Staff; 30 men

Matamoros Battalion (8 companies), 240 men

Aldama Battalion (6 companies, less *Cazadores* and *Granaderos*), 150

Guerrero Battalion (6 companies, less *Cazadores* and *Granaderos*), 150

1st Toluca Battalion (6 companies, less *Cazadores* and *Granaderos*), 150

Guadalajara Battalion (6 companies, less *Cazadores* and *Granaderos*), 150

Granaderos Battalion (5 companies, the *Granaderos* of the *1st Toluca, 1st Mexico, Gerrero, Aldama,* and *Guadalajara Battalions)*, 150-160 men

Cazadores Battalion (*Cazadores* of the *1st Toluca, 1st Mexico, Gerrero, Aldama,* and *Guadalajara Battalions*), 150-160 men
   Escort Squadron, 60 men
   Artillery, 20 men, 1 6-pounder

The numbers engaged are rather imprecise, but it appears that the two armies were not greatly disparate in number. Although Houston reported that he had only 783 engaged in the battle, his actual strength appears to have been about 800-850 men. The uncertainty is due to the fact that some men may have been counted twice or omitted entirely. The medical personnel, for example, were all officially attached to the different regiments present, while eight of the men assigned to the artillery were on secondment from the Regular Battalion. His paper strength, shown in brackets, was about 1150 men, but this apparently includes the troops left behind at Harrisburg, who comprised two companies of infantry (50 and 25 men respectively) and one of cavalry (25 men), plus about 150 non-effective men and recruits. Note that the 2nd Volunteer Regiment actually consisted of six companies of infantry, plus the cavalry troop, but had attached to it three independent companies, including Juan Seguin's 20-man strong *Tejano* contingent.

Mexican figures are confused by the fact that Santa Anna arrived on the field on April 20, with the *Matamoros Battalion* and the converged *Granaderos* and *Cazadores* from five different battalions, plus his escort and the one artillery piece, for a total of 600-700 men, while Cos arrived early on the morning of the 21st with the balance of the *1st Toluca, Aldama,* and *Guadalajara Battalions,* totalling about another 600. So the Mexican Army probably totalled at least 1200 men, and possibly as many as 1300.

Guide for the Interested Layman

What follows is intended not as an intensive scholarly bibliography on the Alamo and the Texas War for Independence, but rather as a guide for those interested in pursuing the subject or particular aspects of it.

Recommended Reading

Two good general works on Texas are T.R. Fehrenbach, *Lone Star: A History of Texas and Texans* (New York: 1983) and David Nevin, *The Texans* (New York, 1975). Fehrenbach's *Fire and Blood: A History of Mexico* (New York: 1973) provides useful background on Mexico.

Eugene C. Barker's *Mexico and Texas, 1821-1835* (Dallas: 1928) provides the most useful treatment of the American settlement in Texas and the origins of the war.

Works on the Texas Revolution or various aspects of it are rather numerous. The best is still probably Walter Lord's *A Time to Stand* (New York, 1963). Jeff Long's *Duel of Eagles: The Mexican and U.S. Fight for the Alamo* (New York: 1990) displays a good deal of cynicism, considerable "political correctness," and a serious lack of knowledge of the military history and practice of the period, but does have some useful things to say about race relations and the possible motivations of some of the people involved. William C. Binkley's *The Texas Revolution* (Baton Rouge: 1952) is also of interest. Aside from some memoirs, there is little available in English that presents the Mexican perspective, Richard G. Santos' *Santa Anna's Campaign Against Texas, 1835-1836* (Waco: 1968) is quite interesting. There are only a few works in Spanish which usefully deal with the campaign, notably Jose C. Valades' *Mexico, Santa Anna, y la guerra de Texas* (Mexico: 1979), and Francisco Bulnes's old *Las grandes mentiras de nuestra historia* (Mexico: 1904), which has a chapter on the subject.

The literature on the Alamo is voluminous. The earliest, and in many ways still one of the most useful works, is Reuben Marmaduke Potter's "The Fall of the Alamo," originally published in *The Magazine of American History* in 1878, and since reprinted several times. Potter managed to interview most of the survivors of the Alamo, and for a time even had Francisco Becerra in his employ. Lon Tinkle's *Thirteen Days of Glory* (New York: 1958) provides an excellent day-by-day narrative, plus some thoughtful notes, and John Myers *The Alamo* (New York: 1973) is also quite useful. Miguel A. Sanchez Lamego's *The Siege and Taking of the Alamo*, translated by Consuelo Velasco (Santa Fe, 1968), provides a look at the siege from the Mexican perspective; albeit that the translation leaves much to be desired.

Susan Prendergast Schoelwar's *Alamo Images: Changing Perceptions of a Texas Experience* (Dallas: 1985) provides a fascinating look at the history of how we have perceived the Alamo in art, literature, and history itself.

Frank X. Tolbert's *The Day of San Jacinto* (New York: 1959) treats that battle in some detail, though with some errors.

The best work on the naval aspects of the Revolution remains Jim Dale Hill's *The Texas Navy: In Forgotten Battles and Shirtsleeve Diplomacy* (Chicago, 1937), which is seriously outdated. There is no comparable work on the Texas Army, aside from some articles in journals, but Philip Haythornwaite's, *The Alamo and the War of Texan Independence, 1835-1836* (London: 1986), a volume in the "Osprey Men-at-Arms Series," contains some material of interest.

Two journals are immensely valuable for this subject, *Southwestern History Quarterly* and *The Military History of the Southwest*. Excruciatingly scholarly, both nevertheless regularly contain well-written, carefully researched, and thoughtful articles on the Texas Revolution, as well as newly discovered letters and other documents of relevence. Though rare, the publications of the *Alamo Lore and Myth Organization* are frequently of considerable value.

Considering how few people were actually involved, the number of diaries, memoirs, and personal accounts of the War of the Texas Revolution is remarkable. Both sides are well represented, and many of the works in question are very valuable. The best first hand account from the Mexican perspective is that of Col. Jose Enrique de la Peña, *With Santa Anna in Texas* (College Station, Tex: 1975), which caused a sensation when it was originally published in Mexico in 1955 and once again upon the appearence of the English version, containing, as it does, the story of Crockett's capture and subsequent execution. Carlos E. Castañeda, translator and editor, *The Mexican Side of the Texas Revolution* (Dallas: 1928) contains excerpts from a number of memoirs and diaries. Santa Anna's memoirs, translated as *The Eagle* (Austin: 1967), are amusing. Other valuable memoirs from Mexican soldiers are Juan N. Almonte, "The Private Journal of Juan Nepomuceno Almonte, February 1-April 16, 1836," *Southwestern History Quarterly*, Vol. 48, No. 1 (July 1944); Francisco Becerra, *A Mexican Sergeant's Recollections of the Alamo and San Jacinto* (Austin: 1980); Vicente Filisola, *The History of the War in Texas* (Austin: 1985), which actually translates only one of the two works on the Texas War by Filisola; and Jose Juan Sanchez Navarro, *La Guerra de Tejas* (Mexico: 1938). Memoirs by Texans abound. Some of the more interesting are: James T. DeShields, *Tall Men with Long Rifles: The Glamorous Story of the Texas Revolution as Told by Captain Creed Taylor* (San Antonio: 1935); Herman Ehrenberg, *With Milam and Fannin: The Adven-*

tures of a German Boy in the Texas Revolution (Dallas: 1935), William Fairfax Gray, *From Virginia to Texas, 1935* (Houston: 1965); Mirabeau B. Lamar, "Mirabeau B. Lamar's Texas Journal," *Southwestern History Quarterly*, Vol. 64, No. 2 (October 1980) and No. 3 (January 1981); Juan N. Seguin, *Personal Memoirs of John N. Seguin* (San Antonio: 1858); John Sutherland, *The Fall of the Alamo* (San Antonio: 1936); and William P. Zuber, *My Eighty Years in Texas* (Austin: 1971).

Several of the participants are the subject of interesting biographies. These have been listed by the name of the subject, rather than the author. Eugene C. Barker, *Life of Stephen F. Austin* (Austin: 1985); Evelyn Brogan, *James Bowie: A Hero of the Alamo* (San Antonio: 1922) is suitably reverent, while C. L. Douglas' *James Bowie: The Life of a Bravo* (Dallas: 1944) is rather less so; James W. Burke, *David Crockett: Man Behind the Myth* (Austin: 1984); Michael A. Lofaro, *Davy Crockett: The Man, The Legend, The Legacy* (Knoxville: 1985); C. Richard King's *Susanna Dickinson* (Austin: 1976) is interesting, but badly proofread; Jean Flynn, *Remember Goliad: James W. Fannin* (Austin: 1984); Llerne B. Friend, *Sam Houston: The Great Designer* (Austin: 1985) is less valuable than James Marquis' *The Raven: A Biography of Sam Houston* (St. Simon, Ga: 1981); Oakah L. Jones, *Santa Anna* (New York: 1968); Martha A. Turner, *William Barret Travis: His Sword and his Pen* (Waco: 1972); Lawrence D. Williams, Jr., *Deaf Smith* (San Antonio: 1964).

For events after the war for Texas, the best works are *The Republic of Texas* (Palo Alto: 1968), edited by Stephen B. Oates, Joseph M. Nance's *After San Jacinto: The Texas-Mexican Frontier, 1836-1841* (Austin: 1963) and *Attack and Counterattack: The Texas-Mexican Frontier, 1842* (Austin: 1964), and William Ranson Hogan's *The Texas Republic: A Social and Economic History* (Austin: 1969).

Films

The Alamo and the Texas War for Independence figures at

least peripherally in some three dozen motion pictures and television programs.

The earliest Alamo movie was *The Immortal Alamo*, filmed in San Antonio by Gaston Melies, brother of the famed French film pioneer George Melies. In this pioneering work, which is lost save for some stills, the role of Davy Crockett was played by Francis Ford, the brother of John Ford. In 1915 D.W. Griffith produced *The Heroes of the Alamo*. Long thought lost, the film was restored in 1977.

Only one reel survives of *Davy Crockett and the Fall of the Alamo* (1926), which retold the tale with all the myths intact. Portions of this film were used in the 1937 *The Heroes of the Alamo*, which oddly focusses on Almeron Dickinson. Another odd film is the 1953 *The Man from the Alamo*, which takes as its focus a character loosely based on the quasi-mythic figure of Louis Rose.

Walt Disney's *Davy Crockett: King of the Wild Frontier* (1955), was the first television Alamo. Staring Fess Parker, it repeated most of the myths, and created a few new ones, such as the "good Indian" who chose to die at Crockett's side.

Although it too repeats many of the myths, including Travis' line in the dirt, *The Last Command* (1955) is probably artistically the best of all the Alamo films. In contrast, John Wayne's *The Alamo* (1959), although far more accurate historically, within the demands of dramatic license, tried too hard to be heroic and, although wonderfully spectacular, is artistically flat.

There have since been several good, historically fairly accurate films dealing with the Alamo, none of which have quite matched the artistic success of *The Last Command* or the spectacle of *The Alamo*. These are *Houston—Legend of Texas* (1986), *Thirteen Days to Glory* (1986), perhaps the most historically correct film about the Alamo, and *Alamo: The Price of Freedom* (1987). *Seguin*, a 1980 PBS effort, takes an interesting look at the Texas Revolution from the perspective of its most famous *Tejano* hero.

A film featuring the Alamo, but not dealing with the events

of 1836 is *Viva Max!* (1969), a comedy in which Peter Ustinov portrays a bumbling Mexican general who tries to retake the Alamo in order to impress his girlfriend.

APPENDIX

The Alamo and Other Revolutionary Shrines

There are several important historic sites associated with the Texas Revolution which may be visited.

The surviving structures of the Alamo in San Antonio are in the care of the Daughters of the Republic of Texas. Although there is not much left of the original fort, a visit to the church and the museum and library which the D.R.T. maintain nearby can be very rewarding. Rather than merely preserve what is left of the Alamo, the D.R.T. have established a fairly good library and archive devoted to the Texas Revolution, with specific reference to the defense of the Alamo. Among the many valuable materials are files containing personal information on each of the defenders and many others associated with the events of 1836. They also have an extremely good book store. Moreover, the staff is enormously helpful and friendly.

The Presidio La Bahia at Goliad is open to the public, and presents a pretty good idea of what a proper early nineteenth century fort looked like. The Coleto Creek battlefield, about ten miles away, has not changed much in the more than 150 years since Fannin surrendered, and a visit provides much food for thought.

Similarly virtually unchanged save for some monuments is the San Jacinto battlefield, which is not far from Houston. A

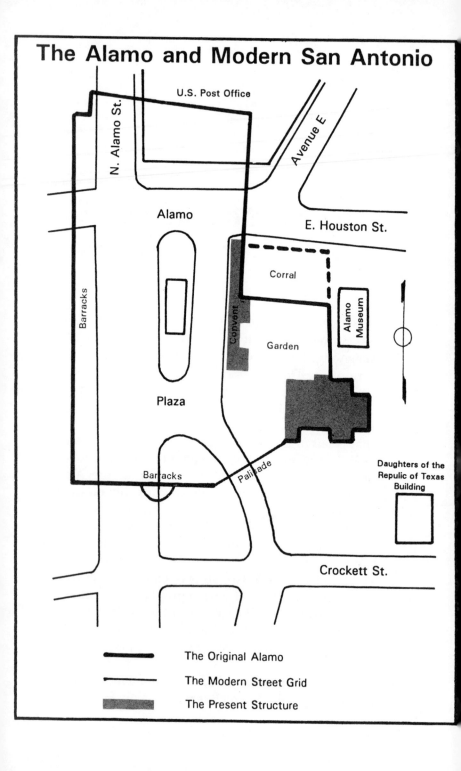

The Alamo and Modern San Antonio

U.S. Post Office

N. Alamo St.

Avenue E

Alamo

E. Houston St.

Barracks

Convent

Corral

Alamo Museum

Garden

Plaza

Barracks

Palisade

Daughters of the Repulic of Texas Building

Crockett St.

——— The Original Alamo

——— The Modern Street Grid

▓▓▓ The Present Structure

walk around the battlefield gives a very good notion of how small the armies involved were. The entire field can be traversed in an hour or so. Such a visit is doubly rewarding if one drops in on the old U.S.S. *Texas*, the only surviving dreadnought battleship in the world, laid down in 1911, which is preserved nearby.

Anyone seriously interested in the story of the Alamo should not miss a visit to the small town of Brackettville, about 120 miles southwest of San Antonio. There can be found the Alamo Village, site of the Alamo movie set originally erected for John Wayne's 1959 film. Based on meticulous research, the set is about as close an approximation of the size and appearance of the original structures as it is possible to make. The only deliberately ahistorical features are the "hump" atop the facade of the church, necessitated by generations of tradition, and some differences on the northern side, where the corral was in the historical structure.

Index

The storming of the Alamo as depicted by artist Theodore Gentilz in 1885. Although executed a half-century after the events, this is generally regarded as a very reliable rendering of the Alamo in 1836. Among the details, note the *Delores Cavalry Regiment*, shown posted in the fields beyond the Alamo, and the men of the *Second Column*, shown pouring into the courtyard through the breach in the northern wall. However, note that the

Mexican troops in the right foreground,
Col. Juan Morales' converged battalion of
Cazadores, are depicted too close to the
breastworks. By the time the *Second
Column* had gained entry into the
courtyard, these troops had sidled across
the front of the Alamo to storm up the
southeastern corner of the post. *Courtesy
of the Daughters of the Republic of Texas
Library.*